Storr Hill Side 1870-1980

Storr Hill Side 1870-1980

by

Donald Barker

The Pentland Press Limited
Edinburgh · Cambridge · Durham

First published in 1994 by
The Pentland Press Ltd.
1 Hutton Close
South Church
Bishop Auckland
Durham

ISBN 1 85821 124 7

Typeset by Elite Typesetting Techniques, Southampton.
Printed and bound by Antony Rowe Ltd., Chippenham.

Contents

Acknowledgements

My indebtedness to my brother Geoffrey Barker and his wife Margaret, Joan and Laurence Barrett, John and Colleen Nicoll, Frank and May Wilkinson, is greater than I can express in a few words, and they are given more extensive introductions in the appropriate place.

The help I received from the staff of the Reference Section of Bradford Central Library, in particular Mr Bob Duckett and Miss Elvira Wilmott, was extremely encouraging, as was the prompt support of Stanley Ellis. I am also indebted to the staff of the Bradford Industrial Museum; Ms. P Chrystall and the staff of the Irby Branch of the Wirral Public Libraries; and the interest in my work and helpful suggestions of Grace and Leslie Carter. I am grateful to Pentland Press, in the persons of Daniel Russell and Meg Ross, who have so ably given my work a form fit to be seen in public.

The most important contribution to this book, however, has been that of my wife, Sylvia, whose patient help and support has never flagged.

Introduction

In reality, the annals of the poor never have been short and simple, but until our day there has been no demand for them. They contained nothing of interest to either antiquarian or publisher and were consequently rarely documented in a form that could serve later specialist historians as sources. History concerned only a few privileged and educated people, who liked to identify with people of the past who had wielded power, wealth or rank, or who had led epoch-making revolutions. The only people who might have been interested were mostly illiterate, and those who were literate were not interested. In the last hundred years or thereabouts, people without social position or pretensions have become interested in *their* forerunners and how they lived. My original intention of writing an oral-history introduction to a linguistic work I have had to abandon, for a number of reasons, and I now find it necessary to place my story accurately and securely, as far as I am able, in the context of national developments in technology, economics, education and general outlook.

Being able to say that one went to tea with a primary-school friend who lived in a row of houses called Short Row, and also with another friend who lived in the Long Row, is an intimate little item of nostalgia, but to learn from books that both these rows of small houses were built by the Low Moor Company before 1841 for their skilled workers is exciting history.[1] Equally exciting might be the history of the Patent Hammer Inn, where Sarannah is supposed to have played polo with a long brush on a pig's snout. It was built by the Low Moor Company, named after one of their great steam hammers, and well into the twentieth century its licence allowed it to open from 6 a.m. to cater for men coming off the night shift in the Forge Yard.

The speed of change in the last hundred years has made it possible for ordinary people with elementary formal education to reach back into a living past that was relevant to them and yet totally different. One can capture the imagination of some members of Generation IV by showing them where Bullet lived and Dont ran on the top of the outside toilets of Ivy Bank; and tell them tales of another epoch when knockers-up really and truly existed and the lamplighter, Mr Healey, leaned his ladder on the arm of the gas lamp at our side gate.

I shall never forget the following conversation that took place some time during the war in Wyke Recreation Ground. Four or five old men were sitting on the seats in front of the veteran's hut, just talking and watching the bowls, while I sat there waiting for Seth. The conversation went:

Old Cock 1:'Wheea's Billy? A emt seen 'im fer days.'
Old Cock 2: 'A dun't knaw. 'Appen 'i's nuen sa weel. 'I'll bi gerrin on a bit nah, will Billy. Owder ner me, onniways.'
Old Cock 3: 'Ah can tell yer, if yer can tell ma when t'last public 'anging wor i' Leeds. I' telled me 'at i' wo'nt born but i wor theear – in 'is mother's belly!'

This hanging took place on 10th September 1864, the only one to take place at Armley Gaol. Public hangings were officially abolished in 1868. Billy, therefore, was born within nine months of Seth, and, as I was waiting for Seth to play bowls with him, the story was perfectly feasible.

I quote this incident as but one of several recorded in this book to vindicate three basic contentions:

1. As Professor Hoskins consistently maintained, history is about people, and my history is about ordinary people.
2. By listening to our parents and their parents talking to their contemporaries, we could all be capable of recording at least a selection from a hundred years of local history.
3. All too often when reading the work of academic and professional historians I lose interest and recall the following passage from *Tristram Shandy*: 'Tell me, ye learned, shall we for ever be adding so much to the *bulk* – so little to the *stock*?

'Shall we for ever make new books, as apothecaries make new mixtures, by pouring only out of one vessel into another?

'Are we forever to be twisting and untwisting the same rope? – forever in the same track – forever at the same pace?

'Who made MAN, with powers which dart him from earth to heaven in a moment – that great, that most excellent and most noble creature of the world . . . to go sneaking on at this pitiful – pimping – pettifogging rate?'[2]

So, I started with the intention of attaching the minimum of bibliographical paraphernalia to the following chapters and aiming at retaining the flavour of the 'call-'oil', the bowling green edge and the queue in the Co-op as far as possible, but many dates and references have crept in, not entirely for the benefit of the reader, but because I became fascinated by the subject and wanted to know more myself.

My original intention was to write an historical account of the dialect of Storr Hill Side during the period of Billy's lifetime, roughly from 1870 to 1950. The most important of my basic framework concepts was to have been the distinction between Great Tradition and Little Tradition, as I had found it in the work of Robert Redfield, a concept I had used in teaching the sociology of dialect for at least twenty-five years.[3] I have since recognised the need to simplify this contrast and have substituted the terms *progressive* and *conservative*, without any political reference whatsoever, although the terms Great Tradition and Little Tradition may have survived in some passages. The difference between the two Traditions is difficult to define in detail, and Redfield himself does not attempt a firm distinction. The two columns of the list which follows merely offer pointers.

Great Tradition	**Little Tradition**
Sophisticated	Unsophisticated
Educated	Uneducated
Logical Thinking	Associative Thinking
Leaders	Masses
Upper Classes	Lower Classes
Ambitious	Unambitious
Creative	Receptive
Progressive	Conservative
Urban	Rural
Versatile	Non-versatile

None of these contrasts is absolute in any way. They are terms which come to mind when attempting a definition and the priorities from this selection would, of course, differ from observer to observer. Nor do they, as lists, constitute anything like a definition of any single member of the community.

It is the connection with the dialect that, in the following pages, produces the leaning towards the character, outlook, hopes and ambitions of people rather than dates, statistics, leaders of society and institutions. These, however, may not be ignored as they are essential as a framework for my history, and to link it with the events and influences of the greater, national society. To save their own sanity, historians have always invested dates and epochs with significance which often did not exist, and the classification of my characters according to generation is also far from precise, if measured against a rigid time-scale. Of my collaborators, Frank only belongs to Generation II, the rest of us to Generation III, even though there is a gap of twenty years between myself and John. And Laurence, early Generation III, has two sons who also belong to Generation III.

It cannot be said with too much emphasis, that the responsibility for the following pages rests entirely with me; the *authority* for the contents I share with my willing friends and helpers.

In alphabetical order *we* are:

1. Myself, Donald Barker, referred to in the first person singular, whose qualifications for this undertaking are, briefly stated, as follows: Born 1922 in Temperance Field, Wyke and moved to Elizabeth Street, Wyke at Easter 1925. I considered Wyke my home until the age of 27, and from Elizabeth Street attended Belle Vue High School, 1 mile north of city centre. My academic education included university courses in German philology, phonetics and historical linguistics and subsequently lecturing in these subjects, the German dialects and Dutch. My real qualification for this purpose, however, consists in having grown up as a member of the community in question, in close and intimate contact with representatives of all the generations concerned in this account of Storr Hill Side.

2. My brother, Geoffrey Barker (Geoffrey), born 1927 in Elizabeth Street. His education was identical in all respects to my own. He returned to the West Riding and, until retirement, taught German and French in a school some 12 miles from Wyke as the crow flies. When it came to checking phonetic script, Geoffrey was invaluable.

3. Laurence Barrett (Laurence), born 1922, grew up as a neighbour in Elizabeth Street from the age of 2 and is thus my oldest friend. He went to Carr Lane School all the time that I was there and then, for his last three years of school, to the Board School, as it was known, at Wyke. He later lived down Wilson Road and then in Low Moor. After serving an apprenticeship at the Airedale Electrical Works at the top of Carr Lane, he

Plate 1. Frank Wilkinson aged 79.

worked for several years at Rigby's Wire Mill as a maintenance man. He is now living at the other side of Bradford but still very much in contact with Storr Hill Side.

4. I had no contact whatever with John and Colleen Nicoll (John, Colleen), until 1983, or thereabouts. John is a native of Storr Hill, received his primary education at Carr Lane, and has lived and worked all his life within a mile of it. As very dedicated local historians, they have supplied a great deal of material for this project in the form of maps, photographs and tapes, as well as some timely corrections.

5. The doyen of my helpers is Frank Wilkinson (Frank), who was born in 1912 halfway down Storr Hill, in the house next door to where my mother and her parents were then living. He grew up there and, apart from war service, he has never left Storr Hill Side. For a few years he kept the fish and chip shop near the top of Storr Hill and then turned painter and decorator.

Other members of the Storr Hill Side community whom I have mentioned by their first names are: Seth Shaw, my maternal grandfather; Annie Barker, his daughter, my mother; Ephraim Barker, my father; Sarannah, adopted daughter of my mother's uncle, Edwin Lightowler; Bullet, whose real name was Walter Lightowler. Other characters are described, sometimes at length, in my text.

My first generation (Generation I) was born before 1890. In my experience, those born before about 1890 represented in my native community the last culturally naive generation, the last generation whose stamp derived from within the community. Most of them could read and write and were able to adjust, to various degrees, to Standard English, when they thought the situation demanded it, but their habitual, domestic speech remained in essence that of preceding centuries. Seth Shaw, 1865-1947, with whom I lived in close contact until well into my twenties, and his numerous friends and acquaintances, bricklayers, colliers, foundrymen, weavers, who kept pigs and poultry, whippets, greyhounds, fighting cocks and ferrets, constitute my anonymous sources of Generation I. They were virtually self sufficient as far as culture in its wider sense goes, having their own traditional and inherited standards, which were virtually proof against the national élite and the influence it wielded, just as the villagers that Laurie Lee left behind in the thirties insisted on their own standards:

> For village honours are still severely local. They include life-long success on the village dartboard, sharp wits in the cattle market, skill at growing whopping but useless vegetable marrows, weight lifting, spitting, ringing bells, trapping foxes, cheating at draughts, winning at whist-drives or working one's way up to be postman or gravedigger.
>
> Outside things don't count – and why should they? Take a train home, go to the pub, hand round cigarettes and remark that you've just been made Inspector of Inkwells at the Ministry of Boil and Trouble, and what reaction do you get? They stick your cigarettes behind their ears, and then there's a silence, and then they say: 'Ah, but d'you 'ear about young Jim Hogg, then? 'E's done well for isself, too. Caught three dozen rabbits last week in the vicarage grounds, an' sold back a dozen to the vicar. 'E's a lad. Har, har.[4]

This was the source of the unshakeable dignity that once distinguished all representatives of my older generations, even the 'wrong 'uns'. Your present day guide round miners' or farm labourers' cottages, the sociologists who stress their stoical endurance and frugality, the long hours and lack of decent housing, education, medical attention, etc., the politician pointing to the improvement in material conditions during his party's period of power, all miss the essence, the signature, of those simple people, namely, an immense dignity in adversity. *Outside things didn't matter*. Those of us who knew that generation are still unable fully to understand why headlines, front pages of newspapers and television screens are dominated by national and international politicians and their unconvincing antics.

My second generation (Generation II) was born roughly between 1890 and 1920. For the language as well as the social outlook of this generation the decisive years came before the end of the First World War. This generation was distinguished from Generation I by being more literate and many more of them earned their living in non-manual jobs. They had enjoyed sound schooling in elementary subjects up to the age of 12-13, read newspapers and fiction and were well aware of a national élite tradition and the power it wielded. This combination produced incentives and aspirations towards both the local leadership and the National Élite. Such incentives were not part of the outlook of Generation I. Generation II discarded much of the rural conservatism which Generation I had retained, in spite of the industrial nature of their occupations, and they made great strides towards cultural change and progress. According to the degree of progress in this direction of each individual, they became bilin-

Plate 2. Three Generations: Walter Armitage Barker, Ephraim Armitage Barker, Donald Barker.

gual. This generation was composed of those who were responsible for the upbringing, the norms and standards of the present author, and included my parents and their working-class friends, my teachers and bosses, those who taught me my job in a factory, mechanics, mill-workers and all those who kept me in order and shaped my future character and ability at an age when learning was an unconscious process.

Generation III was born between 1920 and 1950. Just as Generation I had secured the provision of elementary education for Generation II, so did this generation demand, establish and support higher education for Generation III. For this latter generation, given the support of their parents, there was no limit to their reasonable aspirations. There were for them no barriers to their aspiring to political, social and financial prominence on the local scene, and many breaches in the preserves of the National Élite were discovered and enlarged by them. Increasingly, as the industrial prosperity of the area was eroded, young people found better lives and careers away from Storr Hill Side.

The life of Storr Hill Side now revolves around a Generation IV, about whom I am incompetent to report as people, although details of modern education and employment, etc. are necessary to my account.

As this account progressed, I became more and more aware of a bias towards the north, to Carr Lane and Low Moor, in my selection of material. So many of my characters and their doings belonged to Carr Lane, Morley Carr and even Low Moor, while almost none derive from Town Gate or Lower Wyke, which are no further away, that I have been led to look for reasons for this. It is largely due to the geographical distribution of our family and their friends, but also to the fact that almost all of us concerned with this work went to Carr Lane School which, to be strictly accurate, lies in Low Moor. We had to go to Wyke for our doctors, banks, chemists, pensions, etc., but our friends of all ages and generations lived down Storr Hill and up Carr Lane. It was rather as though we were in the gallery, looking out and down on the rest of the community to which we belonged.

Plate 3. View from our field to Odsal Top. (1953)

Chapter 1

The Location and Climate of Storr Hill Side

Storr Hill and New Road Side, which together provide the title *Storr Hill Side* for my project, lie some three and a half miles to the south of Bradford Town Hall on the way to Huddersfield. On many of the older maps the whole area of settlement concerned is labelled 'New Road Side'. The correct postal name of what is known as New Road Side is Huddersfield Road. The two roads meet at the Junction Inn, which is still there, opposite where Elizabeth Street and Barraclough Square used to stand. Across the road is the Crown Hotel which, although it has all the marks of a coaching hotel, prominent stables and the shelter (the 'elm' or 'ellum', in the vernacular), was not built until 1865-6 and not fully licensed until 1867.

These two roads and the streets leading off them form the small focus of this study, but the wider peripheries reach as far as all parts of Low Moor, Judy Woods, Norwood Green, Wyke Church and Oakenshaw (Map 1). The postal address of Storr Hill Side was, and still is, 'Wyke, Bradford', the area having been absorbed into the Bradford conurbation and local government area in 1899, along with all the other localities which had previously belonged to the North Bierley Local District Board.

Storr Hill climbs steeply up an escarpment, 1:3 in places, out of the broad, flat lowland which comprises Carr Lane, Morley Carr and part of Low Moor. The old name for Low Moor, Wibsey Low Moor, demonstrates both the ancient priority of Wibsey (Domesday *Wibetese* = Wigbald's island) as a centre of trade and industry and the geographical relationship in which Carr Lane bottom lies about 350 feet below the centre of Wibsey. The 600 ft. contour runs through what was our hen-run, while the 500 ft. contour runs through what was Carr Lane Tide Field. At the age of five we, Laurence, Geoffrey and myself, twice a day descended and climbed a hundred feet in little more than two hundred yards as we went to Carr Lane School! To the west and north of Carr Lane and Morley Carr lies Low Moor and to the east and south are Wyke and Oakenshaw.

The local histories of the area give very little information about the making or the age of a road up Storr Hill. They are, however, unanimous in saying that, until the 1820s, the main route from Bradford to Huddersfield and Halifax came down Carr Lane as far as the school and then turned up to the right past Hollin Hall (always Holly Hall to us), as though there was at that time no road up Storr Hill. There is no trace of part of the Hollin Hall route ever having been wide enough for vehicles. James Parker's account[1] is brief and makes sense:

> The old pack-horse road, leading from Carr Lane to Wike, before the present Stor Hill Road was made, went along Carr Lane, up past 'Hollin Hall', across what is now called New Roadside, or Huddersfield Road, past the Quiet Woman Inn, forward to Carr House Lane, then turned to the left at what is now Old Stor Hill, then forward into High Fernley Lane, past the handsome residence of Mr Gathorne Barraclough, whose house is erected on the site of an ancient homestead. It then went along what is now the Huddersfield Road, and joined up to Wike Town Gate, then forward to Lower Wike, etc. The word 'Stor' means a severe or steep hill. The word 'Carr' means low lands liable to be flooded, lands below the hills. At what period the New Storr Hill Road was made we have no data, but we can imagine what a fearful road the Old Carr Lane, past Hollin Hall, would be to travel for either man or beast, especially in winter time.

His other account of this route,[2] as it was in 1822, does include Storr Hill, but does not attempt a date. That there seems to be no account of the building of what in those days must have been a good, wide waggon road that was urgently needed and eventually produced so many houses and side-streets, is really remarkable. Perhaps it just grew, for, even in our day, it was surfaced with nothing more than hard-packed dross and clinker with some ironstone in the surface.

As for New Road Side, Percy Nudds[3] provides an excellent, brief account: 'In 1823 a Bill was passed in Parliament conferring powers to make a road through Truncliffe to Odsal, past Odsal House and in front of

Low Moor House, past Wright's Shop[4] at Low Moor and so to the top of Storr Hill. Hence the name of "New Road Side". The road was begun on 1st October 1823 and was opened in 1825.' James Parker devotes a lot of space to this road and provides some fascinating information about its building and inception.[5] The most relevant information for my purpose is on p.247 : 'Copy of Contract, 1824. – for making the New Road from the left hand side of Storr Hill, Wike, along what is now called New Road Side, took place at the Swan Inn, Brighouse, on the 19th day of January, 1824, the route being to Low Moor Iron Works, and the whole distance being 154 roods in length.' Detailed specifications are given about the width of the road, the drains, the flagstones and the dross for covering the road, with prices and cartage. The price of the land necessary for the diversions, along with the names of the vendors, is also given.

The origin of the name Wyke has given rise to much debate and popular speculation, so much and so wild, in fact, that I cannot help thinking of what the great historian of the early Saxon settlements in this country had to say on the subject: 'No subject has attracted more misguided enthusiasts and ignorant amateurs than the study of place names, and it is essential to beware of any suggested etymologies that are not securely based on the informed collation of all available early forms.'[6] This manner of speculation depends so much on personal imagination and seems to ignore many factors, the most obvious of which is that there are so many 'wikes', 'wykes', 'wicks' all over northern Europe, that it must denote a certain type of settlement. The *Oxford Dictionary of English Place Names*[7] under the lemma Old English (OE) *wíc* gives: 'an early loan-word from Latin *vícus* means "dwelling, dwelling-place"; "village", "hamlet", "town"; "street" in a town; "farm", esp. "a dairy-farm" . . . it is impossible to distinguish neatly between the various senses . . . probably the most common meaning is "dairy farm". *wíc* alone is the source of the pl. ns. WEEK, WICK, WYKE, WIX, also of WICKEN, ASHWICKEN, WYCOMB, WYKEN.' So, perhaps Wyke did originally develop round a dairy farm, but the meaning of 'town', 'settlement' appears to me to be more likely; our word 'vicinity' has a very general application and can refer to any kind of place. The 6 inch map of 1852 shows quite clearly a nucleus of dwellings along the sides of Town Gate, i.e. 'Main Street', each with a narrow burgage plot stretching away from the house and the road. Particularly in the lands of northern Europe, this word, in various guises, denotes a settlement of traders and artisans which became permanent in the earlier Middle Ages and survived only because it was close to and dependent on the fortified castle of some lord or bishop who put it under the administration of an official, hence 'bailiwick'. Many of them later secured independence from the lord or prelate, and drew up an urban constitution with a mayor or provost and a council of aldermen. The written compilation of this constitution was called the '*Weichbild*' = literally 'the form', 'the shape', of the *vícus*. This was the predominant pattern on the continent, but in this country many smaller lords and gentlemen encouraged such settlements on their manorial estates for the sake of the taxes. The exact manner of the founding and development of our Wyke would be pure speculation, but there is little doubt about the origin of the name.

Physically, this part of the West Riding is distinguished by wide, sweeping valleys and plateaus at a height of 500 to 800 feet – the eastern reaches of the Pennines. Some five miles to the west, however, around Halifax, the steeper-sided pockets and the narrower, more tortuous valleys of the Pennines proper begin. From our house one could see for about five miles, across part of Low Moor, Oakenshaw and Bierley to Drighlington. At that time, between the wars, the view included some woodlands, lots of rough grazing, an occasional field of oats or potatoes, woollen mills with their tall chimneys, pit head gear, slag heaps, station sidings, blast furnaces and strangely isolated blocks or clusters of simple and severe, stone-built dwellings. It was a strange kind of green industrial slum, for large areas were still green and cultivated between the pits, weaving and spinning sheds and foundries. Almost everybody I knew, men and women alike, worked in either a factory of some kind, the pit or on the railway, but most of them divided their spare time between their pigs and poultry, gardens and allotments on the one hand and the pub, club, cinema, dance hall or the football ground on the other.

Those who called themselves farmers, living off 30 to 80 acres of fairly rough grazing, were mostly poor men. They made ends meet by operating their own small milk round or acting as general carriers. Out of a population sample of more than 1,500 on Storr Hill Side in 1881, not more than four individuals were engaged in farming. This is a little surprising as, until World War II, there were still large areas of green fields all around on which there grazed small, non-pedigree milking herds of 12-20 cows. We all knew by name at least half-a-dozen farms. Older people, especially, used these farm names and pub names as points of location. When I come to talk about the outlook and initiative of the people of Storr Hill Side, and the way they used their free time, this open aspect will be shown to be of great importance.

Until 1899 the district was part of the North Bierley Union, which had been constituted as a District Council in 1894. In that year huge areas: Thornton, Tong, Idle, Eccleshill in addition to North Bierley, were incorporated into the City of Bradford. Within ten years the connection between these new areas and the city was made firm and permanent by the introduction of electric tramways. There had been a steam tramway from the centre of Bradford to Wyke for several years, but on 1st February 1902 electric tramways as far as Bankfoot were introduced, and on 3rd May of that year the line was extended to Low Moor and Wyke. Henceforward the people of Wyke and Low Moor not only paid Bradford rates and told strangers that they came from Bradford, they shopped for everything except their daily requirements in Bradford, sent their children to Bradford high schools and supported Bradford football teams, cinemas and music halls.

The best description of the climate that comes to mind is that it is cold, wet and windy in winter, but warmer in summer than the western side of Britain, because it is sheltered from the prevailing west winds. Although the great snowfall of 1933 described below was unique in our experience, snow up to nine inches was not infrequent and frost each morning, often lasting the whole day, was not unusual throughout the winter months. The vegetation revived late there, and burst and frozen-up water pipes, particularly in the outside toilets, were normal if adequate precautions were not taken, as was the need to break the ice on the water-troughs of poultry and livestock. Winds from the north and east were really bitter, and, as we lads never under any circumstances got into long trousers under the age of thirteen, walking down Wilson Road against an east wind inevitably produced bright red, chapped and cracked knees. Our land was on a north-facing slope, which led Ephraim to stock up with White Wyandotte poultry only, because he believed that this breed stood up to the cold wind without going off their lay better than any other.

Below the appropriate weather map, Fig. 60,[8] Prof. Manley writes: '0700 hrs., 25th February 1933. Very heavy orographic snowfall in N.E. and N. England and in N.E. Ireland associated with a low which moved westwards; snow 6 inches deep in Durham but 30 inches deep in Teesdale at 800 ft.'

This snowfall started on a Friday afternoon and had not really got going when I came home from school. Now, we used to have our footwear repaired by a man who, either because there was no work for him or on account of bad health, had started to repair footwear in a wooden hut not far from the church at Scholes. His charges were very reasonable, so, to a family like ours, it was worth walking twenty minutes each way. As soon as I got in from school, Mother told me that I was to fetch a consignment of shoes from Scholes after tea. There was a bus which left the end of Worthinghead Road every hour and went through Scholes, so I was given my bus-fare and I set out for the 6 p.m. bus. It was snowing quite merrily, but I was cosy enough in a lot of woollen clothes, and I remember enjoying the play of the street-lighting on the lovely white surfaces by the Temperance Hall and Wyke Infants School.

The bus came, but it had 'Morley' on the destination board, so I let it go, thinking that the right bus for me would display 'Cleckheaton via Scholes' – or something like that. After a while, I asked a bystander about the bus for Scholes and was told that it had gone, and that the Morley bus was the one I wanted. So there was nothing for it but to walk. At the age of ten there was nothing daunting about either the distance or the conditions. I remember how the road into Scholes from the cross-roads at the Westfield Hotel was bounded by a low wall on my right over which the driven snow slashed into my 'neck-'oil' like a knife.

In his little hut the cobbler had a paraffin stove and it was really cosy. I took my time in packing the shoes into a carpet-bag with which I had been provided and in paying for them. When I asked about the time of the next bus back to Wyke, he told me that it would be at least half an hour and I could be home on foot in that time. So I walked, and even though walking through 3-4 inches of snow took a little longer, I was home and warm again well before eight o'clock.

During the next twelve hours, though, that snowstorm broke all records for our part of Yorkshire. Being Saturday next day, I was all set to have an extra half-hour in bed, but Geoffrey and I were bawled out of bed by eight o'clock, Mother arguing that all chores would take a little longer under such conditions. There was more snow than we had ever seen before! It was piled up against our front gate and hedge some 4 ft. high and only the tips of Uram Garside's hen-pen fence were to be seen. The snow had drifted against the houses on Ivy Bank until it was more than halfway up the doors and windows.

As we ate breakfast I remembered my bantam. She was the only survivor of a hatching of Black Wyandotte bantams which had been put out into a bottomless coop at a day old, straight onto the grass. The method raised healthy, sound poultry and was well tried. But this time I had inadvertently placed the coop in a hollow in the ground, and after a heavy rainfall two or three days later the hollow held 2-3 inches of water, and all my chickens were drowned except this one. She grew up into a little dull-

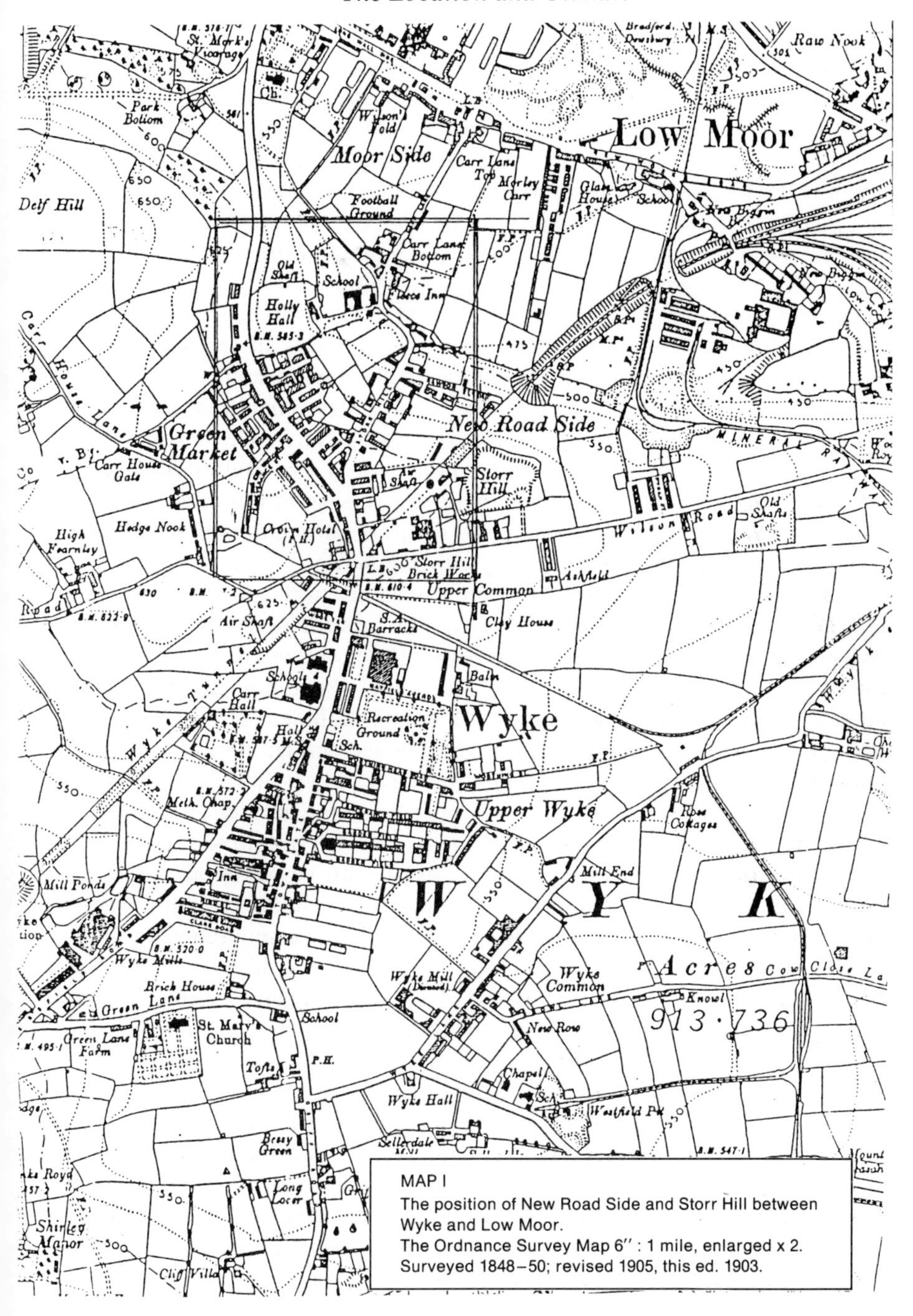

MAP I
The position of New Road Side and Storr Hill between Wyke and Low Moor.
The Ordnance Survey Map 6″ : 1 mile, enlarged x 2.
Surveyed 1848–50; revised 1905, this ed. 1903.

combed, lack-lustre and mis-shapen bantam hen, but the toughest and most independent little character imaginable. She had a breast-bone bent like a sickle, which gave the impression that she always walked sideways, and she seemed to know that she was the ugly duckling of our flock because she would never sleep in a hut with the other birds. First she slept up one of the stunted hawthorn trees, the remnants of an old hedge at the bottom of our field, and then she took to sleeping on the top of the lime-barrel which we kept in the angle of two hen-huts.

She had been on top of this barrel all night, and I was sure she would be a goner this time. However, before I was allowed to wade through the 35 yards of deep snow from our back door to the lime-barrel, I had a few little chores to do, which included digging out Mrs Woodhead who lived by herself, a widow, in the house nearest to us on Ivy Bank. 'If you don't, all that snow will fall straight into the house [i.e. living-room] as soon as she opens the door,' said Mother, and there was no arguing with a case like that. To be precise, as far as the menfolk of the family were concerned, there never was any arguing with Mother.

As soon as that was done, however, I was off to the lime-barrel. The pile of snow on top was some 2ft. 6ins. high, almost exactly the size and shape of the barrel itself. I found something to stand on and looked at the top of the mound of snow and there was a hole about the size of a pencil all that way up through the snow – a breathing-hole that had kept her alive. I removed the snow carefully, and she had enough life left in her to peck me as I lifted her up. I shut her up in a tea-chest in a warm, dry hut with food, drink and plenty of peat litter and didn't let her out until the snow had gone, which didn't take long, as it turned out. It was as though nothing had happened to her, and she lived with us for another two or three years before I sold her at a ripe old age for 9*d.* to my mother's Uncle Fred who was collecting a few assorted bantams for a neighbour's grand-child!

Laurence's memory of that snowfall is of more snow falling on the Friday afternoon and early evening than I can recollect. He can remember throwing snowballs in 9-10 ins. of snow on his way home from school. But his most significant memory of this event is of discovering the next day that Donald Macaulay in Barraclough Square had built an igloo at the end of the street in which he could stand upright. But Laurence had been forbidden to play with him because he used bad language!

Even though the snow did not take long to disappear, it caused major upset in the routine of the district. Old people could not get to the shops and younger people could not get to work. In those days, of course, most of the working population worked on Saturday mornings, starting at 7.30 a.m., and the efforts of many of them to get to work were truly heroic. The trams managed to get as far as Bankfoot, where there was a tram-shed, and Ephraim walked through the slush and the drifts for two miles to get to the trams on his way to work. Harry Dalby's sons dug a path for half a mile in the dark so that their sisters could get to their work in the mill. As for me, I got out of cleaning out the hen-huts that weekend; for once they had to go a fortnight!

Primitive, outdoor working conditions, however, became intolerable in bad weather. It might occur that men on a building site had to work a full day through rain to meet a deadline; or a road-gang had to mend a burst main under such conditions. Such jobs were really punishing, as the term 'waterproof' applied to clothing had in those days only a relative significance. One scene is imprinted indelibly on my mind. The Delf, as we called it, the source of clay for Birkby's bricks, was a huge crater by the nineteen thirties, such as might have served for a film set of a lost world. On the distant bottom men worked to fill the little trucks that an endless chain hauled up to the works at a slow walking pace. When it rained heavily, the men's feet disappeared in sticky, yellow mud, and from the top these diminished figures, swathed in sacks and leggings of all kinds, seemed to crawl about like beetles, or like the popular film impression of the Volga Boatmen.

But it was not really a bad climate and there were many compensations for the pall of smoke and the smell of industrial pollution. Storr Hill Side lies partly in the rain-shadow of the Pennines, and summers were relatively dry and warm.

I have mentioned elsewhere that the cabbage-stuffing scene in Walter Brook's garden took place on an 'old fashioned summer's afternoon'. They were still and warm. On an old-fashioned afternoon in the thirties there was next to no noise from internal combustion engines and no transistors or amplifiers, no electric lawn mowers and no pneumatic drills. A train coming out of Wyke Tunnel about a quarter of a mile away, was merely a dignified background attribute against which the men would check their watches, entirely different from the din and the frantic brashness of the modern appliances I have just mentioned. People not at work proceeded leisurely and had time to be jovial and polite to their friends and acquaintances. These were afternoons when not even the fumes from the myriad of coal fires could obscure the smells of the countryside, grass, hen-muck and old clothes on relatively rarely washed bodies. Hens laid and cocks crowed and fought; the sun usually shone, and men took their time to walk home for their tea. Even in the evenings men would be gossiping over the garden walls and from one top front step to another without their jackets. Normally they removed their jackets only to go to bed and to work. Their wives would be doing the same in their best summer blouses and their tireless children would still be playing their active games.

On one of these really hot days of summer in the middle of the thirties, I was sent down to Sarannah's with some groceries. Going down Storr Hill was bad enough, but even a puddler would have been uncomfortable coming up. At that time Annie made a very fizzy but refreshing drink that she called 'Boston Gingerbeer' or 'Boston Stone Ginger' (I have no idea whether either of them was correct). With a new bottle, it took at least five minutes of turning the cork in the quart bottle an eighth of an inch at a time to avoid drenching oneself and the ceiling! By the time I got home my tongue was dry and hanging out for a draught of this life-saving beverage. But there was nobody at home at either house; they had all gone out and every door was locked.

After a little hesitation on account of getting my clothes dirty, I got down through the coal-grate in the end wall, prised open the door of the coal-cellar with an old spade and reached my objective. But for the state of my clothes, Annie and Sarah would never have believed that I had got down that grate, and nowadays I can't believe it myself, having seen the same grate as recently as 1985.

Cleaning out hen-huts in warmer weather was also no joke. The perches and dropping-boards, however well they were washed in paraffin one Saturday morning, would be crawling with red mite by the next. So would one's trousers or shorts, and I would be made to strip off everything on the back step, get into a bath already waiting and dump all my clothes into the water as I got out.

Chapter 2

Work on Storr Hill Side

My Generation I lived through the golden years of British industrial success. The variety and enterprise of industry in Wyke and Low Moor during the last forty years of the nineteenth century was a wonderful microcosmic example of the national, or more accurately the northern, industrial achievement as a whole. For two of its industrial products the wider district in which the people of Storr Hill Side earned their living was known throughout the world: the production of wrought iron and every aspect of the production of worsted cloth. To be more precise, it was the Low Moor Company that made Storr Hill Side and defined its character down to World War II. The Census Returns of 1881 offer striking evidence of this.

The Census of 1881[1]

The households examined were described as being situated as follows: New Road Side 78, Green Market 45, Storr Hill 23, Storr Hill Top 11, Perseverance Street 26, Temperance Street 22, Butcher Street 17, School Place 15, Rawson Street 15, Church Street 19, Barraclough Square 8, Birkby Street 5, Bell Street 4, Holdsworth Street 3, Huddersfield Road 1 (Crown Hotel), Crown Cottage 1.

Total 293

These contained a total population of:	1353
– made up as follows:	
Infants not yet at school	163
Scholars	281
Housewives with no occupation	227

Mill hands of all kinds – weavers, spinners, sorters, drawers, doffers, reelers, card-setters, winders	169
Coal-miners, hurriers, etc.	109
Iron-workers – miners, forgemen, puddlers, labourers	107
Total	1056

Other occupations: General labourers 41; Carters 10, Painters 6, Plasterers 2, Joiners and Cabinet-Makers 10, Blacksmiths 4, Bricklayers 4, Brick-moulders 3, Brick-burner 1, Contractor 1 (employs 4 labourers & 2 boys); Engine-smiths 3, -fitters 2, -tenters 9, -cleaners 2, -minder 1, -man 1, -wright (coal-mine) 1, Engineer 1; Railway-goods checker 1, -collectors 2, -clerk 1, -driver 1; Stone miners 2, Stone-masons 3, labourer 1; Sawyer 1; Plumbers and Gasfitters 2, Cotton-winders 2, Brass-picker 1, Brass-moulder 1, Wood-turner 1, Safety-lamp maker 1, Steam-boiler maker 1, Factory-hand 1, Warehouse-man 1, -boy 1, Errand-boys 3, Night-watchman 1; Doctor's Assistant 1, Police-constable 1; Tax Collector for Local Board 1, School Staff 10, Landscape Gardeners 2; Licensed Victuallers and Beersellers 5, Butchers' Assistants 2; Broker.

Retired 7, Annuitants 3, 'No occupation' 5, 'Unemployed' 2.

Dressmakers 18, Domestic servants 16, Housekeepers 5, Laundress 1, Waiting-Nurse 1.

Shopkeepers and Traders: Grocers 3 (+ 1 Assistant), Grocer and Joiner 2, Grocer and Vegetable Seller 1, Greengrocers 3, Baker 1, Spice-seller (sweets) 1, Tripe-dressers 2, Boot and Shoe Maker 1, Cordwainer 1, Master Clogger (employs 2 boys) 1, Saddler 1; Coal-dealer 1, -merchant 1, Ironmonger 1 (2 apprentices), Drapers 4, Draper & Milliner 1, Shopkeeper 1, Watchmakers (father, two sons, one apprentice) 4; Joiner, Organist & Choirmaster 1.

Grand Total 1310

An analysis of these Census Returns yields the following data: 114 inhabitants aged 50 and over, or 11.5%. These divided exactly equally between the sexes. By contrast, 'scholars' and infants amounted to 32.8% of the population.

32 widows, aged between 26 and 73; and 15 widowers, the youngest aged 30.

54 unmarried daughters aged between 17 and 30, most of them working in the mill, and 9 spinsters aged over 30.

227 housewives did not have any other occupation; only 11, almost all of them young wives with no young children, are given as working in the mill. Of the 169 mill hands of all categories only 25 were men.

There were a number of girls in the mill at the age of 13, but only 3 (10, 11 and 12) below this age. In the pit there is 1 boy given as 'hurrier' at the age of 10, 2 at 11 and 3 at 12. One of the eleven-year-olds is designated as a half-timer; this practice seems to have been rare at that time; none are given as half-timers in the mill, but most of the women born 1875-1895 whom we knew talked about when they were half-timers. Both my parents were half-timers from the age of twelve, and we have the original certificate of Ephraim's age in 1904, which had to be obtained to allow him to go on half-time. There were only 2 as young as 13 at the Forge.

Most four-year-olds are returned as scholars, 8 only as not yet being in school. Notwithstanding the ages of the young workers given above, there were some 'scholars' aged 14 and even 15. Some members of Generation I were as ambitious as any other for their children.

Storr Hill Side was predominantly a coal-mining and iron-working neighbourhood at the time of its most rapid expansion. Excluding those whom I take to be self-employed, the working population of both sexes represented in my samples numbered 527 and of these 216, or 40.99%, were miners or iron-workers. If 169 mill workers, or 32% of the total, are added, the result is a total of 72% of the work force engaged in production manufacturing. This is the really significant result of a comparison of the economy of 1881 with the present day. Our microcosmic study of the history of Perseverance Street since 1881 shows not only a drop in total residents from 133 in 1881 to 92 around 1930 and to 60 in 1986, there was also a drop in the manufacturing work force in the same period from 60 to 7 and then to 2 at present.

The discrepancy in the totals results from the enumerator having omitted some occupations, or having been given no information. One of the tripe-dressers had daughters aged 22 and 23, and the enumerator probably thought that there was no need to specify their occupations. Margaret Rawson, Entry No. 6 for Storr Hill Side, had daughters of 18 and 16 for whom no occupations are given, her son, aged 20 was returned as 'Doctor's Assistant (out of Employ)', and there are two younger sons given as 'scholars'. One gets a picture of relative affluence, perhaps a private income. Some of the widows and widowers living with married children have no occupation specified; some omissions seem to be inexplicable, while the enumerator's enthusiasm for the abbreviation 'do' (ditto) leads to scholars aged 2 and, possibly, to the coal-hurrier aged 10.

It seems to me that the designation 'Storr Hill Top' must refer to the first nine houses on Elizabeth Street and the first two on the right hand side going down Storr Hill, just below the fish and chip shop. The latter was certainly not there in 1881, but appears on the 24" map of 1893.

The staff of the school was made up as follows: 1 headmaster, 1 teacher, 3 schoolmistresses, 4 pupil teachers and 1 monitress.

Those specified as 'retired' comprised: 1 waterworks manager, 2 beersellers/licensed victuallers, 1 ironstone miner, 1 engine-man, 1 mill stoker, 1 worsted spinner (the only female).

The presence of 3 brick-moulders, 1 brick-burner, 1 brickworks labourer seems to convey that Birkby's brickworks were in production, but we cannot think of a single house on Storr Hill Side of that age that was built of brick. Even fifty years later our houses, Nos. 17 and 19 Elizabeth Street, and the short row of houses at the end of Rawson Street, which may have been built much later, were the only ones we can recall, although, by that time, there were in the vicinity several mills and the swimming-baths built of brick.

The ages of the two butchers, 15 and 23, seem to preclude a butcher's shop, which we find very surprising when one considers the insistence of my Generation I on plenty of meat. There are no fish and chip shops as against three in our day.

Throughout the nineteenth century the whole development of Storr Hill Side and Carr Lane was initiated and controlled by the Low Moor Company. Unlike those parts of Bradford further north, which are depicted in local histories as essentially textile in character, our area was shaped and dominated until the beginning of World War II by miners and iron workers employed by the Low Moor Company. During these years this company claimed to be the producer of the best wrought-iron in the world and it appears that there were very few people who thought it worth while to dispute this assertion. Its reputation was such (and German wartime intelligence so poor – or it might have been just bluff?) that 'Lord Haw-Haw', in his propaganda broadcasts from Nazi Germany twenty years after the demise of the Low Moor Company, threatened to bring Britain to her knees by bombing the Low Moor Company! Even after World War II, local newspapers featured reports and letters in which the existence of Low Moor wrought iron sheets still in use on Chinese river boats and South American railways was recorded.

The history and achievements of the Low Moor Company have been exhaustively recorded in many sources, and Bradford Central Libraries have a collection of original documents. Here, I am really concerned only with the fluctuating fortunes of the Company as they affected the lives of the inhabitants of Storr Hill Side and Carr Lane.

In 1789 the Royds Hall estate with collieries and several farms was auctioned at the Sun Inn, Bradford, and it fell to Mr John Hardy for £33,220. Hardy was acting for a consortium which comprised the Rev. Joseph Dawson, minister of Idle Independent Chapel; Richard Hird, a woolstapler of Rawdon; John Jarratt of Little Horton, a draper; and himself, a solicitor of Horsforth. It was the reverend gentleman, Joseph Dawson, who realised that the estate was not only rich in coal but in iron-ore as well, and he became the first manager of the Low Moor Company. He moved first to Low Moor House and then to Royds Hall, where successive managers of the Company lived until 1928. We used to look over the wall and see Royds Hall house from a distance, through the trees, when we were young, but we had no idea at that time of any historical significance attached to it. The home farm behind it was more important and interesting to us, and the thing we all remember most is the cricket field a little distance away from the front of the house.

The Company was formed in 1790 and from 1795 to 1798 it turned out 2,000 tons of iron per year. When we went past the Harold Club and the old main entrance to the Company's Forge Yard, its original nucleus, on the trams on our way to school, we noticed casually and took for granted the two huge, old cannons which served as gateposts. We had no idea that they had been made in that yard for the Napoleonic Wars and dated back to 1794. They are now in Bradford's Industrial Museum.[2]

If one takes the 6" Ordnance Survey Map, drawn 1846-1850 and published 1852, and measures one square mile with the south side being the present Halifax Road, the SE corner being Odsal Top and the NW corner the top of Pickles Hill, that square mile shows 37 recorded pits, of which 24 are labelled 'Coal and Ironstone Pit'. Two special railway lines to Low Moor Iron Works cross this area. There were several of these lines linking the Company's pits with the works,[3] and, even in the 1930s, one might see a little old locomotive chugging slowly across Huddersfield Road at the top of Long Wall Side or crossing the bottom of Wilson Road just before it joined Wyke Lane. But such sights were rare by that time. The pit shafts were tiny when compared with those of modern mines, and it appears reasonable to assume that they had only a short working life. Of the thirty-seven mentioned above, nine only do not bear the prefix 'Old'. The

Company was already having to seek land for mining purposes to the south and east, a movement in the mining industry that has continued to this day. It also seems as though, at about this time, pit installations were becoming bigger and more comprehensive, perhaps to increase the effectiveness of the Company's private railways. Five of the active pits shown are closely grouped round the centre of Wibsey. Among these are the only two that are named on the map: North Field Pit and Acre Lane Pit.

Such a concentration of pits belonging to the Low Moor Company was equally dense for miles around. The truncated, circular, brick structures that remained of these old pits were familiar to us in our young days; one to the right near the top of the Monkey Steps, which led down to the Newbiggin from Wilson Road, always made me a little fearful and uneasy. Some of them had been filled in after a fashion. In some cases the filling had sunk and the Company had put a rough fence round the top, but it was not sufficient to keep out the more adventurous children and one or two lost their lives, because it was always on this forbidden ground that the most luscious blackberries grew. Carr Lane School and St. Mark's young men played football in a field on the left up Carr Lane. It was on this pitch that I and many others played our first proper team matches, proudly wearing a school jersey and real football boots. On p.22 of *Low Moor in Times Past*, there is a photograph of some men and women standing in a muddy field and looking down a hole in the ground. The accompanying text reads: 'In the background of the picture the large field still remains as Carr Lane Football Field, while the other fields are now occupied by Markfield Estate. It was during a match in the football field on January 31st 1948 that the ground opened to reveal one of the Low Moor Company's former coal pits, which was later found to be 190 feet deep.' This account does not mention that a young man had just crossed the ball before he fell down the hole which opened up under his feet, but he was saved by a balk of timber that had stuck some 20 feet down the shaft! On the map of 1852 there is the word 'Shaft' at just about the same place.

For my present purpose, the following paragraph from Dodsworth is important:

> Although the Low Moor Ironworks were a well-established industrial concern by the end of the [eighteenth] century yet the partners continued to run the estate, acting jointly as 'squires'; thus the manor court was held as usual, the joint lords of the manor fixing rents and making leases to their tenants for farm and

> pit workings. This feudal procedure (much of the common was still unenclosed) was kept until late in the following century and developed into that industrial paternalism that marked some of the great enterprises of British industry.[4]

Unlike many of the textile magnates, who mostly built mansions at some distance from their factories and operated through managers, the directors of the Low Moor Company lived locally, Dawson at Royds Hall, Hird at Low Moor House and Hardy at Odsal House. They remained in touch, in control and available.

This paternalism, in which John Hardy seems to have played the leading part, was evidenced throughout the nineteenth century. As early as 1851 it had 400 company-owned houses;[5] fifteen pubs[6] (in contrast to the principles of Sir Titus Salt!), and had founded and endowed three schools. (See chapter on Education.) Its workers and their families got free medical attention.

By this date, however, the Company was already having to look for new sources of coal and ironstone. While there were still large areas as yet unworked in Wibsey, and the Company was able to make good purchases in 1828 and 1831, it was now necessary to look further afield, and land was acquired at Beeston in the Leeds area as early as 1834. Land was bought in the Wyke area in 1838, when the Wyke Colliery was bought from the manor of Bierley. Over the next seventy years, it was in this area, Wyke, Scholes, Cleckheaton, Hartshead, that the Low Moor narrow-gauge railway was developed.[7] The pits that we heard of in conversation from old miners of Storr Hill Side, lay along this 'tramline', as it is called on the 6" Map: Westfield Pit, Drake Pit, Coates Pit, Chairbarrows (they pronounced it 'Cheerbarrows') and Hartshead. The other pit of which we heard that was not on this line was Norwood Green Pit, which, after a brief interval, continued working until into the fifties. Thus, the mining of this combination of Better Bed Coal and Black Bed Ironstone started its southward journey, and I am told that the same seam is now being mined in the Barnsley area.

It was this development, the move of the supply of the right kind of coal to the south, that accounted for the enormous expansion of our neighbourhood after 1850. Storr Hill Side lay between the Old Works, the New Works and the new and larger pits. Of the 293 houses featured in my analysis of the 1881 Census Returns, only about 50 appear on the 6" Map of 1852.

As is often the case, an industrial enterprise, like a culture or civilisation, is at the height of its wealth and power when its competitive, commercial, creative strength is beginning to fade. The Low Moor Company had made pipes for the new gas industry since the 1820s; it had profited from the developments in railways and marine engineering; and when required it made armaments for the British forces. Its output of finished iron goods in 1835 was 21,600 tons per annum, and in 1836 it was found necessary to open new works on the Newbiggin site with two new blast-furnaces capable of producing 70-80 tons each per week.

In 1860 it was still working 51 pits, 16 of them being 'open work' pits. Nineteen of these were still at Wibsey and no doubt employed some miners from Storr Hill Side and possibly, a little later, my grandfather from Great Horton. Acreage in Wyke had been extended and pits near Brighouse were being worked by 1862. From 1858-1870 the Company was working some of the Farnley Iron Co.'s reserves at Beeston. In 1863 the work force totalled 3,600, composed of 1,993 miners, 770 forgemen, 420 furnacemen, 323 engineers and 94 agents and miners.

But its methods and plant were becoming more and more out of date. It had failed to profit from the introduction of mild steel after about 1855 and had to charge for its plate iron two to three times the price of mild steel. It was buying in coal at 16*s*.5*d*. per ton against its own production at 14*s*. In spite of all this, government departments were still important customers, and the Company continued on something approaching its old scale until the First World War. Indeed, during that war profits from shells exceeded the annual surplus of the works for any year since 1888.

The end was not far away. In November 1919 the Low Moor works were amalgamated with the larger firm of Robert Heath & Sons, of Biddulph Valley Ironworks. The prospectus was designed to make it look as though the Low Moor Company was taking over Heath's, but in fact it was the other way round, and the Low Moor Company had to be heavily subsidised from Biddulph. A large consignment of Yorkshire bars was sent back from Canada, as not being up to standard. In 1928 a receiver was appointed, from whom Thos. Ward bought the firm. They closed down all the mines at Leeds, Wyke and Bradford, and 36 miles of the Company's narrow-gauge railway were dismantled.

The demise of the Low Moor Company and the almost total disappearance of working miners on Storr Hill Side between the wars was not merely a local phenomenon; it was part of the national pattern. After the war, as Marion Yass says:

> French, German, Dutch, Belgian and Polish mines not only recovered but were modernised. Equipment in the British mines – as in

> the mills – was older and less efficient. Production was slow and expensive. Annual coal exports between the wars averaged less than half the pre-war figure. By 1925 one quarter of British miners were out of work.[8]

From the point of view of my own recollections, the important thing is that those two 70 ft. blast furnaces of 1892 at New Works (we always called it the Newbiggin), which produced a grade that commanded a price two and even three times the price of ordinary pig-iron, remained in blast under the differing vicissitudes of the firm until 1936, when the last pig-iron was made at Low Moor. When they were in blast, even though my room faced away from the Newbiggin, I needed no light to get into bed; the glow gave a bit of mystery and romance to the usually unwelcome termination of play. Anyway, we had electricity in the house by the time they closed down and reading in bed had become possible!

Between the wars there were so many middle-aged men on Storr Hill Side with apparently no occupation, standing in groups talking, passing a Woodbine from one to the other, lounging in shirt-sleeves on their door-steps, making a drink last a long time in a pub, that we as youngsters never knew how they had been employed. Even now, and after consultation with my old friends, I am unable to say what some men on Elizabeth Street did or had done for a living. But, we agree that there were at least three men, possibly four, colliers on Elizabeth Street who never had regular work in the pit between 1920 and 1940. They lived on the dole, eked out by odd jobs and the earnings of their wives and children. Among the older people on Storr Hill Side the expression 'on t' Lloyd George' was frequently heard. This derived from Lloyd George's great fight of 1911 to secure some form of national insurance for the workers.

The colliers suffered much more severely than the textile operatives. As I have said, not only were the seams relatively narrow and uneconomical in our district, and not only was there a drop in the general demand for coal as export outlets were closed, but in addition, the Low Moor Company was being run down as a major producer of wrought iron and its pits were no longer as necessary as before to produce high grade coking coal for its hearths and furnaces. For several years after the First World War there was work to be had in the Low Moor Company's forge yard. They no longer worked shifts, though, and the Patent Hammer's licence to open at six a.m., to serve the night-shift as they came off, was no longer necessary. Frank Hall, who lived on Elizabeth Street, had been a turner at the Forge, but, as a result of the General Strike, he never worked at his own trade again after that. His brother Harry, who lived next door with their father, was luckier. He continued to earn good money as a clerk for the Low Moor Company and eventually owned some houses. Some, but not many, colliers got labouring jobs in the mill or other jobs, both skilled and unskilled.

One collier, who got occasional work in the pit, and whom we used to see shovelling in a ton of free coal from time to time, got a nasty spot on his hand while at work which refused to heal up properly. The thought that it was malignant and that he would never be able to work again so preyed on his mind that he threw himself down a deep well in a neighbour's hen-pen and drowned himself. His grown-up son repeatedly threw a rope down to him but he ignored it.

The climax of the colliers' unhappiness came with the General Strike of 1928. One of my earliest memories – I was aged four at the time – is of being taken for a walk by my mother into what we called The Big Wood (Royds Hall Great Wood on the map of 1852). This is a steep and narrow ravine with the stream, Judy Beck, at the bottom for most of its length. We walked up The Mountain, the steep rise on the Norwood Green side that had been cleared of trees during the First World War. People said that this had been done to fire the Low Moor Company's furnaces during the war. Perhaps to make charcoal? The steepest bank of the whole ravine was just opposite us, and I can remember seeing two men standing on a flat ledge which, as I decided when I was a good bit older, was about ten feet above the level of the beck. There was a hole in the hillside, perhaps 2ft. square, and one of the men held the end of a rope which issued from this hole. All of a sudden the two men started to haul on the rope and, after what seemed to be quite a long time, a tin bath full of small coal emerged. There was probably a small pile of coal nearby from previous bathfuls, but I didn't notice that because I had realised that the bath must have been filled by a man working under that enormous weight of hillside and I was terrified at the thought of what would happen to him if the tunnel caved in.

These men were probably anticipating a serious shortage of coal for domestic purposes, should the strike last long. They were not the only ones who reacted to the same idea. People who owned an acre or two of land sometimes had a shaft sunk on their land by 'blackleg' miners in the hope of eventually taking advantage of a black market in coal. One such was sunk behind what we called 't' big 'aas', Cambridge House, on the low side of Worsnop Buildings down Storr Hill. Frank had just started work at the age of fourteen and remembers vividly how some orthodox, striking, miners came and threw the primitive pulley on a tripod, some picks, shovels and a wheelbarrow that was lying at the top of the shaft, down on to the men working below. Frank was afraid that they would never get up again! *Plus ça change*! – the miners of the Midlands and the North were divided in much the same way during the last decade. With the same intention, also during the General Strike, coal was got from a gallery driven into the steep escarpment below Rawson Street on which Herbert Dickinson had his smallholding.

So much for coal, iron and the Low Moor Company. The other industry which dominated the economy of Storr Hill Side was the textile industry, as will be clear from my analysis of the 1881 Census. In this analysis I have not itemised the different occupations within the industry of the people recorded, although they are recorded in the Returns for the most part, but have been content to designate spinners, weavers, combers, drawers, winders, sorters, etc. as 'mill-workers'. Nor have I listed the different textile products on which they were engaged at the time, as this might change more or less frequently for some of them. At the time, Bradford was recognised as the world headquarters of the trade in wool and the manufacture of worsted cloth. The latter was, however, a very wide category of different cloths, defined by Cudworth[9] as follows: 'The term *worsted* is applied to all wool fabrics which in the process of manufacture are not fulled after being woven, whether it be confined to the product of the long staple or mixed with cotton, silk, or other textile material.' It was precisely the development of new methods by which stronger and, often, cheaper yarns, such as cotton, silk, alpaca, mohair, etc. could be combined with long-staple wool by astute and adventurous Bradford mill-owners that resulted in the enormous expansion and prosperity of Bradford in the second half of the nineteenth century. The word 'worsted' derives from Worste(a)d (the place of wool), a little town in Norfolk.

The following brief history of the worsted trade in Bradford in the nineteenth century is culled largely from Cudworth's excellent little book. It is intended merely as explanatory background to the presence on Storr Hill Side of 167 worsted mill operatives out of a total population of all ages of 1,353. The percentage is higher when one remembers that of this total 11.5% were aged 50 and over while 32.8% were aged 14 and under; it works out at 2 out of 9 of the working population in a neighbourhood that was essentially geared to coal and iron.

The first steam-driven textile factory in the town of Bradford was built in 1800 in Thornton Road. This was a spinning shed and it was followed in 1801 by another and in 1902 by yet another in Horton Lane. 1826 saw the introduction of the first power looms and in 1827 the first combing machines. Workers' opposition to the introduction of machinery, culminating in the Luddite Riots, did not leave Bradford and district unscathed. The attack on Rawfold's Mill, Liversedge, so vividly described in Charlotte Bronte's *Shirley* and the murder of the mill-owner, John Horsfall, on Crosland Moor testify to this. According to Cudworth: 'For these diabolical outrages, seventeen persons, including the three murderers of Mr. Horsfall, were hung in York and many were transported for life.'[10]

From Cudworth's account it is clear that the enormous expansion and prosperity of Bradford and district in the subsequent decades was the result of inspired application to the production of yarn by new combing and spinning methods, which allowed the exploitation of fibres previously thought to be either unmanageable or uneconomical. It was the several combinations of cotton, long-staple wool, alpaca, mohair and silk that produced 'Worstedopolis' as Cudworth knew it, and as we knew it in our young days. 'Cotton warps were introduced into Bradford in 1834, and produced a revolution in the manufacture of the district. From this point may be dated the most rapid growth, both of the trade and the town.'[11] Previously the manufacture of Bradford had been a 'pure manufacture' – the fabrics were alike in warp and weft. The traditional stuffs, based on the long staple of pure merino wool, had been, on account of the scarcity of the raw material, too expensive for all but the very wealthy.

The first commercial consignment of Australian wool to this country amounted to 167 lbs in 1811. In 1850 it totalled 39,018,221 lbs and in 1880, the crop that our operatives of the 1881 Census would be working on, the amount was 300,240,128 lbs. In 1811 the home crop of wool amounted to 138,574,672 lbs, of which 14,076,300 lbs was exported as raw wool, leaving 124,498,372 lbs for home consumption. The total for 1800 had been 83,040,000 lbs![12]

Here are some further statistics as explanatory background to our worsted operatives of Storr Hill Side. They are the figures for the whole of the United Kingdom, but are more applicable to Bradford and District than to anywhere else in the country.[13]

The Value of Imports of Woollen and Worsted Yarns:

1865 £ 998,784
1870 £1,635,154
1880 £1,842,135
1890 £1,935,061

1900 £2,163,873
1910 £2,795,574

The Value of Exports of British Manufactured Woollen and Worsted Yarns:

1865 £5,429,504
1870 £5,182,926
1880 £4,222,693
1890 £5,260,925
1900 £6,123,349
1910 £9,046,394

The Value of Imports of Manufactures of Wool:

1865 £1,910,758
1870 £3,096,257
1880 £7,079,848
1890 £7,938,918
1900 £8,504,782
1910 £5,653,321

The Value of Exports of Woollen and Worsted Goods Wholly or Partly Manufactured:

1865 £26,669,636
1870 £27,664,051
1880 £23,934,541
1890 £29,175,898
1900 £25,946,037
1910 £42,659,823

The value of imported Mohair, Alpaca, Vicuna, etc. rose from £715,000 in 1860 to £1,409,000 in 1875 and to £2,158,000 in 1910.

Parallel to these trade figures, the population of Bradford (Allerton, Bowling, Bradford proper, Eccleshill, Heaton, Horton and Manningham) rose from 73,210 in 1841 to 156,280 in 1871. With the incorporation of Thornbury and Tyersal (1882), Allerton (1882), North Bierley, Tong and Thornton (1899), the population had risen to 279,767 in 1901. In ten years, from 1871 to 1881, the population of Wyke, then not yet incorporated into Bradford, rose from 4,186 to 5,315. About three-quarters of the houses of Storr Hill Side shown on the 1908 25" Ordnance Survey map, which is the basis of my general maps, had been built between 1850 and 1880. Cudworth, writing in 1876, observes, 'It is about Wyke Common, and towards that portion known as New Roadside, that the greatest increase has taken place in working-class dwellings.'[14] The populations of Wyke and Low Moor are not included in the figures for Bradford as they formed part of North Bierley, which was not incorporated into Bradford until 1899.

Given that workers of the 1880s were prepared to walk two miles and more each way to and from work – and work a ten-hour shift in between! – the following mills could have provided employment for our mill-hands of the 1881 Census: Bateman Mills (which became Rigby's Wire Works) opened 1777; Coll Mills, Odsal Top, 1825; Folly Hall, Wibsey, 1836; Victoria Mills, Low Moor, 1845 (occupied by Hind's in 1854); Buttershaw Mills 1852; Wilson's, New Works, 1855; Fountain Reid, Oakenshaw, 1862; Perseverance Mills, Wibsey, 1873; Slack Side, Wibsey, 1873; Ben Wright, Wibsey 1865.[15] The nearest mill to Storr Hill, Morton's, started trading in 1903; Carter's at Low Moor in 1910. Quite a bit later Calverley's Mill was built on what had been the Wyke Tide Field, behind the Zion Chapel that became the Wyke Hippodrome Cinema. Further down Huddersfield Road there were Pepper Lee's, Goodman Abbot's, Benson Turner's and, still well within a two-mile radius, the famous Firth's carpet mills at Bailiff Bridge.

The nearest mills to where we lived were Hind's Mill up High Fernley and the mill on Mayfield Terrace, called by us the City Shed, which had also been founded by the Hind family but belonged to Berglas Brothers in our day and is labelled as a silk mill on the map of 1908. The Hind family played a leading role in the textile trade in our part of Wyke. According to Percy Nudds's rather garbled account,[16] the family had started business in Tyersal and then had moved to the Victoria Mill in Low Moor, about 1854. Nudds then claims that 'according to James Parker's book a company was formed in 1867 at Wyke called the Wyke Mill Co. This company built the first mill for the carrying on of the textile trade in Wyke.' Parker, in a paragraph dated February 1904, gives details of the recent launching and financing of a company to be known as John Hind & Co at Wike Mills which is to supersede the business of silk manufacturing 'hereto before carried on by I. (Irvine) Hind at Wike Mills'.[17] None of our sources locates the Wyke Mills mentioned in all of them. There follows a disjointed account of the business activities of the various members of the Hind family. The City Shed, he claims, was built by Fred Hind in 1899, but the mill up High Fernley, which stood on the site where High Fernley First School now stands, is not mentioned in his account. There is no doubt, however, about the accuracy of his statement that 'The Hind family were held in high regard and esteem in the village of Wyke, not only as model employers but as kind-hearted gentlemen.'

The range of fabrics manufactured appears incredible to us today. Cudworth lists and describes: the older fabrics having the same wool warps and wefts: bays, says, shalloons and serges; these, along with the soft yarn goods like Coburg merinos, gave way to the hard, shiny, mixed goods (i.e. different yarns in warp and weft) about 1850. 'At this period of manufacturing development all the tendencies appeared to be in the direction of harsh, or, as it was called, "aske" feel or handle, with metallic lustre.'[18] Of these 'Orleans' was a piece-dyed fabric, in imitation of the more expensive Alpaca and Brilliantine cloths. Cotton was not only used for warps; poplin 'competed very strongly with goods of a more expensive but similar character manufactured in Roubaix . . . and made up handsomely in the dress.' He goes on to describe balerno, cashmere and repp, all terms which we heard frequently from the women of our families without understanding them. There were special materials for worsted coatings (we wore a lot of this stuff both for coats and suits when young), for trouserings, linings, what was called stockingette for jerseys or bodices for ladies; there were Albert serges and Victoria twills and ulster cloth 'for ladies' mantles'. For anybody interested in materials or fashion Cudworth's review of Bradford trade from *c.* 1840 to *c.* 1890 is a revelation.[19]

In a directory of Chester and North Wales for 1874[20] a certain Edward Smith, Milliner and Dressmaker of 36 High Street, Wrexham has a full-page advertisement tastefully laid out in a great variety of fonts in the manner of the day. Part of this advertisement has the following contents:

> The Family Mourning Department is replete with the Newest Fabrics of the most approved manufacture, dyed by Ripley's Patent, and includes: Coburgs, French Twills, French Merinos, Dress Russells, Pat. Wp. Paramattas, Silk Wp. Paramattas, Pat. Wp. Baratheas, Balmoral Crepes, Demi Lustres, Alpaca Lustres, Persian Cords, Arabian Cords, Sedan Cords, Reversible Cords, Crapes, &c. This Patent secures great fulness and Durability of Colour, and being free from oil does not retain dust.

In spite of the exotic names and the foreign provenances indicated, it is a safe bet in the light of Cudworth's account that almost all of these fabrics, with the exception of those of French provenance,[21] were made in Bradford and district. 'Ripley's Patent' is perhaps more interesting. Frank's first job (1926) was at Ripley's Dyeworks (Bowling Dyeworks, then part of the Bradford Dyers' Association – BDA) and there was still a special 'shop' in these works devoted to this patent. It had been patented in the first place because these dyes were based on the revolutionary new substance of those days, aniline.

There were other dyeworks much closer to Storr Hill Side: Sharp's,[22] the RNO[23] and the BDA all had works within easy walking distance, and, from what we remember of the occupations of our neighbours and acquaintances in the 1920s and 1930s, this branch of the textile trade seems to have remained active in the district for some time after the others were in decline.

I have devoted so much attention to the local textile industry because, unlike the Low Moor Company, it survived, although in a modified form, well into our own day and was the one common ground of the whole population. It would be safe to say that, although there were undoubtedly individuals (like ourselves!) who had no experience of working in a mill, there was no family without at least one such member. Especially among the women, there was scarcely a conversation in our younger days in which there was no mention of mills and mill-work, be it Minnie D –'s new job at 'Old Johnny's' (the vernacular name for John Robertshaw's Coll Mills), or what they were paying weavers at the City Shed, or what shoddy stuff they were turning out at another. This took place with such casual familiarity of reference that the outsider never could follow the full story; it remained a closed book to us outsiders. My own memories, gathered when I was sent with a message on behalf of a neighbour to one of the nearest mills, are of the tremendous clatter of picking-sticks, the oily smell of wool and the frantic bustle of machines, belts and countershafts. Against the blur of all this, human figures in working clothes moved with machine-like, detached preoccupation. It was only when one of them came to the door to see what your errand was that you realised that they were normal human beings who made sense to you. One of our operatives of the 1881 Census was a 'worsted mill furnace stoker', others were 'engine tenters', etc., and there were still people doing exactly the same jobs in the same boiler-rooms fifty years later. When you were taken into a 'boiler-'oil' by a relative who had a message for the boiler man – or simply felt like a little gossip – the heat that came out of the open doors of the big Lancashire boilers was frightening to a child, but down the side of the boiler was a nice place to be on a frosty day. In those days the heavy coke-fumes meant nothing to children brought up in houses heated by unlimited coal and, very often, lighted by gas. After World War I, a bigger proportion of the men worked in the mill than are indicated in the 1881 Census Returns. The wives of miners and ironworkers had encouraged sons to go into the mill, as it was a far more respectable and clean job while paying almost as well as getting coal or working at the forge.

It will be noted that these were not the only occupations available to the population of Storr Hill Side in the nineteenth century, although they accounted for the vast majority of the working population. The particular sample of the 1881 Census returns that I have analysed above shows a surprising absence of dye-works operatives, railway workers and brick makers. Writing some five years before the Census quoted above, Cudworth[24] says: 'As to employment, there is abundance for the male portion of the community, chiefly in the numerous collieries with which the countryside is honeycombed, and at Low Moor Ironworks. Then there are Messrs. J. & J. Sharp's dyeworks at Pickle Bridge, Messrs. Stott's cotton works at Bailiffe Bridge, Messrs. Sellers' card works, the brick works of Messrs. Birkby, &c.' There follows yet another vague reference to the business activities of the Hinds, followed by something we had never heard of: 'Another limited company established in 1870 the Waterworks, the supply being obtained from the Bradford Corporation.'[25] We never heard mention of this, nor of the manner of payment; it would, however, be just in time to profit from the enormous expansion of Storr Hill Side.

The staple occupations on Storr Hill Side, mining, iron-production and textiles, remained almost as reflected by the 1881 Census down to the First World War. There were minor economic depressions, some short time periods and some industrial unrest before the war, and the Bradford wool trade had already adapted to a new pattern of operation; they now concentrated on buying and selling wool and similar fibres from all over the world, combing and spinning them and sending them back to all corners of the world ready for weaving. This was not enough to change the patterns of life and employment in our neighbourhood; there was still a lot of weaving carried out in the local mills. It was after 1920 that the real depression had effect, and I include here, as a background and framework to the twenties and thirties on Storr Hill Side, some events and statistics describing the national situation. These are culled mainly from the pages of Marion Yass.[26]

Although cotton had been the most important textile export in 1913, when Britain had provided 65% of the world's textiles, the share of the Bradford wool trade amounted to enormous sums of money and was by far the largest field of employment in our area. During the war, while Britain continued to over-produce on out-dated machinery and with out-dated processes and use of labour, Japan and India invested in modern cotton machinery, and on the continent of Europe industrialists were much quicker to modernise and extend their production of wool and synthetic fibres than was the case in the West Riding. Although there was a great boom immediately after the war, because everybody wanted new clothes, blankets and furnishing materials, this was over by 1921 and nearly one-third of British mill-workers found themselves without jobs and many more were on short time.

Yass proceeds:[27]

> By December, 1920 over 800,000 men had lost their jobs. The figure rose to over a million in January and had doubled to more than two million by July 1921. The 1920 extension of the unemployment benefit scheme introduced for demobbed soldiers was quite inadequate to meet this situation. Although it covered twelve million people earning under £250 a year, it did not touch domestic servants or agricultural workers. Moreover, the scheme now became contributory, which meant that those unemployed who had not contributed got nothing. Weekly payments were made to cover the benefits of 15*s*. (75p) a week for a man and 12*s*. (60p) for a woman. Worst of all, benefit could only be claimed for fifteen weeks in any one year. The scheme had not been designed to alleviate anything but short-term unemployment. In 1921 provision had to be made for men to continue to draw benefit after they had used up their fifteen weeks allowance. This benefit was paid by local Poor Law Guardians, not by the government, so that pressure was naturally greatest on those local authorities in poorer areas who could least afford to pay the benefits. It became known as 'the dole'. Being 'on the dole' soon came to mean merely being unemployed.

In the textile industry there was some unemployment and a lot of short-time; three days a week was common. It all depended on the order-book. Many, like Frank in the dye-works, might work a week or two and then be on the dole for a couple of months. Most textile firms had what were called in the vernacular 'laikin lists', operatives who could be laid off or put on short time as the occasion demanded. Certain groups, overlookers, youths and girls from the ages of 14 to 18, for instance, were not on the 'laikin list'. But there was no closing down of factories and all the old divisions of the industry remained well represented in the area. There were still working weavers, carpet-weavers, spinning hands, rovers, tenters, carders, wool-combers, woolsorters, burlers and menders and dyers living on Storr Hill Side, but the number engaged in full-time, regular work was much reduced. On the whole, factories were employing fewer hands, and this was not due to any appreciable degree to improvements in the technology of the trade; also, many young people in their teens were staying longer at school than had been the case in 1881. In addition, as our analysis of the history of Perseverance Street shows, there was a marked decline in the numbers of the population, especially of youths and girls under twenty.

We remember people from our neighbourhood working at the following places of employment between the wars: New Biggin Blast Furnaces and the Low Moor Best Yorkshire Iron Co., the remains of the Low Moor Company and, on the old premises of the Low Moor Company Forge, Low Moor Steel Alloys Ltd. The following mills still offered employment, although perhaps to a reduced work-force and with some short-time periods: Buttershaw Mills, John Robertshaw's at Odsal, the Band Mill at Oakenshaw, Hind's Mill up High Fernley as well as their old mill on Mayfield Terrace, known as the City Shed, then owned by Berglas Bros.; Pepper Lee's, Goodman Abbot's and Benson Turner's further down Wyke; Morton's Mill in Carr Lane; the Carpet Mill, Firth's at Bailiffe Bridge and the mill behind the Brown Cow, near Wyke Hippodrome Cinema, Calverley's Mill. The above were of importance to the people of Storr Hill Side, notwithstanding the opportunities of employment offered at a greater distance by improved means of transport. The Low Moor Company and these mills had special associations for them, for many of those working there in the thirties had followed parents and possibly grandparents as well as neighbours and other relatives. They had often been found their jobs by people whom they had known all their lives and whose presence while at work denoted a kind of security and help. Before the pattern of local employment had been totally changed by efficient and cheap public transport, Generations I and II had worked at these places, walking both ways and many of them coming home for dinner at midday. They were part of the very fabric of the community.

The same applied to Rigby's wire mill, near Holy Trinity Church, Birkby's Brick Works down Wilson Road, Low Moor Station and its Locomotive Sheds, dye-works like Sharpe's and Hunsworth Dyeworks, both B.D.A. concerns, and the R.N.O. Dyeworks at the far end of Town Gate. Other places of employment, although some of them might employ no more than half a dozen hands, were: Airedale Electric Co., the Oakenshaw Filter Beds, the Chain Bar Rope Works, Marks' Chemical Works down Wyke Lane, from which men came home with bright yellow faces from the picric acid used there, the maintenance of Parks and Playing Fields, Ramsden's Corn Mill and the haulage firm of Ernest Bailey, founded before World War I.

We can remember people on Storr Hill Side who worked in the mill as their parents and grandparents had done. My grandmother Shaw had been a burler and mender, and both her daughters became burlers and menders. In the thirties my mother, Annie, tried to bring in a few shillings more by having pieces to mend in our house. The only large dining table we had was pushed under the front window and the piece lay on the floor between the window wall and the table legs. Mother pulled it foot by foot towards herself, across the table while her trained eyes spotted every missing thread, every snag and every slub. All these were rectified by hand. Sometimes a single thread had to be put in under and over, under and over, like a process of invisible mending for half the length of the piece. Faulty threads of all kinds were removed with pointed tweezers called burling irons, made of fine steel, hardened and tempered. I still have a small pair which belonged to my mother. But this work did not last long as her health could no longer cope with it. Four or five burlers and menders in a relatively small room, anywhere with roof-lights, working on commission, were relatively common. The upper story above John Foster's workshop was one and the room above the Crown Stores was another. I remember quite vividly the scenes that occurred when she took me to buy clothes and a salesman tried to tell her that the composition of the cloth was of such and such a quality when she knew full well that it was not. On such occasions she was Seth's daughter, all four foot ten of her!

Morton's Mill, up Carr Lane, started trading in 1903, and continued to weave worsteds in the same mill down to the Second World War. John Morton had acquired the land to the south of his mill, nearer to the nucleus of Carr Lane, and decided to extend his mill onto this land during the thirties. Seth worked alone on this job, laying bricks when it suited him, for quite a few years, for there was no urgency. Trade was slack and

John Morton was banking either on a revival of the wool trade or on an advantageous sale of his premises. When the war came, the extension was finished in a hurry and occupied by English Electric, working at high pressure on war-work. For a few years after the war this situation continued, textiles in the older part and engineering in the new part. At present, in the old part, kits of car accessories are made up, while greetings cards are manufactured in the new part. The fairly large car park is always full during working hours; no factory draws the whole of its labour force, nor even the majority, from the immediate vicinity nowadays. None of the mills mentioned above is still manufacturing except Benson Turners in Lower Wyke, and, of course, it is no longer woollen cloth that they produce.

On what we called the dross hills, because there the Low Moor Company had tipped enormous, craggy loads of clinker and slag from its furnaces, there is now an industrial estate devoted in the main to the warehousing of chemicals. On part of the old nucleus of the Low Moor Company there is a firm making specialised alloy steels: Low Moor Fine Steels. Not far away is a firm called K. V. Engineering; and also quite near is an aluminium scrap-yard. There is a depot of British Road Services nearby. Almost opposite the site of the old Patent Hammer, there is a yard which supplies reclaimed stone, of which there must have been thousands of tons available when the district went into decline. All this is on the flat land between the bottom of Storr Hill, starting in the old Carr Lane Tide Field, and stretching northwards as far as the Guide Post.

The sample I offer in the form of the residents of Perseverance Street gives a clear picture of the decline of manufacturing on Storr Hill Side. In 1987 the residents comprised: 3 widows living alone; 3 retired couples, and one pair of retired spinsters, a retired butcher and a retired welfare nurse; 2 textile workers and a carpet-weaver; 3 motor-mechanics and a lorry driver; a building contractor, a builder, a builder's mate and a plumber; a social worker (man), a nurse, a child-minder, a school-cleaner; a representative for a paper firm and another driving a van; a man and wife who run a fish shop situated some seven miles away; a part-time shop assistant and a part-time office worker. In addition there are 5 housewives who do not go out to work and 9 children of school age or under.

Looking back, it seems to me that the alleviating factors on Storr Hill Side during the depression of the twenties and thirties were as follows:

1. Unlike the centre of Bradford, Wyke had so many different enterprises manufacturing a wide variety of textile goods. If one mill had to lay

people off because there was a pause in the demand for its products, there would often be another not far away that was setting on a few hands.

2. The technical side of all the traditional occupations of the area had developed and there was a new demand for both manufacturing and maintenance engineers as well as for electricians. Public transport in the shape of trains, buses, trams and trolley-buses provided many skilled jobs – and all of them required unskilled labourers. Cars and lorries were beginning to make their mark, and although the Crown Garage employed only the owner and his apprentice, it was a sign of things to come. A number of small engineering workshops started on contract work and the Airedale Electric firm at the top of Carr Lane, where Laurence served his apprenticeship, was also a new employer. One notable feature of the 1881 Census is the relative absence of railway workers; one would have expected more in the light of the importance of Low Moor Station as a major junction in the West Riding network.[28]

3. In addition to the various kinds of public transport themselves offering labour, there is also the fact that, through its help, people were able to accept jobs much further away than could their parents and grandparents. For forty years my father travelled on trams and buses to his work in Thornbury, which required a change of vehicle in the centre of Bradford. Likewise, Frank Wilkinson was able to accept a job at Ripley's Bowling Dyeworks at the age of fourteen in 1926.

4. There was also plenty to occupy the minds and bodies of the poor and unemployed. They were not penned up in dingy, filthy hovels in dreary dark streets as they are normally represented in accounts of the depression in the industrial north.

Almost all of us on Storr Hill Side lived within 150 yards of open, green land, and everybody who so wished and possessed a modicum of understanding could keep poultry, sometimes geese and pigs, or grow vegetables and soft fruit on an allotment. Their ventures and products in these fields were something they could be proud of and they gave men and women subjects of conversation among one another which never palled. So, all in all, Storr Hill Side was spared the worst effects of the depression between the wars. They lived in straitened circumstances but were not poverty-stricken and demoralised. Most of them managed to retain their personal pride and dignity; they remained active and hopeful and they helped one another.

They really did help one another. Laurence, still in his mid teens, was made into a steward of the Low Moor St. Marks Sunday Schools' Sick Club. He sat for half an hour every Sunday before the school started taking the subscriptions of 1½*d*. per adult per week, and ½*d*. per week for children. They had to subscribe for a year before they were in benefit; they then drew 4*s*.6*d*. per week for 13 weeks and 2*s*.3*d*. after that. Children were paid 1*s*.9*d*. per week when sick. This was an organised bit of help involving money payments, but there were many other unofficial practices, small in themselves, which nevertheless reassured the recipients that they belonged to the neighbourhood and somebody had them in mind. A certain joiner, Herbert Ackroyd, who had helped with the building of our houses on Elizabeth Street and refused all payment, had to have a cock-chicken for his Christmas dinner as long as we kept poultry. Ephraim sometimes hefted on his hand a boiling fowl after he had killed it and said something like: 'Nay, A can't sell that. Tak' it on ta D–, 'is wife's nooan sa weel.' This spirit of neighbourliness survives. Early in 1990 Frank and May, aged nearly eighty, left Perseverance Street to go to an almshouse up Abb Scott Lane. A young wife from the new bungalows opposite their old house presented them with a cake as a farewell present and their new milkman up Abb Scott Lane gave them their first week's milk free!

In the following account of the wages and conditions of work on Storr Hill Side, I have concentrated on the local aspect and have tried to pay minimum attention to national and regional circumstances, which are well documented elsewhere.

Cudworth's account of the life of the miner and his family in the early days of the Low Moor Company, although long before the days of my Generation I, is very relevant. He describes lads of six and seven years having to be carried to work on the backs of their mothers, who also worked down the pits, and working from 7 a.m. to 6 p.m. with an hour's stoppage for lunch (if they got any!). For this, day in day out, week in week out, they received 1*s*.6*d*. to 2*s*. a week. A man's wages for getting the coal amounted to only 15*s*. for a full week. Conditions were even worse for the hurrier lads – 'Conditions were of a very different description from the well-drained and ventilated roadways of the present time' – and there were no tramways and no wheeled corves, but a kind of scoop that was pushed along by main force. He goes on to say that 'the coals were drawn up and landed by women, who worked "double shifts", their wages being about 7*s*. per week.'[29]

Mr Scriven's Report of 1842 on child labour in the collieries of the West Riding gives the age and physical details of hurriers in the Low

Moor Company's pits and of those in neighbouring pits of other proprietors, including 'Messrs. Akroyd and Co's New Road Side Pit'. He is particularly appalled to find young girls among them, although he lists none down the Low Moor Company's pits. I can do no better than quote a short sequence from his Report:

Item 102. 'Margaret Gormley (No. 9) says: I would rather set cards at 5*d*. a-day than work in pit.'

Item 103. 'Patience Kershaw (No. 26) says: I wear a belt and chain at the workings to get the corves out. The getters are naked except their caps; they pull off all their clothes. I see them at work when I go up. They sometimes beat me if I am not quick enough, with their hands; they strike me upon my back. The boys take liberties with me sometimes; they pull me about. I am the *only girl* in the pit. There are 20 boys and 15 men. All the men are naked. I would rather work in the mill than in the coal pit.'

Item 104. 'A deplorable object, barely removed from idiotcy [sic!]; her family receiving 2*l*. 19*s*. 6*d*. a week.'[30]

The facts and comments of Mr Scriven's Report, along with other such reports, must have touched the conscience of the government of the day sufficiently for them to pass an act forbidding the employment of women and girls underground in the very same year. To put these conditions into perspective: there is every possibility that the parents of some of my Generation I were among those listed by Mr Scriven.

According to Dodsworth, the wage bill of the Low Moor Company in 1851 was £1,800 weekly, with 3,000 hands on the payroll. Mr Wickham stated at this time that, although the average wage was 12*s*., a forgeman could earn as much as £6 while a skilled craftsman received £3 10*s*. Truly elite workers![31]

Wages and conditions were often worse for textile workers. Cudworth tells how, before his day, combing of the wool by hand was carried out on a domestic basis:

> It [combing] was formerly performed in the houses of the operatives – generally, indeed, in their bedchambers – and was all done by hand. It was necessary that the combs should be heated, and for this purpose they were placed in an earthenware stove, or 'pot', as it was called, which was kept at a high temperature by burning charcoal in it. The wool was oiled to render it more

> pliable. The vapours generated by the charcoal were deleterious in the extreme. Nor was the occupation hurtful to the bodily health merely. Dirt and stench produced moral as well as physical degeneracy; and the combers too often sought relief from the nausea of their work-rooms in the excesses of the ale-house.[32]

In Cudworth's time, a sorter, on piece work, earned 'about five shillings a pack or one farthing per pound for his work.'[33] When he comes to his own day, he cannot refrain from an enthusiastic comparison of the conditions and wages of the 1880s with the above: 'In other words, one combing machine turns off work equal to seventy-five hand combers. Men's wages vary from 15*s*. to 20*s*. per week, the former wages being given to old men who are not fit for other labour.' He is quite lyrical when he comes to describe conditions and pay in the spinning sheds of his own day: 'Under the provisions of the Factory Act, the spinning rooms are well whitewashed and ventilated; their ordinary temperature is the moderate and healthy one of 65. The calling is a clean and active one and secures the spinners (mostly girls) to be well fed and clothed. According to the age and excellence of the spinner the earnings average from four to nine shillings a week.'

The section devoted to wages, rents and housing of Bradford in the report of an enquiry by the Board of Trade in 1908[34] gives a clear and concise picture of the facts that interest us here. The weekly rate of wages, for an ordinary week in summer of 49½ hours, was for the following: bricklayers, masons and plumbers; fitters, turners, smiths, pattern-makers, platers, rivetters; cabinet-makers, french polishers, upholsterers and printing compositors, all skilled men, between 33*s*. and 38*s*. In the woollen industry, wages were noticeably lower; only wool-sorters, warp-dressers and twisters exceeded 30*s*., the highest being a possible 33*s*. by drawers. Weavers, spinners and combers earned markedly less, not exceeding 17*s*., but in the case of the last, this was probably a basic wage that was enhanced with piece-work. Compared with the 4*s*. to 9*s*. for spinners recorded by Cudworth in 1888, those of 1908 got 8*s*. to 11*s*. Labourers in the building trades earned 24*s*. 9*d*. and in the engineering trade 22*s*. to 24*s*.

In the building trades, the wages of skilled men are given an index of 83 compared with 100 in London, their labourers an index of 85; for the engineering trade the equivalent grades were 87 and 96; in the printing trade it was 85 for skilled men and in the furnishing trade 83.

The same report gives rents as 3*s*. to 4*s*. for a two-roomed back-to-back; 4*s*. to 5*s*. for a three-roomed house and 5*s*. to 6*s*. 6*d*. for a small 'through' house. No house prices are given; working men did not buy houses in 1908.

Retail prices of foodstuffs were: tea 1*s*. 6*d*. per lb; loaf-sugar was 2¼*d*. to 2½*d*. per lb. while demerara was 2½*d*.; the cheapest was something called 'moist' at 1¾*d*. Four grades of bacon were quoted, ranging from 'collar' at 5*d*. to 6½*d*. per lb. to 'roll' at 6*d*. to 9*d*. per lb. You could get 12 to 14 eggs for a shilling. American cheddar cheese was 6½*d*. per lb.; Colonial and Irish butter both sold at 1*s*. per lb., but Danish was 1*s*. 2*d*. Potatoes cost 2¾*d*. to 3*d*. for half a stone; household flour was 7½*d*. to 8*d*. half a stone; a four-pound loaf cost 5*d*.; milk was 3*d*. a quart; coal 11*d*. per cwt. and paraffin 7*d*.-8*d*. per gallon.

The economy of the country prior to World War I and just after remained remarkably stable. There were sufficient increases in prices to make my Generation I and early Generation II complain bitterly about the cost of living, but, seen from to-day, they appear negligible.

The earnings of factory workers between the wars varied enormously according to occupation and status. Frank started work in 1926 at the age of fourteen at Ripley's Bowling Dyeworks. He got up at 4 a.m., walked up Storr Hill to catch the first tram of the day at 5.20 a.m., got off the tram at the Carlton Cinema and walked along St. Stephen's Road to start at 6 a.m. His day's work finished at 6 p.m., when he did the same journey in reverse. For sixty hours a week in the factory, fifty-five of them working, he was paid the, for those days, very good wage of £2 2*s*. 6*d*. By comparison, Laurence started at fourteen, ten years later, at the Airedale Electric, where the day started at 7.15 a.m. and finished at 4 p.m. in winter (to save on lighting!) and at 4.30 p.m. in summer. He earned 10*s*. a week with a rise of 6*d*. every six months, and Jack Rhodes started in 1938 for 16*s*. 8*d*. per week. Men were getting up to £8 at Ripley's but only £2 to £2 10*s*. 10*d*. at the Airedale Electric. Jack's father, a miner, earned £1 18*s*. a week for a 40-hour week. Setting capstan lathes for the G.E.C. during the war, I received £8 5*s*. for working a night-shift of 61 hours when I had reached the age of 21, and appreciably less for doing exactly the same job before that. Wages were slow to rise after the war, and it was not until the mid-sixties that there was a great increase; I am told that somebody doing the job that I did at the G.E.C. now (1987) earns £210 per week.

By this time, there was usually a canteen at the place of work. At Ripley's there was a separate section for the staff. Laurence rates the canteens at both the Airedale and at Rigby's as 'decent, with sound, warm meals'. Nevertheless, most men took sandwiches and a 'mashin', i.e. tea and sugar in a tin box. Both Frank and Laurence were 'mashin' lads' in their early wage-earning days; their job was to collect the tea, sugar and pot from each man in advance, brew the tea and serve it during the dinner hour. Laurence can still remember the name of the man who took condensed milk as well as tea and sugar – just to complicate an already complicated job for a lad!

The canteen of a factory on essential war work was quite different; they enjoyed special catering rations, which meant that many men and women were able to eat, at a very reasonable price, meals at least as good, if not better, than they could get at home. We had an hour for a proper meal from midnight to one o'clock and a further break of half an hour at 4 a.m. Between the breaks the canteen staff baked delicious cakes, which we could eat warm during the short break!

At the beginning of my period, there were no facilities for washing in any works or mines, as far as I have been able to find out. There were no pit head baths and no place to hang their clothes when they stripped off to go down the pit. Even in the nineteen-twenties and thirties, it was possible to see men coming home in their pit clothes with their faces blackened with coal-dust. At home, all they had was the old tin bath in front of the fire and hot water ladled in with the piggin out of the fireside boiler. By this time, however, almost all factories and workshops had lavatories, but, on the whole they were kept in such a disgusting condition that a large proportion of the workers could not bring themselves to use them. Frank is convinced that toilets such as he saw at Ripley's were so disgusting that many workers there, by refusing to use them, induced serious complaints in later life. A rather decrepit pensioner was paid to look after them, which meant that they were always filthy. Laurence makes the point that it all depended on the age of the premises; in the Old Mill at Rigby's they were primitive in the extreme, but good in the New Mill. Helliwell's, a patent glazing firm at Brighouse, where he worked for a few weeks, had toilets which discharged into the beck outside. Sarannah, who, like Annie, always managed to have the last word, collected the excrement that she found in her coal on a little coal shovel and put it back on the coal-man's waggon the next time he called!

Chapter 3

Education on Storr Hill Side

Before and throughout my First Generation, the workers had, for the most part, learned their jobs and trades without the use of language. They observed and imitated what their master or their seniors did while performing some auxiliary, unskilled task for him. The farmer and farm-labourer had acquired the necessary skills and lore through always being on the spot from the day they could toddle. Likewise, the execution of the great engineering feats of the early and mid-Victorian age was carried out by men – smiths, foundrymen, machinists – who had learned by watching and the barest minimum of verbal instruction from masters who were themselves not very articulate. This applied not only to artisans and élite workers, every skilled man and woman learned their trade in this way: 'Mawe [author of an impenetrable manual on gardening] might have turned out a few excellent pruners but it is hardly surprising that most garden apprentices learned by watching the foreman or head gardener. Let loose to prune and tie-in by themselves, they then had their work inspected and were often made to undo and painstakingly re-tie to the head gardener's satisfaction.'[1] This is exactly what happened in the factories and workshops of the West Riding as late as the beginning of our century. It is tempting to think that the technological explosion of the last hundred years is the result of this system being allied to a highly developed use of language and theory in formal education. Whereas Napoleon, just like Hannibal two thousand years earlier, had to use animal traction to take an army over the Alps, the last hundred years of technological and scientific advancement have not only made man independent of animal traction but have enabled him to move freely in space and outer-space.

Of my Generation I on Storr Hill Side, the more intelligent learned from their parents, their teachers at Sunday School, later at primary school, but more often from their slightly older fellows, to measure and weigh things and check their wages. They could fix a right-angle by what Seth called 'threes, fours and fives', and he used to claim that a good navvy could dig out a cellar true to a quarter of an inch using only notches on his pick-handle and a line-band. As long as there were genuine wheelwrights working, probably even today, the length of iron bar needed to hoop a cart wheel was calculated by running a toothed wheel, like a large, metal pastry-cutter, round the assembled felloes rather than doing a difficult and, when done under working conditions, less accurate calculation with π.

But throughout the nineteenth century, local industry, like British industry as a whole, created more and more clerical and supervisory jobs for which efficient reading, writing and arithmetic were absolutely essential requirements. The outside world came much nearer as knowledge of the sources of materials, distant and foreign customers, and written contact with both of these became more and more necessary. From the evidence of marriage certificates in the local archives, it would appear that around 1860 slightly more young people were able to sign their names than were still making a cross. Seth's father, Shadrach, signed his name but his mother, Martha, made a cross.

As far as Storr Hill Side and the district around was concerned, significant provision for elementary education had been increasing throughout the nineteenth century. In this the Low Moor Company and the churches, Anglican as well as Nonconformist, sometimes acting together, had led the way.[2]

As early as 1791, the Low Moor Company built a low building in Abb Scot Lane (which, at the time of writing, was still standing and in use as two cottages) as a school for boys of the district. The boys worked during the week and only went to school on Sundays, but in addition to the Bible, the three R's were taught there. In 1821 the Wesleyans of Wibsey founded the Village School, which thrived under the headship of Mr Joseph Wright (not the great linguist!) from 1828 to 1861. Seth most likely had his early education at this school. James Parker, writing *circa* 1902, says 'it is now spoken of today as "Wright's School".'[3]

There were three schools connected with Holy Trinity Church in the nineteenth century: Central School, which we knew as 'Scott's School', deriving its popular name from a long-serving headmaster of the nineteenth century, was built by the Low Moor Company in 1814, and not closed until 1975, during the great reorganisation of education in the area that took place during the 1970s. I can remember playing football at the age of ten for Carr Lane School against Scott's on the Carr Lane field. The other schools were at Raw Nook and Hill Top. For the latter the Low Moor Company gave the land and built the school in 1846, intending it for infants only. It is still there, albeit not exactly on the same site, and now integrated into the comprehensive education system of the Bradford authority.

To come to our more immediate neighbourhood: Going down New Road Side, the side-streets on the right immediately after Bell Street were named School Place and School Street, but there was no sign of a school ever having been there, and when I started to enquire about these names not even the oldest native I consulted could explain them. The problem was solved by James Parker, like so many other problems of our local history. We knew the New Road Side Wesleyan Chapel, which stood at the corner of Perseverance Street and New Road Side, directly opposite the end of School Street, but we had no idea that it had once been a day school.[4] Sunday schools were of immense importance for the education of my Generations I and II, for most of them started when they were the only schools in the area and offered the rudiments of a general education.

Plate 4. Carr Lane School.

Carr Lane School,[5] a church school attached to St. Mark's Church, was built in 1863 and closed in 1962. This school was the link between myself and my helpers, as we were all at different times pupils there until the age of eleven and Frank had the whole of his schooling there, leaving at the age of fourteen. It is now a meat-packing warehouse, surrounded by barbed-wire entanglements. In the twenties and thirties the headmaster of Carr Lane School was Mr Frank Russell, who was so much part of the school for such a long time that, had he been the head in the nineteenth century, the school would most likely have acquired the name 'Russell's School'. Other teachers who taught us between the wars were: Miss Fletcher, Miss Butterworth (mentioned in Grace Carter's *Wiche is Wyke*),

Plate 5. Carr Lane School Boys, 1922.
Back row, l. to r. William Haley, Stanley Hopkinson, Reggie Terry, Fred Emmett. ? ?, ? ?, John Rowley.
Row 2: Miss Wilson, Cyril Britton, Ronnie Greenwood, Harry Wilkinson, Hubert Ormonroyd, ? Haley, Harry Wilkinson, William Hurley.
Row 3: Ivor Ormondroyd, Reg Cooper, Thomas Wilkinson, Harry Rackham, Ronnie Harker, ? ?, Harry Murphy, Sergeant Emmett.
Seated: Frank Wilkinson, Ernest Clough, Wilf Jones, Irvine Holdsworth, Edgar Mitchell, George Hollis.
Front row: Laurie Craven, Arthur Holdsworth, Jack Clarkson, Ernest Kellett, Willie Chapman, Harry MacLean, Irwin Barraclough.

Miss White, Miss Blowers, Mr Faulkner, and Mr Gill. I also remember a Miss Holdsworth in the Infants' School. Laurence and I started there together in 1927.

New Works School[6] was also built by the Low Moor Company in 1872 as an Infants' school for the children of workers at the Newbiggin and the New Forge. It was closed in 1885, when the teachers and children were transferred to Carr Lane. In 1886 it was re-opened as a girls' school with Miss Anne Briggs as headmistress. Miss Briggs remained at the school until 1913 and was a highly respected member of the community. My mother, Annie Shaw, was a pupil of Miss Briggs around the turn of the century. According to the rules of the school, which were listed clearly and precisely, each girl paid one penny every Monday morning.

At the other end of Wyke, towards Bailiff Bridge, the Moravian Brethren had founded a community and a church as early as 1753, and had offered a Sunday school and infants' school until the school attached to St. Mary's church was founded, which then assimilated the Moravian school. The school attached to Wyke Church, at Green Lane, founded in 1850,[7] and similar in status to Carr Lane, was rather too far away to affect us. In fact, I can't recall any acquaintance ever mentioning that he or she had attended it, although I must have known one or two. The little school at the corner of Worthinghead Road and Town Gate, which we always knew as Wyke Infants and which is now a Welfare Clinic, was opened in 1876.

The Bradford School Board seems to have made no effort to provide any other school for Wyke proper (i.e. near the nucleus of the old township represented by Town Gate) until 1902, which was the year in which the old School Boards were disbanded and the responsibility for education given over to the municipal authorities. James Parker, writing in 1904, says:

> The site for a new Board School at Wike was purchased in November 1901, of J. Harpin, at 5*s.* per square yard. 372 yards of this land has been purchased by the Bradford City Improvements Committee to widen the road at front of the school, at 5*s.* 3*d.* per yard. The total estimated cost of the School, including site is £19,170, for which amount a loan has been obtained at 3½ per cent. from the Prudential Assurance Company, repayable in 50 years.[8]

He then goes on to list the principal contractors and the amount of each contract. In an earlier book, he had announced the estimated cost as £12,500. This school was the most modern and best equipped school in

Plate 6. Carr Lane School Boys, 1933.

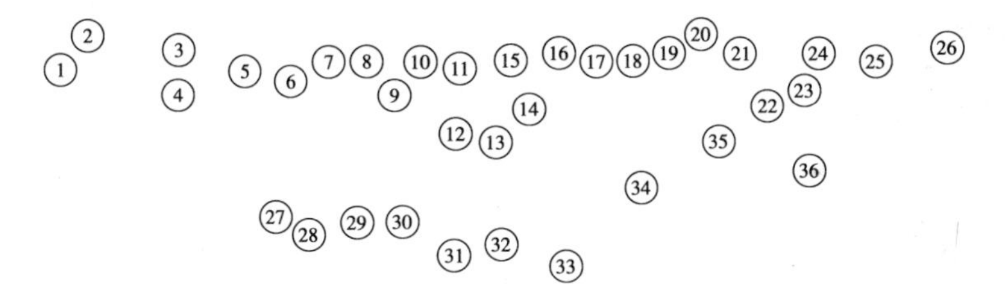

1. Jack Wainwright 2. ? ? 3. Jack Wormald 4. Tom Rowan 5. Bentham Cornwell 6. Jack Wilkinson 7. Fred Brayshaw 8. Roy Widdop 9. Douglas Fawcett 10. Laurence Barrett 11. Stanley Bower 12. Fred Murphy 13. Frank Spencer 14. Leonard Benn 15. Jack Garside 16. Eric Berry 17. Billie Lee 18. Edwin Petty 19. Leslie Crampton 20. Albert Bartle 21. Eric Metcalfe 22. Donald Barker 23. Frank Wheeler 24. Ronnie James 25. Herbert Mounsey 26. Kenneth Harker 27. Donald Wooler 28. Harold Worsnop 29. Norman Priestley 30. Frederick Lee 31. ? ? 32. Maxwell Vowells 33. Derek Hirst 34. Bud Sugden 35. James Firth 36. Reynold Summerscales.

the area in our day, underlining the difference made by the authorities between the financing of their schools and the independent and denominational schools. We always referred to it simply as 't' Booerd Skuil'.

When I first went to school, this Board School, Carr Lane School and Scott's (Holy Trinity Central School) were all-age schools. As a result of the Hadow Report of 1926, however, Carr Lane became a primary school, whose pupils left at the age of eleven either to go on to secondary education or to the Wyke Board School for the rest of their schooling. It took some time for the Hadow Report to be implemented in Bradford, and I think it was as late as 1932 before we at Carr Lane experienced the invasion of a lot of new pupils from Wyke Infants and the junior forms of the Board School and in turn lost our senior pupils to the latter. When I went to Belle Vue, Laurence went to the Board School, Wyke Modern School to give it its proper name. In accordance with the recommendations of the Hadow Report, the Modern Schools were expected to make the last three years of schooling for those who did not go on to secondary education more interesting and more applicable to their future working life. At Wyke they had half a day of Woodwork, two sessions of Science, instead of Arithmetic they now did Maths – even learning something about logarithms – and they had a properly equipped gymnasium in which to develop their muscles. Carr Lane had never catered for such things.

At all times, and especially in expanding industrial communities, there have been those who aspired to 'better themselves' and those who did not, and the people of Storr Hill Side were no exception to this. The brief outline I have given of the provision of education for Storr Hill Side and neighbourhood throughout the nineteenth century makes it clear that there was plenty of opportunity for my Generation I to learn their three R's. Whether they did so or not and, more important, whether they made use of and developed these skills in their jobs and/or their personal interests in later life, depended, as always, on the individual. These two opposing attitudes were well represented by my two grandfathers. Walter Armitage Barker could write his name and read simple things when need arose, but he had obviously been a most reluctant scholar and he avoided and pretended to despise all contact with the written word. This attitude was, in fact, the typical one of the miner, in whose ethos all ways of life other than his own and all jobs other than that of getting coal were soft and effete. Seth, on the other hand, having an acute, enquiring turn of mind, made great practical use of and took pleasure in reading and writing within the scope of his own interests.

Seth read the newspapers regularly and understood most of what he read. Ephraim used to pick up a *Telegraph & Argus* as he came through Bradford on his way home from work. He would read his bits on the tram and a little after tea, until he fell asleep in the easy chair. It would then be passed on to my mother, but, by seven o'clock, Seth would come in from next door, looking for the paper, which he would then read until bedtime. Sometimes, but not always, my grandmother would get a look at it that evening but more often she had to wait until the morning.

Not many of his generation were able to get as much out of the newspapers as Seth was, but the good range of newspapers and periodicals in the public lending library over the baths, entered at the top of Storr Hill, was well used by older men and men out of work. These newspapers were fastened by laths down the centre onto wooden stands set at a slight angle to the walls, so that you had to stand to read most of them. The periodicals lay on large, heavy tables. Some people were there simply to pass the time in a well-heated room; some were there only for the racing or sport pages; others were concerned mainly with the columns announcing births, marriages and deaths; many more went carefully through the adverts, especially in the local papers. They tended to ignore politics and international affairs, even though they were given a prominent position in the papers. The subjects which set them talking for a few days were natural disasters, pit tragedies, plane and train crashes, and the racing and other sporting news.

My collaborators and I are all agreed that educational practice in those days took no account of libraries. The library just mentioned was less than three hundred yards away from Carr Lane School and would be passed twice or four times a day by about half of the pupils of Carr Lane School, but we cannot remember ever being required or encouraged to make use of it by our teachers. For its time, it was well stocked with all kinds of literature, from a juvenile section containing the 'Deerfoot' books of E. S. Ellis and the military adventures of G. A. Henty to the collected works of Tennyson, Keats, Shelley and Byron. I had become acquainted with all these by the time I was sixteen, to say nothing of Butler's *Hudibras* and the *Ingoldsby Legends*! It was the same when I was at Belle Vue; I passed the Bradford Central Library every day that I attended that school (when we didn't run up through Kirkgate Market!), but my teachers never suggested that I might make any use of it. And this at a time when not all homes had wirelesses, to say nothing of television! It is a convenient excuse for the teachers of today to blame the widespread illiteracy of the young today on these two technological snares, although they have undoubtedly played a part. It is also a sad fact, for which the teachers are not to blame, that the assessment methods of those days did not require any reading outside the narrow curriculum; youngsters could do very well for themselves without being interested in reading.

Percy Nudds sums up the history of libraries in Wyke in a couple of short paragraphs.[9] In 1902 a branch of the Bradford City Public Library was opened in Wyke Infants School. The library I have just described above developed out of this from 1904 onwards. With the increase in population and the increase in reading, as well as the more developed demand for public libraries, Bradford City Council replaced the above and the Hill Top Branch with a single, fine, new purpose-built library at the junction of Woodside Road and Huddersfield Road, practically next door to the old Board School. This was opened in 1958.

To return to Seth. Before I was born he had been the secretary of a homing-pigeon society, which had given him not only some sport and a constructive interest, but also some contact with a much wider cross-section of the community. It brought him, if not exactly friendship, the easy acquaintance, of John Morton, owner of the mill up Carr Lane, who at that time lived at Park House. It was probably at least partly through this activity that Seth was fascinated by maps and would sit poring over them for hours, sitting in the cratch with the maps spread out on the top of the old, heavy, deal table. He took in all kinds of information from them and liked to calculate distances. Some facts and figures interesting to him he would jot down in a note-book: the height of Blackpool Tower, the length of the longest tunnel in Yorkshire and when it was built; Wilfred Rhodes's averages (by my time it was Hedley Verity and Herbert Sutcliffe!). His favourite book was a one-volume encyclopaedia, which we had got for him through the special offer of a Sunday newspaper. Many members of that generation who had adopted literacy were fascinated with facts about the physical world both near and far, and encyclopaedias were among their favourite reading matter. I do recall, however, fetching the detective stories of J. S. Fletcher[10] from the library for Seth.

Older women of Generation I who were so inclined read romantic novels, such as those of Ruby M. Ayres and Ethel M. Dell. One rarely found a woman of that generation in the library, however; it was as though they did not trust themselves to find their own books in the library and get them stamped and this was usually done for them by their daughters or younger neighbours. There were women's weeklies and monthlies in those days, but few women bought them as they were regarded as an unnecessary luxury.

An elderly man of Seth's age, badly crippled in his legs (probably with rickets) had told his housekeeper that I was to have his copy of *Harmsworth's Encyclopaedia* of 1908, in eight volumes, when he died. These were handed over the fence which separated our back gardens from

Ivy Bank in due course, and my father then told me that they had originally appeared in weekly instalments and he had pleaded in vain with his father to take them for him. Such was the difference between my two grandfathers.

For the last fifty years or so it has been the experience of most employers that the employees most valuable to him have been those who learned the practical side of *his* business first and then acquired some relevant theory to support the practice. But in some crucial areas of employment, employers had to pay graduates and those with paper qualifications more than those who served them best.

It was the good fortune of my Generation I and most of Generation II that they were offered an education that aimed purely and simply at equipping them for the jobs available locally, and enabled them to rise to positions of responsibility in their line of employment, provided they had the will and the bent to do so. Those who advocated, provided and, for the most part, administered this elementary education were lay philanthropists and practical men of business, a combination that has existed to this degree only in late Victorian society. The industrialists and business men who provided the educational opportunities genuinely wished to improve the lot of the lower orders by equipping them for better jobs; and, obviously, they were also intent upon a more competent, educated work-force to operate their warehouses, factories and shops. Which was exactly what the working people wanted! They, too, were interested only in an education that would lead to a better job. And teachers were, in the eyes of the whole community, doing their job well if they turned out young people who could read orders, descriptions of products and instructions, and be diligent and accurate in all things. If they could also write simple things in legible manuscript, so much the better. But the most important achievement was to be able to do elementary calculations of weight, measure and cost. They learned their tables day in day out and did a lot of simple practical exercises with them. The workaday situations in which this knowledge was to be practised did not, of course, allow time for pencil and paper, so the supreme discipline was mental arithmetic. A private letter from a one-time pupil of Miss Briggs' school tells me that they could go home any time as soon as they had got their mental arithmetic right. My mother, an early Generation II pupil of Miss Briggs, used to check her own and her mother's bills from the Co-op and work out the 'divi' in her head.

Many members of Generation I and older Generation II responded to the insistence in school on good handwriting in the same way as they appreciated good craftsmanship, and this was one of the factors by which they judged the quality of education being offered to their children. When Generation III was compelled by a different approach to education, and secondary education as a further stage, to take notes and write essays at examination speed in whatever handwriting they could achieve, their parents and grandparents often considered that they must be wasting their time in school, doing nothing worthwhile. The fact that so many of the improvements in all aspects of welfare made in their time had been made at the expense of standards of quality declining in so many features of their lives was too immediate for them to grasp. The age in which jobs were done thoroughly and accurately by intensive labour, producing well-constructed and well-finished articles, was coming to an end; that insistence upon quality was giving way to a demand for quantity.

If the more progressive members of Generation I wanted elementary education for their children, then the progressives of Generation II wanted secondary education for theirs. The aspirations of one generation become the norm for the next. Many of those of Generation II who did have these ambitions for their children were unable to grasp all the implications of the educational opportunities offered to them. The slump and the General Strike, even though our area was not so badly hit as many industrial areas and those who had regular work were better off than their class had ever been, had the effect of increasing the demand for education. By the end of World War I they had a better standard of living, better working conditions and their children had better job-prospects than they themselves had enjoyed. The slump and the General Strike, while it had a serious effect on the life of many of our parents, did not prevent them from insisting on a better education for their children. Moreover, they were still satisfied with their lot because they were still prepared to work hard and be happy in manual jobs. Manual workers were not regarded as failures, but those who made it into the professions were regarded with awe by some and with jealousy by others.

Hence the excellent provision for secondary education in Bradford was welcomed and made full use of by people in all walks of life. There the children of well-to-do wool merchants sat in the same classroom cheek by jowl with the children of day-labourers. They were also treated exactly the same; in my experience, there was no favouritism in any aspect of school life. After the Education Act of 1870, for which the Bradford M.P. E. W. Forster was largely responsible, Bradford set out to build schools at a rate that staggered and sometimes aroused the anger of the ratepayers. There had always been the Grammar School[11] which had admitted a small number of pupils from humble backgrounds, but now the municipal Education Committee built a series of outstanding High Schools: Belle Vue, 1879; Carlton, 1883; Grange, 1905; Hanson, 1890 and a Roman Catholic high school, St. Bede's, 1900. In this enterprise, the city fathers and businessmen spared neither effort nor money. They staffed these schools with teachers on a higher scale of pay than anywhere in the country outside London.

Early in 1933 I was due to sit my 'scholarship' examination for a place at a secondary school or Bradford Grammar School. This exam had for us no other title than 'The Scholarship' and neither we nor our parents understood fully either its workings or its purpose. I was recovering from measles and was still a bit off colour, so my mother was going to keep me at home and not let me sit the exam. It was only the fact that our esteemed family doctor, Dr Brown, persuaded her to let me sit the exam and only then keep me off for a fortnight, if necessary, that got me into the examination room. I qualified, along with four others that year from Carr Lane, for a free place at Bradford Grammar School, but my parents thought that I would be socially out of my depth and were doubtful about being able to maintain me there. Moreover, a great friend of Dad's, from his dog-showing days before I was born, had a boy who had done very well at Belle Vue High School on Manningham Lane, so that settled it. Belle Vue was the furthest Bradford high school from Wyke, but a surprising number of pupils, especially girls, were sent there from Wyke and Low Moor. When my School Certificate results were known, Mr Fisher, headmaster of Belle Vue, still had to convince my mother in an interview that I should go on into the sixth form and eventually to a university. My parents would have had no misgivings if I had ended up as a skilled manual worker, and, indeed, the majority of the people of Wyke and Low Moor at that time were satisfied if their children obtained regular work and were quite happy if they rose above the status of unskilled labourers.

At this time there were more girls than boys from Storr Hill Side in secondary education. Perhaps this was because the demand for women in many non-manual and clerical jobs was increasing much faster than it was for men. Or it might have been that parents were more concerned to protect their girls from hard manual labour in the mill. Of his contemporaries, the only children to go to a high school that Frank, born 1912, can remember were Irwin Barraclough and his brother from Rawson Street. As far as I can remember, the first child to go to a secondary school from Elizabeth Street was Mary Garside, in or about 1931. She grew up in a back-to-back house on Elizabeth Street. Her father, Irvine Garside,[12] had some stabling, a cowshed and a few acres of poor land about a quarter of a mile from the house. He kept cows and had a milk round, but he frequently had to buy milk because his own cows did not yield enough. With his horses he did general carrying. He fetched the bricks, mortar and clinker for hard core (from the Low Moor Company's Dross Hills) when our houses on Elizabeth Street were built. Sometimes he eked out by emptying ashpits and, perhaps, before my time, he was one of the night-soil men of whom I heard tell. Mrs Garside dressed more consistently in Generation I style than anybody I knew, always in a full-length black skirt even in the 1930s. She baked and brewed and there was always, it seemed to me, an earthenware baking-bowl full of beer in the making on a little table under the window. Their son, Stanley, younger than Mary, was a constant playmate of Laurence and myself. I don't remember ever seeing a book in the house, but this was the background from which Mary went forward to secondary education, and was appropriately employed thereafter. Sheila Crossland from New Road Side, whose widowed mother did dressmaking at home, also went to Belle Vue. Marion Hollis, of my own age, went to the newly opened Bolling High School for Girls from a low cottage down Storr Hill. There were other boys beside me going from Wyke and Low Moor, of course, but not from the immediate vicinity.

In the education to which we were subjected from *circa* 1927 to 1940 there were quite a few elements which derived from the nineteenth century. At Carr Lane the three R's were administered to us in the spirit of the 1870 Act, taught, perhaps, by better teachers who were better paid than before the Act. Religious Knowledge (we always called it Scripture) was quite often the subject matter of our reading lessons, in suitably modernised and abbreviated form, of course. As far as I can remember, there was nothing much in the way of geography or history and what was called art was the soul-destroying practising of drawing straight lines freehand with a pencil or, more advanced, attempting to shade a three-dimensional object like a jam-jar. Drawing tolerably straight lines might well have been useful in many manual jobs, but it was definitely not art.

At Belle Vue, although the curriculum was at the time a fashionable one, it was dictated by the academic staff of the northern universities and was designed to relieve them of as much basic teaching as possible. Passing the examinations of the Joint Matriculation Board was only of nominal help to most pupils of these schools who were destined for local businesses, shops, management of factories, etc. The great advantage of such schools, however, was that the insistence upon competition at all costs had not yet started to cripple our schools. Most pupils and teachers did the best they could and both received in return full recognition for any positive contribution to the life of the school, however limited and humble that may have been. So what Belle Vue did achieve with outstanding success was to turn out a body of young men and women with confidence in themselves to do a good job in the field of their choice, yet having the instinct born of experience that it is better to cooperate than to compete. Several of my contemporaries at Belle Vue finished their education at the older universities, quite a few became university lecturers and professors, and one was awarded a life-peerage. But although children like myself profited from these secondary schools, they were never part of the life of Storr Hill Side. These schools lay in the urbanised centre of the city and drew in pupils from a large number of small communities like ours and transformed them into rather different people. Real 'improvements', in the pupils' command of English, literacy and numeracy, as well as in manners, were the work of the local schools.

By the time the Second World War broke out, education had ceased to be a factor in the decline of the dialect. From the linguistic point of view the existing system continued to have the same influence, but was now supported by a wide range of occupations in after life, the shrinkage of a rooted population of manual workers and the increase of a vernacular based on Standard English. From the social point of view there is only the great damage of that monument to sterile élitism, the 1944 Education Act, to report. This was designed purely and simply to fill the universities and other institutions of tertiary education with students for whom the country could then find no suitable posts. It also made clear to a majority of children of eleven and twelve that they were *by law*! rejects, and would attain a respectable position in society and a good, secure job only by working much harder, by starting much lower, than their more fortunate contemporaries or by an unpredictable stroke of fortune. The successful candidates in the 11+ examination could, even at that early age, expect good social standing and a white-collar job. There are plenty of examples of successful men and women with whom it still rankles that they were rejected by examination at the age of eleven: I know a wealthy estate agent, two directors of medium-sized companies, a very successful representative of a firm making textile machinery and a respected university lecturer whose scholarship is internationally recognised. I also know an electrician earning nigh on £40,000 a year who lives opposite a schoolteacher with a degree and a diploma who earns between £9,000 and £10,000 a year at the time of writing. All of these 11+ 'failures' regard the grammar school 'failures' with contempt and, even in middle age, like to see one of the select in straitened circumstances. But most of these are prepared to pay, if necessary, to send their children to grammar or private schools, because, as one of them put it, 'It looks so much better on a job-application form.' I also know parents who have joined one or the other political party to facilitate their children's progress to a grammar school.

These vagaries of the education system after the war had, however, very little effect on the language of the area. While the grammar schools corrected the language of their pupils as part of their social mission, the pupils of the secondary modern schools mostly retained a more up-to-date version of the language of their parents or, after leaving school, adjusted their language to their several jobs and ambitions, while retaining a linguistic basis that was undeniably northern. There is no longer a confrontation between the dialect and Standard English, only one between 'good' and 'bad' S.E.

The great re-planning and re-thinking of education by the Bradford authorities in the sixties and seventies left Wyke as a major centre of local education with mostly new school premises, new facilities and progressive syllabuses. The three-tier system of the Bradford Education Authority is realised in Wyke in the following schools with the following principles and curricula. Quotations in the following paragraphs are from the prospectuses of the respective schools.[13]

High Fernley First School, built opposite the end of Edge Nook, was opened in June 1975. It 'is a county comprehensive First School with Nursery catering for the needs of children from the age of 3 to 9 years' and its professed aim is 'to help each child to develop at his/her own rate and to his/her full potential in all areas of development – intellectually, physically and socially.' Pupils are introduced to English, Maths, Science ('core subjects' of the National Curriculum); and to what are called 'foundation subjects': Technology, Geography, History, Art, Physical Education, Religious Education and Music. There is no formal sex education 'but reference may be made to reproduction through our work with animals in school.'

Parents are encouraged to take a close interest in the education of their children. Curriculum documents are available for parents to read, and the prospectus contains some good advice on parental encouragement. In the Bradford area, ethnic and religious distinctions within the community demand special attention. Religious education now has to be totally different in content to what was taught at Carr Lane. Whereas we learned the basic material foundations and beliefs of Christianity in a most haphazard way, through frequent and lengthy prayer sessions and from stories from the Bible told by the teachers, as well as those used to teach us to read, the modern school now has to formulate its policy and satisfy parents of widely differing religions: 'Following Government regulations, the worship is "broadly and mainly" Christian in content, although we draw on material from other faith groups.' Parents may attend assembly on Thursday morning to satisfy themselves that nothing takes place that offends against their particular beliefs; and they may also apply formally in writing to the Head for exemption from religious activities.

Neither race nor religion was an issue in our schooldays; now both are crucial and have to be formulated precisely in the prospectuses. High Fernley and Wyke Manor both publish a list of seven offences against racial harmony which are unacceptable in the school, and state firmly that 'No incident will be allowed to pass without an immediate response.' Wyke Middle School avers: 'Although we are not a multi-racial school nevertheless we are thoroughly committed to the multicultural and equal opportunities policies of Bradford Education Authority.'

In my analysis of the Census Returns for 1881, out of 288 households on Storr Hill Side there is not a single mother with children of school age going out to work, and school meals were unheard of. Nowadays, even infants and primary school pupils usually stay to lunch. At High Fernley this costs 80p. per day and provides a choice in both courses; milk at £1 per term and biscuits at 12p. per week are also offered. The teachers use this opportunity to teach table manners and the management of cutlery and crockery. At Carr Lane every child, without exception, went home to dinner, however poor and scanty the meal may have been. There was free milk towards the end of my time at Carr Lane: one-third of a pint consumed through a straw from miniature milk bottles. The milk monitor was a very important little person! As my groups of Carr Lane School pupils make very clear, there were absolutely no regulations about clothing. Laurence and I can see in our group of 1932 at least two lads who had to wait each year for the annual handout of a jersey and shorts from the charitable organisation called The Cinderella Club.

Other signs of the working mother occur in the prospectuses: absences require only notification by telephone, although longer absences require a note from the parent and a doctor's note; the teachers will administer medicine, if it is provided with precise instructions about times and dosage.

Wyke Middle School, housed in the old Board School buildings with the addition of some extensions and some temporary accommodation, caters for children in the 9-13 age group. It was integrated into the Comprehensive System for the Wyke and district area in 1974, and proclaims in its prospectus the same ideals as the other two schools: 'We hope to maintain a friendly, happy and productive atmosphere in which all pupils can become aware of their own capabilities and responsibilities. It is important therefore that pupils become involved with their own learning and are not treated as passive receptors.'

At this stage learning becomes a more serious matter and the prospectus describes the school's interpretation of the National Curriculum in some detail. The school obviously takes its educational mission very seriously, laying stress upon the subjects most likely to be required in a normal working life: English, Mathematics, Science and Technology. A secondary tier of subjects contains: History, Geography, Religious Education, Art, French, Music and Physical Education. Concessions to the demands of modern life and its more complex problems are evident in a course on Information Technology, Personal and Social Education, and Home and Family Studies.

Professional help from outside is available for pupils with special problems such as hearing or sight difficulties. A wide variety of visitors, ranging from the Deaconess to the local police constable talk to the pupils about their jobs and experiences. Further provisions and amenities include a School Bank, regular meetings of staff and a Parents' Liaison Group and lays emphasis on Pastoral Care of its pupils.

Given the age group for which a Middle School is responsible, it is not surprising that Wyke Middle School seems to be conscious of a certain lack of purpose beyond its immediate teaching of subject matter. Indeed, whereas High Fernley can take pride in laying important foundations of both academic and social kinds, and Wyke Manor can list external examinations for which it prepares candidates and publish their results in some detail in its prospectus, objectives such as these are not so clearly defined in the case of a Middle School. In accordance with national and local requirements, the school bridges this gap with Records of Achievement. These take the form of a ring-binder into which the child enters his/her achievements both in and out of school; they are kept in school but are available for pupils to add material and for parents to inspect at all times. After leaving the Senior School, these ring-binders become the pupil's personal property. To me, this is where the strength of a school such as this lies. After almost forty years of setting and marking all kinds of examinations from O-level to post-graduate, I and many of my colleagues have come to the conclusion that the traditional form of examination, by itself, is a most unreliable method of assessing ability and usefulness to the community. Properly conducted, such records of achievement are to be preferred every time. I am confident that, given my experience, any intelligent Storr Hill lad would agree, but this is not the place to debate this point. A further step towards enlightened education is the policy of not operating a homework timetable, but expecting pupils to complete assignments in their own time. Homework may be set, however, by parental request.

The senior school, Wyke Manor School, opened as an 11-16 Secondary School in 1959, and since 1968 has been a 13-18 Upper School. It has many points in common with the High Schools attended by some of the children of Storr Hill Side in the twenties and thirties, but reaches out far beyond the scope of anything we knew.

Like the others its prospectus starts with a statement of general policy, for which there would have been no need in our schooldays: 'The aims of the school are to discover and nurture the talent of every child and to inculcate basic quantities of honesty, integrity, industry and tolerance. The pupil who will gain most from Wyke Manor School is the pupil who *gives* most in terms of personal commitment.' I suppose that this has been the aim of all good schools, but, until the present state of competitive education, they did not see the need to formulate it in the tone of an electioneering speech.

Like the other schools above, it is concerned to enlist the help and support of parents in every possible way. Documents concerning pupils are available for parents to see. 'Each pupil's progress and achievement is under continual review by the pupil, her/his Form Teacher and Subject Teachers.' Parents should be encouraged to see that pupils record outside activities. 'Upon leaving school each pupil will receive a file which contains a summary of the total Record of Achievement as well as the Record itself.'

With professional precision the prospectus details the school's services and requirements as regards Assessment, Care and Welfare of Pupils, Discipline, Uniform, Assemblies, Muslim Prayer and Religious Festivals, and its Public Examination Policy.

In School Year Nine (pupils aged 13+) there is no choice of courses: all take the following: English Lang./Lit. (4 periods); Maths (4 periods); Humanities (Geog. 2 periods, Hist. 2 periods); Science (Biol. Chem., Physics, each 2 periods); Modern Language (4 periods); Design Technology (C.D.T., Art, Business Technology, Home Economics, each 2 periods); Physical Education (2 periods); Religious Education (2 periods); Drama (2 periods); Music (2 periods); Library Skills (1 period); Life/ Social Skill (1 period).

In School Years Ten and Eleven (pupils aged 14+ and 15+ respectively) the Curriculum consists of a Common Core comprising: English Lang./ Lit., Mathematics, Science, Physical Education, Foundation Subject Carousel ('modules on Religious Education and Careers Education'!). Common Options are: Humanities, Technological Options, Modern Language Options, plus one free choice of an optional subject.

After this, of course, in what was the Sixth Form in our day, there is no restriction of choice of subjects – other, presumably, than what is imposed by circumstances of staffing and timetabling.

To me, the most encouraging item in the Prospectus, indeed, in the whole of this account of contemporary education on Storr Hill Side, runs as follows:

> From September 1987 Wyke Manor, along with all other Upper Schools within Bradford Local Education Authority have been involved in the Technical and Vocational Education Initiative (T.V.E.I.). This is a major initiative to give young people aged between 14 and 18 a wider richer education in order that:
> more of our students can seek and gain skills and qualifications that will be of direct value to them at work;
> they can apply their skills and qualifications to real life problems;
> they are offered planned work experience and are better prepared for the world of work;
> and there is an emphasis on initiative, motivation, enterprise and other areas of personal development.

The policy embodied in this scheme appears to go a long way towards remedying the weaknesses of school education from about 1920 to 1970. During these years, following the example of the older universities, all assessments and future prospects depended on a display of intelligence (or a good memory and powers of regurgitation) in written examinations. Employers, to their cost, took the easy way out and relied on examination results in subjects which had nothing to do with their business when making appointments. Professors, both in the Arts and in the Sciences, insisted weightily at conferences and on committees that they 'must maintain their standards', which, in practice, simply meant that they were not prepared to consider any change or progress. Parents, wanting only the prospect of a good job for their children, had to go along with the powers that were. The result was a national meritocracy, an élite, that had no contact with, no understanding of, the world in which they were expected to earn their living, that never had to show any success or profit but could continue to make mistake after mistake and failure after failure without ever being made answerable for them. Compared with the rest of Europe, we still have an educated élite of this kind; let us hope that schools like Wyke Manor and education authorities like Bradford can make a significant contribution to remedying this archaic situation.

Chapter 4

Some People

My Generation I was the first to benefit from the Ten Hours Act and the great spate of liberal reforms in the interests of working people promulgated by the country's leaders from the middle of the nineteenth century onwards. Their parents had started life in the bad old days when food was inadequate, housing and sanitary conditions disgusting and working hours hard and long. In my Appendix I, I have given some relevant details from the Reports of a government inquiry of 1842 into the employment of children.[1] These reports contain details of the 'Age, Height and Circumference, Educational Qualification, and Condition of One Hundred and Twenty-Four Hurriers Employed in the Low Moor Company's Coal Pits, Bradford'. Some other pits are included, such as the 'New Road Side Pit of Messrs. Akroyd & Co., depth 285 ft.'. The pit is marked on the map of 1852 and it appears to have been on the spot where there was a gap in Church Street as we knew it. This might well explain why Church Street was so difficult of access from Huddersfield Road. It was a small pit, employing only five hurriers, and it probably did not operate for long as we never heard it mentioned in our time. These hurriers were all boys and had started work at the age of eight or nine. The height of Jesse Butterfield, the eldest at sixteen, was 4 ft. 8$\frac{1}{2}$ ins.; he had worked in the pit for eight years. None of them could either read or write. Although it appears that the Low Moor Company did not employ girls as hurriers there were pits not far away employing girls at the age of nine, which is interesting in the light of the comments of the agent involved and the fact that later in the very same year, 1842, an Act of Parliament forbade the employment of women and children in coal mines. It was a step in the right direction, but the implementation of this particular law was delayed for decades,[2] as much by the greed of parents as of the mineowners.

These factors contributed to a high infant mortality, and an appreciable proportion of older people mentioned in the following pages were survivors of half, or less than half, of the total of children born to their parents. Infant deaths were accepted as inevitable, as the will of God by the more pious, and if they died very young, they tended to be relatively quickly forgotten. If they survived their years of infancy, then malnutrition, cold and damp living quarters on a north-facing slope in the Pennines some 600 feet above sea-level, and long hours of strenuous work often crippled them for the rest of their lives.

Many of their children, my Generation I, lived to a fine old age, for two reasons: the first was that they had needed constitutions of iron and steel to survive at all, and the second was that, as they had grown older and more at the mercy of their afflictions, the conditions of their lives had improved enormously. They were better fed and clothed, there was unlimited cheap coal, but, above all, hours and conditions of work had improved. True, they had not improved sufficiently to make the life of the collier an easy one, but, at least it became tolerable for those born and bred in mining communities such as ours; hard men could now survive to live to an old age. Both men and women had better conditions of work in the mills, as had workers in the iron industry. Although the results came too late for the children listed in Mr Scriven's report, his observations and those of others like him produced an enormous effect on the conscience of the Victorian élite.

Not only were the conditions in the mines a little better, many men who had started off as colliers had taken advantage of alternative occupations offered by the improved general situation. Whereas Edwin Lightowler was returned in the 1871 Census as 'collier, aged 11', he had got out of the pit at a relatively early age and had a comfortable middle age as landlord of the Patent Hammer Inn. This was also the career of Dan Smith, who kept the Rising Sun at Scholes. Walter Brook also got out and worked from about 6 a.m. to about 10.30 a.m. each day, dressing fish and poultry in the Bradford wholesale market. It was the improvement in the general prosperity of the area during the late nineteenth century that created such opportunities for my Generation I and the older end of Generation II.

Being out of work was, however, still serious, especially if a man had a young family to keep. The threat of the workhouse was still real. Both my Generation I and Generation II were apt to deplore an act of laziness or extravagance with: 'Tha'll (Wi s'l) end up i t'warkaas,' or words to that effect. Sometimes, but by no means always, there was the help of a more fortunate member of the family, and old people living alone were sometimes taken in by more fortunate relatives, unless their own pride prevented it. This affected Generation II more than Generation I, however, and will be dealt with in another place. If Generation I people survived into their twenties, they were still exposed to occupational hazards and diseases which have largely disappeared today. Barring these, they had, inevitably, absolutely indestructible constitutions. Of my two grandfathers, one wielded pick and shovel on the pit bottom, often working eighteen-inch seams, for forty-four years (according to his children, anyway!), while the other could work all day with an eight-pound stonemason's hammer, came through typhoid fever in his fifties and survived pneumonia at seventy-five; and this without the benefit of modern drugs and medical treatment.

As I said in my introduction, the prototype figure of my Generation I and, in a sense, the father of this work, was Seth Shaw, my maternal grandfather. He was born on 28th June 1865 to Shadrach and Martha Shaw of Slack Side, Wibsey. His father's occupation is given as 'iron works worker,' but he appears in later census returns as 'mason'; perhaps his main work was in lining furnaces and pits. Seth succeeded him as a mason, a term which included brick-laying when required, but as almost all building was in stone, it is easy to see how the trade-name was adopted in the first place. Seth's parents had three sons and three daughters between 1861 and *c.* 1881. Before Seth was of working age, the family moved down to Barmby Street, down Wilson Road. Both on her marriage certificate and on Seth's birth certificate, Martha made her mark instead of signing her name, and was presumably illiterate. Shadrach could write. We have traced six generations of the Shaws in direct male line of descent born on Wibsey Slack.[3] As far as the sources tell us, they were all miners, labourers or masons; some of them moved from one of these jobs to the other and back again according to the different sources. The last of this line to carry on the name of Shaw was born in Scholes in 1939, grandson of Seth's brother Fred.

Seth married Sarah Lightowler, born in Barraclough Fold, Morley Carr, on 11th July 1891 at the parish church of Oakenshaw-cum-Woodlands. After Barmby Street, perhaps on getting married, Seth and Sarah lived in houses lower down, towards Oakenshaw and Woodlands, and my mother, Annie Shaw, was born on 5th May 1893, at 44 Wyke Lane, which is still standing and looking from outside very much like it did in the 1890s. After that Seth and his family lived in Woodlands and Raw Nook (it was probably from here that Annie attended Miss Brigg's school) before going to 30 Storr Hill, where they lived throughout the First World War. It was from this house that Annie was married in 1920, and it was where I was taken to see my grandparents during the first two years of my life.

At Easter 1925, Seth, Sarah and my Aunt Eva, who was then not yet married, moved to 19 Elizabeth Street, one of the two 'modern', brick-built houses he and my father had built on an acre of land on Elizabeth Street. Here, next door to us, Seth and Sarah lived out their lives, he dying at the age of eighty-one in May 1947 and she in June 1949 at the age of seventy-nine.

When I was tiny, Seth used to run races with me and was disgusted with himself when, at the age of five or six, I could beat him. He always moved rather stiffly; in fact, this was a characteristic of his generation, owing to the life they had been forced to live. When I was a little older, he was a very stern mentor in teaching me how to use hand-tools, especially hammer and chisel ('tha might as weel ewse a stuen!'). He and Ephraim together laid a foundation of everyday artisan lore that remains a source of help and satisfaction in the use of a hammer, a saw, a sharp knife, a chisel, a screwdriver, etc. and learning to understand why a saw or a file cut one way only and which way, I was taught to plug a wall with a 'jumper' chisel and never to address a man working up a ladder; I was given severe warnings against making a friendly approach to a strange dog and against picking up anything in a blacksmith's shop without spitting on it first, and always to turn an empty wheelbarrow to face the way it would go after you had loaded it.

It was, however, as a companion and a pal that Seth left an imprint on me that, according to some, I bear to this day. He came into our house and I went into theirs as though the two houses were one. When I was about fifteen, my grandparents bought a wireless, almost as big as a church organ, with a monumental polished wooden front. We in our house had not yet reached that stage of civilisation (I think that my parents resisted such extravagance for another two years!) and Seth would fetch me into their house if anything good came on. I can remember us huddled close together up to the set, elbow to elbow, to listen to the Benny Lynch v Small Montana fight in 1937.[4]

For quite a few years my Saturday morning job was to clean out the hen huts and I was usually helped and bossed by Seth. Seth and Ephraim in partnership kept about 100 laying hens and all the young birds that go with such a flock, for ours were home-bred and reared. Of course, in those days they were all kept free range, and huts were small and spread out, so

I or Seth pushed a heavy wooden wheelbarrow, with a proper 'turl' hooped with iron, full of wet hen-muck through wet ground. Seth's advice was 'tha mun do like t'navvies – start at a speed tha c'n keep up all day an' get slower.' This is no place to theorise or moralise about the educational benefits I derived from working with Seth. Suffice it to say that they were greater than those I got from Ephraim, simply because the latter did not let me do the job but kept me hanging about just fetching and carrying for him. Presumably this is how he himself had been treated as an apprentice at first.

Although very tolerant and long-suffering as a rule, especially where members of the family were concerned, Seth would occasionally feel spurned and ignored (have little bouts of paranoia, as it would be termed today); on such occasions he would break loose in a brief but very destructive rage, smashing things up with the first hammer that came to hand. Most of the damage, however, was to hen-huts, fencing, water troughs, etc.

He was very devoted to the game of bowls. On his eightieth birthday, a week or two before the General Election of 1945, he suggested to me that we should go to the Harold Club and start bowling at 8 p.m. as the day was so hot. He asked me who I thought we should vote for, listened to what I had to say, asked a few questions, not disagreeing, and then said, 'Aye, A think tha't reight.' Seth was always secure enough in his own dignity to give even a child a fair hearing and his honest opinion; he had so much natural dignity that he never had to stand on it with anybody. It always took him a long time to walk to the Harold Club, and it was quite irksome for me to have to slow down to the same pace, but, once on the green, he could tire me out even when he was eighty.

I never knew why he could not get on with his son, Harry. My mother always told me that Seth treated him with contempt and scorn and he seems to have been a tragic figure whose life was brought to an end at Albert on the Somme in 1916. Annie mourned him deeply, having 'mothered' her younger, timid brother through his early years. Perhaps I can explain the difference between Seth and his son. Seth was decidedly of this world and of the society of mankind, whilst Harry seems to have acquired an orientation at an early age towards the world beyond and became something of a pious prig, too virtuous and God-fearing to work with rough, vulgar men. Apparently he was never satisfied with any job, being unable to get on with his fellows, whilst they in turn rejected him for his 'holier than thou' attitudes. Seth would have none of that! I can remember a picture of Harry in church choir gowns on top of the piano bought for Aunt Eva to learn on. The only surviving likeness I found was a roughly torn-out face crammed into the back of a cameo brooch left by Annie.

So many of the points I have to make about Generation I and the local community as a whole are illustrated with some reference to Seth, that there is little need for me to describe him further here. Anybody who might read these pages should try to combine the natural dignity of the character with the trowel in his hand (Plate 12) with my collection of *The Sayings of Seth.*

At the top of Carr Lane there was the typical, small, stone-built pub called The Patent Hammer. Round the corner and across New Works Road (always known to us as 'Long Wall Side') there was the immense wall that enclosed the Forge Yard of the Low Moor Company, so the name of this pub is readily explained. In the vernacular it was simply T'Patten. It is no longer there; the whole area at the bottom of New Works Road has been razed to make way for modern housing. Throughout my early life the landlord was Edwin Lightowler (Plate 7), brother of my grandmother, Sarah Shaw. To his own generation he was known as Ned Reid, for reasons unknown to me. He was born in 1859 or 1860 and the 1871 Census records him as a miner at the age of eleven. His wife was dead before I was born and he ran the pub practically single handed with the help of an adopted daughter, whom everybody knew as Sarannah (Plate 8). Nobody ever called her anything else until, fairly late in life and after the death of Uncle Edwin, she married a certain Squire Hoyle.[5]

Edwin Lightowler had the reputation of having been a rough sort of lad in his younger days. I heard tales of his greyhound and whippet racing exploits, and he seems to have had a reputation for interfering with the scales on which the dogs were weighed. Matches were made at certain weights and there were no officials or governing bodies to control things. Obviously, there was as much fighting as racing, and Edwin seems to have held his own with the best. Seth told me that he was good at knur and spell in his younger days. He had also done a bit of cock-fighting, and I must have heard the following story three or four times. Sarannah, when a young woman, walked into Cleckheaton one Sunday afternoon with a friend. There, they dropped in on friends of the family for tea; there was no need to announce a visit in advance before the days of the telephone. After tea, their host bethought himself that he had promised Ned Reid a game-cock and he asked Sarannah if she would take it back to the Patent Hammer. He would pay their fare on the train from Cleckheaton to Low Moor. She would not think twice about a small matter like taking a game-

Plate 7. Edwin Lightowler, who kept the Patent Hammer Inn.

cock on the train on a Sunday afternoon. So the two lasses in their Sunday best set off with the cock in a small sack. In the train an affable gentleman asked by way of friendly conversation what was in the sack. 'A gam'-cock,' said Sarannah. 'By God, yer gooa ta e reight Sunda schooil, ye two,' said the man in amazement. And nothing more was said in that compartment until the girls got out at Low Moor.

Sometime after Uncle Edwin's death in 1933 Sarannah married Squire Hoyle and they went to live at the bottom of King Street. This was quite some way from all but the smallest of general shops, and I was told quite frequently at one time by my mother or grandmother to take groceries and other things down to the tiny one-up-and-one-down old stone house. I can remember quite clearly that they kept a shut-up bed of the old type at least until the end of the last war. It was a huge cupboard in the one downstairs room (as far as I can remember, there was no sign of upstairs being used at all), made of solid mahogany with turned corner pillars. She also had a little mongrel terrier dog that would even eat lettuce with salt on it. After performing this party piece for Sarannah's friends and visitors, he was always rewarded with a more congenial titbit, of course. The only thing that Sarannah was afraid of was thunder, and she used to sit on the cellar steps (under the bedroom steps, which were also made of stone) and cuddle the little dog while a thunderstorm was passing over.

During the war, even though in her seventies, she was reluctant to have her meat and provisions sent from the shops on New Road Side, and particularly from the Co-op in Mary Street. She preferred to don her thick shawl, as in my photo of her, and, in bad weather, her clogs, and carry a couple of heavy carpet bags back down to King Street rather than trust the shopkeepers. Many people still alive will remember her as the scourge of the local shopkeepers. I once witnessed her enter a butcher's shop and snap out like an upset terrier dog: 'Ah much is that meit a'v just gotten off tha?'

'Wun en' three awpence a pund, Mrs Hoyle.'

'Tak' it back, then. Tha's dun me en ahns. A'll ev mi brass back! Duen't say nowt! Tak' this meit en gi ma t' brass!'

There were four or five customers in the shop, and she had a voice as penetrating and staccato as a shed full of looms.

How quickly it would go round, then, on the few occasions when she was verbally bested by a shopkeeper. She came up Storr Hill one cold day during the war and ordered a bag full of goods at the Co-op. While the manager, who usually took good care to serve her himself, was making out the cheque, she said with perfect timing: 'A 'ear yo've 'ed

Plate 8. Sarannah Hoyle, adopted daughter of Edwin Lightowler.

sum blackleead, but ye've nuen saved me onny, en a v asst time en time agien.'

'Nou, Mrs Hoyle, A din't kno yer wanted sum.'

'Well A did, en A' s'l 'e te 'ev sum. A 'evn't ed onny for muns en muns en A'v spit en A'v spit wol A can't spit ner mooer.'

'What day do yer blackleead, Mrs Hoyle?'

'Thersda. What for?'

'A'll see if A c'n send t' flahr lad dahn te spit fo yer!'

The name of the victorious manager, eminently worthy of being put on record, was Mr Weston. I was quite elated at being able to take a photo of the old co-op in September 1985 (Plate 9). There were two large rooms (at least, they seemed large to me when I fetched things from it during the thirties), of which the larger was very much like any other grocer's shop of that time. Round three sides there was a very solid counter of which the sides were used for display and the ham and bacon department while the longer middle section was where one got served. At the back there were the usual shelves of tins and jars and little drawers for spices, etc. The smaller room was called 't' flahr 'oil' because it had a row of wooden bins all down one of the longer sides, and from these the 'flour-lad' weighed out stones and half-stones of various grades of flour and grain. There was a vinegar-barrel and a treacle-barrel in one corner and bundles of firewood in another and not much else, apart from a little short counter at right angles to the wall opposite the bins.

I cannot resist telling one more story about Sarannah, which, if not true, is certainly extremely *bien trouvé*. My father loved to tell this one and expected me to vouch for its truth because I was there. And I did, in fact, on occasion, swear that every word was true, although all that I could really remember was once seeing a few new-born piglets in a clothes-basket in front of the kitchen fire in the 'Patten'. It might easily have been a different occasion.

Here is Ephraim's Tale: One dark evening, when I was seven or eight years old, Sarannah rushed up Storr Hill as fast as her hard, bony shins would carry her with the message that a sow was about to farrow that had a bad record of savaging previous litters as they were born. Would Dad come and help?

He didn't wait to have his tea and he took me with him, 'to hold the lamp,' as he said. The most probable reason why I can't remember the details of this story may be because it was only one among many when I 'held the lamp'. We went through the pub to the sties out at the back. Dad looked at the sow and formed his plan. Luckily it was in a low-walled sty

Plate 9. The Co-op. (1985)

within a small building; there was no enclosed sleeping-place that we couldn't see into. The idea was that I was to hold the lamp and Sarannah was to clout its nose with the long brush every time it tried to turn round to savage a newly-dropped piglet, while Dad was to rush into the sty before the sow could recover from Sarannah's polo-mallet blow and retrieve the piglet. This worked quite successfully and it says a lot for Sarannah's prowess and accuracy that Dad lived in good health for quite a long time after that. After a time in the clothes-basket in front of the kitchen fire, the piglets were cautiously re-introduced to their mother and she reared a fair proportion of them.

Some time in 1980, perhaps 1981, I raised a shout of 'Bullet!' in the Local History Section of Bradford Central Library, which caused a few earnest students to raise their heads and give a scornful look or two. Sylvia and I were looking at the 1871 Census Returns for the area Storr Hill, Carr Lane, Morley Carr, and the entry which caused the shout read 'Walter Lightowler, child, aged 1,' and the address was near the top of Storr Hill.

Walter (Bullet) Lightowler was probably my grandmother's cousin, possibly a nephew, but she didn't like to admit it, in fact, she was quite touchy about the relationship, whatever it may have been. Everybody knew Bullet and, just as was the case with Edwin Lightowler, many knew him only by his nickname. Even when I was working as far away as Lidget Green for a short time during the war, there were people who had heard of Bullet and his exploits, usually apocryphal and garbled versions in true folk style. But there was no doubt about his having the reputation of being the roistering roughneck of the neighbourhood. Nobody accused him, however, not even behind his back, of being a gangster, or thug or thief, nor even a compulsive liar, although he might, as many did, embroider outrageously his accounts of his own exploits. What my grandmother had against him was that she was 'respectable' and he was not. She had a husband who would work if he could get work, and they owned their own house which had a bath and an indoor lavatory. In her view, she and Seth 'were something because they had something'. Bullet had nothing and would drink and fight into the bargain. On the whole, when not at work, Seth was expected to keep better company than such as Bullet. Not that Seth ever took much notice of that.

While I was growing up at 17 Elizabeth Street, Bullet was living at 91 Storr Hill, and our respective back doors stared at one another over a distance of about forty yards. He bred dogs for ratting and poaching, which had originated, he claimed, from crossing greyhound and staghound. At all events, they were beautiful dogs of great presence and quality. The best known of these was a certain Dont. Regularly at breakfast time Dont would stroll along the stone-flag tops of the outdoor 'nessies' which marked the boundary between Bullet's garden and Ivy Bank, drop down into our back yard, trot in a relaxed way round our house, take our front garden gate in his stride, and continue on his morning constitutional as though he had nothing more difficult than a bowling-green to negotiate. Technically he was a scruffy mongrel, but in essence he was as thoroughbred and aristocratic as any Derby winner. Bullet claimed that he had only to turn Dont out of the house on a dark night and he was sure to come back with a hare or a rabbit.

Bullet's dogs had to be more than instinctive ratters – they were trained and coached for the job! Here is one little memory: Saturday evening during the war and double summer time; Bullet walking unevenly but only half-drunk down Storr Hill carrying a cage-trap containing five or six half-grown rats, which he had caught in the old stables at the back of the Crown Hotel. There were people going in and out of the little, free-standing fish and chip shop a little higher up Storr Hill from where Bullet lived (still there in 1985, although very dilapidated), and he stopped and announced, 'A'll just see if that young dog o' mine's onny gooid.' He fetched out Paddy, who might have been a son of Dont and was then about ten months old, and then shook out those rats in the middle of Storr Hill. Not one of them reached cover! The dog nipped them once and was away after the next. There was no playing with dead rats or wasting time worrying them for a dog that wanted to get into Bullet's team!

Here is another little memory, just to exhaust the subject of Bullet and ratting. We had a brick cabin at the bottom of our field, in which we kept poultry food and tools. It had a bench made from old sleepers from the tram-shed where Ephraim worked and a free-standing, square, iron stove on legs, well out in the middle of the floor, whence a four-inch iron smoke-pipe went into a chimney in one corner. Next to this cabin, attached to one end, there was an extension about 28 feet long, with a brick back and free end and a slated roof, in which we kept poultry. As it was on a slope, the poultry section was stepped in three levels with the wooden shuttering for the concrete floors left in place, i.e. the 'riser' of each step was a stout wooden board. A pair of rats once chewed their way through one of these boards and made a snug home under the concrete. Seth saw one of them go to ground, looked for other entrances and exits and blocked up the only two he could find. Ephraim came home from work and Bullet was sent for. So, at about 7 p.m. that evening there was

Ephraim, Seth, Bullet, a large dog (not Dont), a creamy white ferret and myself, as usual, holding the storm-lamp in a section of that hen-hut approximately 9 ft. x 9 ft., all bent upon the destruction of two medium-sized 'rattens'.

When Bullet saw what the job was, he was none too happy about it. His ferret was with young, and he didn't want her to stay under and suck her victim's blood for hours, if she should make a kill under all that concrete. Seth said he was worrying like an old woman, and Bullet said he wasn't risking a good ferret for just two rats that Seth could easily smoke out with a few shreds of old car tyre or catch in a trap, anyway. Seth, as usual, prevailed. The ferret went down and soon a rat, the male, emerged; the dog snapped once and retreated two paces. The female just put her nose out, saw the great, fierce-eyed dog and turned back into the run, preferring to face the ferret rather than the dog. There was a few seconds of threshing about under the concrete and then silence. The men looked at one another and waited. Five minutes later the ferret was still under there with her victim, when Seth went to fetch an eight-pound hammer to break up his beautiful concrete floor. He broke a way through to that precious ferret in a manner that brought Bullet out in a cold sweat.

As children and young adults a good half of our walks, and later a lot of our courting, would take us to the wooded area between Wyke Station (closed 1953) and Royds Hall. Each section of these woods had its own name, as given on the map of 1852, but we lumped them all together and called them Judy Woods, the only name we knew for them. The story of how they came by this name is told in James Parker's book[6] and need not be re-told here. Horse Close Bridge, as it is called on all maps, was Judy Bridge to us, and this was the focal point of our rambles. In those days, all these woods were the property of Bradford City Corporation, and were open to the public, just like a present-day country park. Oak and beech trees predominated and some of the latter were fine specimens by West Riding standards. There were extensive beds of tall bracken in some parts and plenty of brambles, but in other parts there was enough grass under the tree-cover to make the scene idyllic, especially in late spring when there was a wonderful carpet of bluebells.

The 'gamekeeper', as he was generally called, of this municipal park was Harry Dalby (Plate 10), who belonged, I should think, to the end of my Generation I. Harry lived in some old cottages which stood in the middle of the fields between Royds Hall and Judy Bridge. Unlike his present-day counterparts, he took a very paternal view of his job. He taught me, as he must have taught a lot of children, the names of the

Plate 10. Harry Dalby.

common woodland trees, plants and birds. At that time, he was trying to keep down the numbers of magpies in Judy Woods, because he regarded them as a threat to the smaller species whose eggs and young they ate. He swore that they could tell the difference between his walking-stick and his gun, as he never saw a magpie when out with his gun but he could get within a few yards of them, even with me with him, when he was carrying only his stick.

Harry's identity in the locality was as the cabbage king. In those days the little shows in the schools, clubs and pubs made much more sophisticated and stringent demands on exhibitors than do the big commercial shows nowadays. They required perfect single specimens rather than extensive displays which are able to absorb and conceal a number of mediocre specimens. In our neighbourhood, judges of cabbages looked for small cabbages of about 1lb. weight, *very* tightly wrapped and with the minimum of stem. Sheer size got you nowhere. The idea of awarding a prize to an *uncut* cabbage, as I have seen at the great Southport Show, would have evoked scathing contempt from Harry and his fellow exhibitors. Harry could grow those small, heavy, close-packed, core-less cabbages better than anybody else for miles around. He saved his own seed, sowed, planted and fed to an esoteric formula of his own and was so successful that the ordinary allotment gardeners of the vicinity stopped competing against him.

I think I must have been in my early teens when, on an old-fashioned summer's afternoon, I was hovering on the edge of the group of men in Walter Brook's garden, spellbound by the plot that was unfolding there. There was to be a show in Wyke Board School the next evening and Walter and some of his friends were determined to stop Harry Dalby from winning the red cabbage class for the umpteenth time in succession. From somewhere they had obtained a red cabbage that looked like a possible winner. The Co-op butcher was one of the company and he had been sent for his best boning knife. Probing with this had revealed that the stalk inside the cabbage was much too big. The cabbage was then clamped between the knees of the local bobby, who always dropped in for anything up to half an hour on such afternoons, just to get his jacket off! The offending core was expertly excised and leaves from another cabbage were rolled like a cigar and pressed hard into the cavity. This one was going to have no stalk at all, and even Harry Dalby couldn't match that! As always there was a lot of relaxed back-chat and genuine fun. This was a genuine, real life and unrehearsed scene of *Last of the Summer Wine* vintage, but the participants were taking it at their own, relaxed speed with long, often significant, silences and expressive but inarticulate sounds. They were not playing to an audience in an impersonal way, and there was no regular spacing of the wisecracks.

There was talk of standing several pints to the judges beforehand, just to help to clinch the coup. For some reason I was unable to go to that show and when I asked Walter next day how they had got on with the cabbage, he just grunted tolerantly and shook his head with a little secretive grin. I bet they chickened out and never even put it on the table, but that issue was, and is, irrelevant. They had had their fun; they did not need success. By this time, some of those present would possess wirelesses, but by no means all of them. For all of them, however, their kind of fun and amusement had been fixed long before there were cars and radios for working men.

Walter Brook (Plate 11), who was also a major figure in my view of Generation I, has been mentioned above. Like Edwin Lightowler, although fully twenty years younger, he had started his working life as a collier but had got out of the pit, either thrown out of work ('made redundant' simply does not fit my Generation I!) or having taken the opportunity when it arose. As long as I knew him, he earned his living dressing and cleaning fish, game and poultry in Bradford wholesale market. He started at about 6 a.m. and got back home about 11.30 a.m. His job was mainly gutting fish, so the real work had to be completed by 7.30, because the men from the fish and chip shops would be there before then. It was a highly skilled job when it was performed with the speed and accuracy that Walter commanded. He once gave a demonstration in our kitchen of boning and trussing a turkey which showed greater skill, to my mind, than that of many of the 'skilled men' engaged on making aircraft radio and radar in the wartime factory where I worked.

Walter lived down Storr Hill, but the tiny bit of land that he rented and used as a garden and poultry run lay just over the fence from our land. As Walter had all his afternoons free and spent most of them in this garden, from which there was a wonderful panoramic view reaching as far as Odsal Top, it was one of the main gossip and relaxation centres of the community, especially as Walter had great need of the company of his fellow men and women. He loved to 'tell the tale' (but not in his own home!), was generous to a fault (with people he got on with!) and he had an enthusiasm that was irresistible when talking about chrysanthemums or Rugby League football. Many of the tales of his early working life began with the formula: 'When Ah wor at t' Brussen Unnion' (When I worked at the Burst Onion Pit), which is a bit more original than 'Once upon a time'.

Plate 11. Walter Brook.

The contents of many of his tales were no doubt as fictional as traditional fairy-tales!

If Harry Dalby was the local cabbage king, then Walter was the self-appointed chrysanthemum king. His little patch of land was as inhospitable to any of the more exotic florist's plants as it could be: 600 feet up on a north-facing slope in the Pennines, and a shallow mixture of red shale and sticky clay required immense dedication to produce any flowers of quality. And indeed, if the truth were told, Walter rarely did produce anything of exhibition quality; his reputation as a chrysanthemum fancier rested on his personal combination of enthusiasm, generosity and entertainment value. He could make friends and keep them without any conscious effort. One of his best friends was George Bacon, who at that time was growing the chrysanthemum trials for the northern section of the National Chrysanthemum Society on his nursery at Eccleshill. George was also an active hybridiser, and Walter was able to grow quite a few of George's creations before they were put on the market. The main chrysanthemum man for Bradford Parks and Gardens, whose name I forget, always made Walter welcome and paid quite deferential attention to Walter's opinions. He had also captivated the owner of a small woollen mill – again, I cannot remember the name – who, three or four times a year, would come with his car and take Walter and his cronies on a Sunday morning trip around the main chrysanthemum fanciers of Bradford and neighbouring parts.

Walter's greenhouse was such a ramshackle affair, made up of old windows and bits of wood that 'fitted where they touched', that I was afraid to go in it if there was any appreciable wind. It got around, of course, that Walter was likely to have the latest releases and was prepared to let people he liked have them cheap, 3*d.* each for rooted cuttings of the latest, for instance. I was once in his greenhouse with him when people he didn't like came into sight round the corner of the snicket that led from Storr Hill. Walter growled something really uncomplimentary, and struck a couple of sharp blows against the glazing-bars of his greenhouse roof, which were treated with the same whitewash as he used on the interior of his hen-hut, causing a shower of tiny white flakes to fall on the massed boxes of chrysanthemum cuttings below. Walter met the visitors a couple of yards from his greenhouse door; they talked and presently made their requests, only to have their attention drawn to the unprecedented attack of white fly on Walter's cuttings! They could see it for themselves! Absolutely covered they were! So the unwelcome visitors commiserated with Walter and left without chrysanths. It was not easy to get rid of white-fly in those days!

Walter was also a great devotee of Rugby League and had played in a junior team when younger. Ephraim, Walter and myself, sometimes also Geoffrey, regularly walked up to Odsal Top to watch Bradford Northern from about 1939 to 1950. Walter had a select group of friends and acquaintances who always stood in the same place, and their comments, criticisms and repartee were as good an entertainment as the game itself – often better! One gem of wisdom contributed by this group has remained in my mind ever since. A visiting player, noted for over-vigorous and downright dirty play, had committed one of his typical offences and the crowd was baying, 'Send 'im off! Send 'im off!' Now, there was one of our group who had been a sergeant-major during the First World War, and, some thirty years later, had lost none of his vocal power. With perfect timing, he waited until the crowd was drawing breath and bellowed, 'Leave the bugger on an' kill 'im!' On a few occasions, when there was talk of sending down an unworthy, really naughty, student, I have recalled this advice!

The characters and life-style represented in this account give the impression of an idyllic, carefree existence. This is quite misleading. Theirs was a life-style founded on the working hours and conditions described in the Report on the Employment of Children and in Cudworth's dramatic description of a tour of the Low Moor Company's forges and furnaces.[7]

More People

As Generation I gave way to Generation II, there was still a sufficiently close sense of community in the district, and the numbers involved were still so relatively small, that all levels of society were in touch with one another. This was particularly evident in the relationship between employer and employee. They still passed one another in the street, shopped at the same shops and, most important, owner-manager and labourer made out their cases and stated their minds to one another *face to face*. Workers of both sexes showed deference to the bosses, and very often expressed genuine admiration of a sort for them. In turn, most of the millowners and the managers of the Low Moor Company were of local stock, and it came natural to them to devote themselves to the improvement of the district and the well-being of its inhabitants. None of them would have left his own enterprise to be run entirely by managers and retired to a fine mansion in a more salubrious part of the country. They would never have conceded that a paid understudy could do the job as well as they could;

they were sure that there was no quicker way to bankruptcy than that! From the days of Ancient Greece and Rome, I can find in history no flourishing society capable of growth that has ignored this principle.[8] They often retired at an age that suited them when there was a capable son, or son-in-law, to take over, but control had to remain in the family.

The philanthropic efforts of the mill-owners and other entrepreneurs of Wyke and district are a constant feature of the histories of James Parker, writing at the beginning of this century. Although Parker shows the same sycophantic attitude to successful business men as the majority of late Victorian provincial historians, there is sufficient hard fact in his accounts to convince us of the involvement of its local entrepreneurs in the social life of the district. To start with Henry Birkby. He started Storr Hill Brickworks, down Wilson Road, in 1869. Not only did he make up Wilson Road for the distance of half a mile, but he was responsible for the building of several mills and similar premises in various parts of Bradford and district. Parker, writing in 1902, says:

> He retired from business some years ago, and the firm is carried on by his sons under the old name . . . Mr Birkby has taken an active part in the public life of Wike for a great number of years, being one of the first members for Wike when it was included in the area of the North Bierley Local Board in 1876, and remained a member of the Board until it was made into a District Council in 1894, and continued to sit as one of the members for Wike, till it was annexed to Bradford in 1889. He has been Poor Law Guardian for Wike on the North Bierley Board of Guardians for eight years. He was also a member for three years of the North Bierley Joint Hospital. Mr Birkby has taken a great interest in the welfare of Wike and district and has rendered yeoman's service to the district in getting many improvements, including, along with others, the Recreation Ground. He was returned as Councillor for Wike Ward to the City Council, in 1899, for three years, and which he now represents.[9]

Such was the Great Tradition view of Henry Birkby. But he was a larger-than-life folk hero to the Little Tradition and many stories were told about him with great relish and not a little artistic embroidery. The popular name for him was Harry Slasher, deriving from his fiery temper which led to frequent threats to slash somebody. A friend of Seth's was a slater, and he was once employed to slate the roof of one of the Birkby barns, the one nearest the tunnel ventilator shaft. As was the practice of good, skilled slaters, this man was hitting the nails only once as he drove them into the laths to fix the slates. Down below, on a tour of inspection, Harry Slasher observed this, and shouted up to him, 'Ah long is them nails tha't ewsin'?' The answer was, 'A gooid inch.' Whereupon Harry sent the slater's lad to fetch some 1 inch nails. They still went in with one blow. So Harry, thinking that the slater was shirking effort and that he, Harry, was getting an inferior job from him, sent the lad to the joiner's shop for some 2 inch nails. The slater, who had up to then proceeded with his job without comment, decided that it was time to stop this nonsense, and shouted down to Harry: 'Tha c'n tell 'im ter fotch six inch nails an' ah'll bray 'em in i' wun!' So Harry gave it up and went away.

Once he joined two or three old men sitting on the low dry-stone wall at the top of Wilson Road – where later a police-box stood. He was getting on a bit by then and, by way of letting the others know how well off he was, he talked about his problems as regards how to leave his money and his property. They listened in respectful silence, but finally one of them, who had a wooden leg and was consequently not at all well off, said: 'Aye, well, ther's wun thing. My lot wants me ter live as long as A can, bud thine can't wait for thee ter dee!' Harry would be silenced on this occasion, but it wouldn't stop him from sitting on that wall again, in the same company, whenever it pleased him.

Harry did not lose every round, though. The story went round that, while sitting on either the Local Board or the District Council, he pressed for the widening of Worthinghead Road. There would have been only one contractor in the running, if it had been approved. Another member of the committee demurred, and thought it quite wide enough for the traffic it carried. Harry exploded: 'Wide? Wide? A could piss across it!' The chairman thumped: 'Mr Birkby! Mr Birkby! You are out of order!' Harry trumped: 'Aye, Ah kno' A'm aht av order – else A could piss *twice* across it!'

This was a difficult act to follow, as they say. His sons seem to have left the business to free-wheel during the inter-war years. Nor did they play any part in local politics. The only one we ever knew was Albert, who lived at the old family house, tended some exotic plants in his conservatory, where he also kept a monkey, and who had a steel hook in place of one of his hands, just like Captain Hook in *Peter Pan*.

John Morton, owner of the mill up Carr Lane, was a totally different type of local tycoon. He played no part in local politics, nor in the local folk-lore, but he was every bit as close to the Little Tradition as Harry

Slasher. For he was a 'fancier' – and a genial and generous man into the bargain. I am not sure, but I think that he had become acquainted with Seth when they were both members of the same homing society, as the pigeon racing clubs were called. Seth had been secretary of such a club before I was born and maps from which he could calculate distances and the time it would take a pigeon to fly from X to Storr Hill fascinated him for the rest of his life. John Morton was not a dedicated competitor, as were most 'fanciers', but he was interested in all 'fur and feather' subjects as well as in the usual florist's plants. The first time I ever saw goldfish in an ornamental pond in a conservatory was when Seth took me at an early age to visit John Morton at Park House. John Morton's son, Edgar, was a real 'fancier', however, and I believe that he made fur and feather exhibiting, judging and trading his full-time job. I remember seeing Edgar judging at Bingley Show and at Brighouse Show. He went to live at Priestley Green, so I am told.

When Seth began to feel the strain of working a full day laying bricks, at the age of about seventy, John Morton had just started an extension to his mill. He intended this to be a long-term investment, apparently, for once it had been marked out and the foundations laid, he told Seth that he could go when it pleased him, lay as many bricks as he wanted and he, John, would pay him so much per thousand bricks. For weeks on end during the mid and late thirties, Seth and Frank's father, Arthur Wilkinson, would be the only figures on the site, just laying bricks at their own pace in fine weather. The photo of Seth (Plate 12), much enlarged from a contact print of a negative produced by a primitive Box Brownie, was taken whilst he was doing this work. As soon as the war started, the supply of wool from Australia dried up and, like many another woollen mill in the neighbourhood, Carr Lane Mill was turned over to munitions and acquired by the English Electric Company. It seemed to us that Seth's building was finished overnight by a horde of frantic men driving hysterical machines.

These are the two examples of local industrialists best known to me. But even a cursory reading of James Parker's book should convince any reader that they were typical examples. The great landmark at Odsal Top, Coll Mills, founded 1825, was owned just before our day by one John Robertshaw, so the mill was known, not without a certain amount of affection for the owner, as 'Owd Johnny's'. The local employers found that it paid them, within reason, to look after and encourage good workers; nobody worried about the other kind. After Walter Brook had a slight heart attack, the owner of the wholesale fish, fowl and game business

Plate 12. Seth Shaw, aged about 70.

where he worked sent a car to pick him up every morning at 5.30 a.m. This kind of 'industrial relations' was common down to World War II.

Inevitably, there were early Generation II characters, who could have held their own with the best personalities of my Generation I. Gladys Garside lived down one of the old streets off New Road Side until she was past ninety. She had a home help, with whom she got on very well. One morning, as they sat together at their 'elevenses', Gladys mused, 'Well lass, A can't grummel. A've 'ed a gooid innins, an' it can't last much longer. Bud A s'l be alreight if the' find ma a soft, warm spot i' St. Mark's churchyard. Sumwier wier A san't get disturbed, tha knaws.'

To which the younger woman replied, 'Ee, A come through thier ivery mornin' to mi wark. A s'l say "Mornin, Gladys, nooan a bad day terday".'

Promptly came the reply: 'Aye, do that, lass. Bud dooan't wait fer a answer, er tha'll bi lat' fer wark!'

Harry Broomhead, whom Seth persisted in calling 'Brusheead', was a smallish, wiry, slightly bowlegged man of early Generation II. He earned his living as a general dealer, and sometimes he would do a 'flitting' for poorer people whose belongings would fit on his flat cart. On the corner of his modest flat cart, Harry sat as though he had sprouted from it, totally relaxed and comfortable. Frank's drawing of the bottom end of New Road Side in the thirties, showing a flat cart and a tramcar, has captured Harry perfectly. His shop, next door to the Mitchell brothers' butcher's shop, was full of the most uninviting furniture and bric-à-brac that one can imagine, and, at the time, we were told that he slept among his wares at the back of the shop because the living quarters further back were packed full of junk.

There were very few men of that age who did not like a drop to drink, especially the unmarried ones like Harry, and he was no exception. Which introduces one of my favourite tales, for which I can vouch absolutely.

Donald's Tale: Ephraim liked to offer pasturage to any kind of livestock that would help to keep the grass down in our field and thus diminish the chances of our hens getting crop-bound. At various times, we boarded sheep or stirks for Jim Mitchell until it was their turn to be slaughtered, or a plump, proud, entire pony for David Christie, the chimney-sweep, and, one summer during the war, the rather aged galloway that pulled Harry's flat cart.

One Saturday evening in summer, just as the day began to fade, Harry turned up, more than a little the worse for wear, with the purpose of saying 'goodnight' to his horse. He held out an empty hand that did not fool the horse for one second and called indistinct endearments. As Harry held out a friendly hand to the front end of the horse, it turned and, with what was for it an enormous effort, managed to lift its hind legs eighteen inches from the ground and tipple Harry off his feet. There was no real danger; the horse was so old and decrepit that it could not get its feet any higher! A pile of second-hand floor-boards lay nearby, so Harry seized one and whirled it round his head with venomous intent. He missed, of course, lost his footing and finished up on his face.

It was at this point that Annie fetched me to our front door to see the fun. Seth, also a little the worse for wear, had appeared on his own front step that was raised some two feet higher than the path and provided a fine miniature grandstand. There he was, solemnly dragging the gold-plated watch that was his pride and joy from his waistcoat pocket and proclaiming: 'First rahnd ta t'os.' The battle went on, with Seth intoning at appropriate intervals: 'Second rahnd ta t'os an all,' or 'Third rahnd ta Brusheead.' The truth of this one I can vouch for. They could make fun, good, clean fun, out of nothing!

There were personalities on Storr Hill Side who were well known for other talents and characteristics than these originals described above. Between the wars the shopkeepers and small tradesmen formed the most obvious backbone of the community. For one thing, everybody knew them.

About halfway down Storr Hill there lived and worked John Foster, a third generation wheelwright. John and his wife Mollie still live there and the old workshop and forge premises have been modernised and enlarged by his son, Lionel, who carries on the family tradition of fine craftsmanship in the field of general engineering. I can bear witness to John's amazing versatility, as his workshop was another meeting place, a 'call-'oil' for a small group of friends and neighbours, just like my description of Tom Hoyle's clogger's shop. The only time John's bench was tidied was when Walter Brook had dropped in for a chat and a warm at the old stove; Ephraim had his first heart attack while threading studding rods on a primitive machine there. John's craftsmanship comprised at least three distinct trades: he was a fine worker of the most durable hardwoods from which he constructed carts from scratch; in his little forge he could make and apply the iron hoops that served as tyres on all carts when we were young; he then became a signwriter and finished the cart off with the most accurate and delicate of lettering and lined patterns. We have seen genuine gipsy *vardos* done up there as well as wealthy butchers' fancy show traps. When such work was not forthcoming he made hooks for a bacon factory or wrought iron gates, even wrought iron staircases for the wealthy. The most elaborate and tasteful designs and scrolls were simply chalked on the stone floor of the shop and the glowing rods of iron beaten on the anvil until they matched them. It was probably in his little lean-to forge that, at a fairly young age, I was given the valuable advice: 'Nivver pick owt up in a blacksmith's shop baht spitting on it first!'

Above the shop he kept a loft of pigeons; he was a fancier who did not compete. Before I knew him, his Sunday morning recreation had been the sport of ratting! When the West Riding Folk Museum at Shibden was opened, a wheelwright's shop was set up there. John was asked if he had any old, traditional tools of the craft and this led to him being asked to demonstrate the hooping of a wheel in that shop for a Yorkshire Television programme for schools. On one occasion, when she had been marched into the wrong classroom in her primary school on the Wirral of Cheshire, where an educational programme on the television was just finishing, my elder daughter, then aged six or seven, shouted, 'That's Uncle John Foster!' She had been carried up the ladder by him to look at his pigeons on more than one occasion.

Being sent shopping at an early age was our introduction to society and the wider world. On my Map III, I list over twenty-five small shops on New Road Side, well within two hundred yards of our house. They were all kept by different people of different personalities and principles. As children, it was of course the sweet shops where we could spend our tiny dole of pocket money that most concerned us. There were many of them, for both children and adults indulged to excess in sweets in those days, but four come to mind as being specialists, selling nothing but sweets and tobacco. Leonard Atack, at the end of Barraclough Square, who also sold some soft drinks, some pills and some popular remedies; Mr Jones in his wooden hut next to the Crown Hotel stables; Mrs Healey, whom Laurence and I rated as the best for range and quality and whose husband was the lamplighter for the area; and, as the 'tuck shop' for Carr Lane School, Mrs Benn, whose one large living-room in a pre-1850 house had been converted into a little shop by the introduction of an interior 'porch' about four feet square and provided with a flap across the inner doorway to act as a counter. We soon learned how to react to all of these different personalities, and they were all experts at dealing with us. We were sent at an early age to the three fish and chip shops, learning to queue in a confined space and patiently wait our turn. They each not only produced different types and qualities of fish and chips, they, too, had their different personalities, to whom we had to adapt our behaviour.

Plate 13. The top of New Road Side. The window on the right belongs to the Junction Inn. The sign 'Clipper and Comb' indicates the shop where we had our hair cut in the twenties. Tom Jagger kept it during World War I and for fifteen years after. (1985)

With experience, one came to size up shopkeepers by the appearance of their premises. At a glance one reacted unfavourably to a dingy, smelly, badly stocked and untidy shop, even though at that age we could not express our reaction. Nathan Garside's greengrocer's shop (which was selling video recordings in 1985!) always smelled of earth from the permanent carpet of soil that dropped through potato sacks and was never swept up. By the look of them, the fruit and vegetables on the shelves might well have come out of the same sacks. It was naturally produced food, though, and the housewives of those days were accustomed to lots of dressing and washing of natural produce. If they took off the outer layers or pods and found bad food inside, they simply took it back.

On my picture of the top end of the right hand side of New Road Side, just decipherable, is the sign 'Clipper and Comb', announcing that those premises are still used as a barber's shop (I suppose I should say 'hairdresser's shop' nowadays) as they were during World War I and probably earlier. In those days it consisted of one room with a stone floor, a stove and a wash-basin, a single chair and a mirror, with a few seats and a bench for waiting customers. Throughout the nineteen-twenties we had our hair cut there by Tom Jagger,[10] who was the epitome of a New Road Side tradesman of those days: of medium height, sturdy build, pretty bald with a greying military moustache; he always wore a grey, linen jacket as his working uniform. There were still many men who, probably because they could not keep a cut-throat razor in good condition, relied on a barber to shave them, and Tom charged 1½*d.* per week to shave them daily, usually in the evening. We paid 3*d.* for a haircut. There was no cutting of hair on a Friday evening; that was reserved for shaving men who had one shave a week and wanted to be smart and clean for the weekend.

He was followed in the shop by Arthur Roebuck, a pleasant, younger man of well-cared-for appearance: good complexion, well-brilliantined black hair and a smart white overall. The shop also looked cleaner and smarter with some modern tools of the trade and new plumbing. Tom's one and only 'short [very short] back and sides' style gave way to a little more fashionable and varied repertoire.

The name of the present business, 'Clipper and Comb' completes perfectly the three periods that those premises have seen: the age of the cut-throat razor, the age of the safety-razor and brilliantine, and the age of shaving and hairdressing with electrical apparatus.

During the lifetime of my Generation II, just now coming to an end, there took place the greatest transition in all walks of life that Storr Hill Side has undergone in its relatively short history. We are here dealing with personality; other features of this transition will be dealt with in the appropriate places. From the beginning of the century, this kind of people and the conditions in which they thrived began to be whittled away. Many of my Generation II were cast in exactly the same mould as their forefathers, and did not change much to the end of their lives. They maintained the same resilience in adversity, the same ability to cut their coat according to their cloth, the same indifference to the world outside, the same sense of duty and the same brand of humour. Bit by bit, however, Generation II and their children, Generation III, lost the dignity in adversity, the indifference to the world outside and the sense of humour that had distinguished Generation I. They were no longer as keen on gambling on their own prowess or on any chance occurrence; they no longer used their fists on one another with the same insouciance as before. Perhaps it was the feeling of insecurity and uncertainty engendered by World War I and the slump that followed that made them more concerned with material provision for the future and hence more dependent on social and economic conditions.

Conversation on Storr Hill Side centred more and more on dare-devils on motor-bikes, on local and national football teams and their 'stars' (although these 'stars' still had to be able to play football – the stage when large transfer fees alone could draw the crowds was quite some way off), on race-horses and jockeys. Horse-racing offered the perfect stage for the know-alls; every factory and every tap-room had its would-be tipster. The women remained as voluble and catty as ever, but talked more about fashion and planned more shopping forays and coach-trips; they talked less about local scandals and the prices of things and more about the progress of their children at school. The latter was very important to them once they had become aware of the opportunities to 'better thersens' offered by education.

Pondering the reasons for these changes, it had occurred to me that apart from the universal developments that can be discerned throughout the nation, one vital factor has been the lack of direct contact with their fellow men, the lack of hearers who could answer back. As long as neighbours and friends, masters and men, audience and entertainers met face to face, both able to state their mind and take up a stance on the spot, there was a far better chance of understanding one another than is normal nowadays, when all conversation, all opinions and recommendations that matter are conveyed in a strange language by people the receivers have never met, and by a totally impersonal medium that can be immediately switched off and ignored. The ability to reason with human beings in a language shared by both parties, to fully explore a subject of interest, to hone one's own powers of expression and sense of humour, have been almost totally destroyed by the all-pervasive influence of a medium that is about as natural and healthy as a diet of nothing but canned beans. What the media concocts has now come to be regarded as reality; for many, any problem that cannot be solved by pressing a button is totally insoluble; trying again, rehearsing is not featured in the media, so perseverance has almost disappeared. Arising from this, teachers, in particular, have an enormous problem which afflicts them day after day throughout their career.

Chapter 5

Housing on Storr Hill Side

From all the evidence it is clear that the workers of Storr Hill Side in the late nineteenth century did not belong to the class of 'Victorian poor' as described by the standard histories of the period. The area I have defined as Storr Hill Side was a late nineteenth century workers' dormitory; there was no pit, factory or blast furnace in the immediate vicinity and it was surrounded by open, green land on which many of the inhabitants kept poultry and pigs. In spite of the considerable contribution of the Low Moor Company, it was not a planned, regimented settlement provided by philanthropic employers, like Saltaire, Ackroydon or Port Sunlight. It was the product of small, local entrepreneurs and builders and the dwellings had in consequence a wide range of size, plan and quality. Although some of the property, especially the low cottages of the Rock Side and the Green Market, built before 1850, were, by the standards of the period between the wars, crude, inadequate and insanitary, something like half of the property represented in our 1881 Census is still standing and, with few alterations and a little maintenance, is perfectly habitable.

The majority of dwellings built before 1850 on Storr Hill Side seem to have been single-storey 'low houses'. Most of these have gone, but enough of them have survived, still occupied although usually enlarged, to give us a good idea of what they were like when first built. Good examples of them survive on the left going down Storr Hill (Plate 15 and Fig.1) and in what is left of the Green Market at the time of writing (Plates 16, 17 and Fig.1a). The plans of dwellings offered in the following paragraphs are drawn from memory, with a lot of help from Frank and Laurence, and consequently dimensions and proportions may not be strictly accurate.

The three low cottages, Nos. 68, 70, 72 Storr Hill Side, have been known to all of us since childhood. Originally they comprised five dwellings, and, in fact still housed four families down to the end of World War II. They have since been given new doors and window-frames and fancy imitation stone roofs and have been made more weatherproof and brighter in appearance by rendering the outside walls. At the time of my photograph of 1985, the top cottage and the bottom one had assimilated their neighbours, leaving the middle dwelling at its original size. Before World War I the bottom cottage, No. 68 (Fig.1), had been extended at the back to accommodate a scullery and a very small 'parlour' which was used as a bedroom. The history of this cottage is complicated; apparently it had originally had two stories, i.e. a 'chaymer-'eight', but at the time of which I am writing the original bedroom was being used by the family next door. It was not unusual for a family to allow neighbours to use a bedroom for which they had no pressing need.

One went down a few steps to enter the front door, which led directly into the one room in which the family lived, ate and slept. In the twenties and thirties the family included parents and a son and a daughter, both grown up. It was normal in most of the houses of the neighbourhood for children of both sexes to sleep in the same room, depending on the size of the family and the size of the house. In a 'chaymer-'eight' house, if there was a large bedroom it might be divided into two with a flimsy wooden partition.[1] The loft was not left open to the slates, there was a kind of cockloft, but the beams supporting the bedroom floors were left uncovered, i.e. they were not underdrawn. They had running water to a tap that was often enclosed in a cupboard, and by our time they had gas and outside water closets. These examples stood well back from Storr Hill, and their gardens were large enough to produce useful vegetable crops. Ike Hollis, living in what had been originally the top two cottages, No. 72, used to sell rhubarb. His daughter, Marion, went to Bolling High School for Girls in 1933.

Unlike those of Storr Hill, the pre-1850 low houses of Smith Street (Plate 17) and Main Street (Plate 16) in the Green Market did not stand in gardens big enough to add to their practical usefulness and general amenities, and it is little wonder that those of Smith Street were in 1980 functioning as garages or small workshops. The only adaptation necessary was new fronts constructed of brick pillars supporting rolled steel joists to hold up the roof and a pair of wooden doors big enough to admit a car. Frank had one of these as his paint-store at one time and has supplied the details given in Fig.1a. A minute bedroom had been partitioned off the main living room, and from this a flight of steps led down to a cellar. It

Plate 14. The Junction Inn. The door used to be at the front of the porch, now walled up. (1985)

Plate 15. Low cottages. Nos. 68-72 Storr Hill, pre 1850. There were then five dwellings, now three. The Hollis family lived in the one nearest to the camera, the one with the jazzy new roof! (1985)

Plate 16. Looking down Main Street to New Road Side. Pre-1850, low, one-room housing. Vincent Smith's on left at bottom. (John Nicoll)

Plate 17. Same kind of dwellings of the same age in Smith Street, made into garages. (John Nicoll)

Plate 18. Front of Short Row. (1986)

Plate 19. Back of Short Row. (1986)

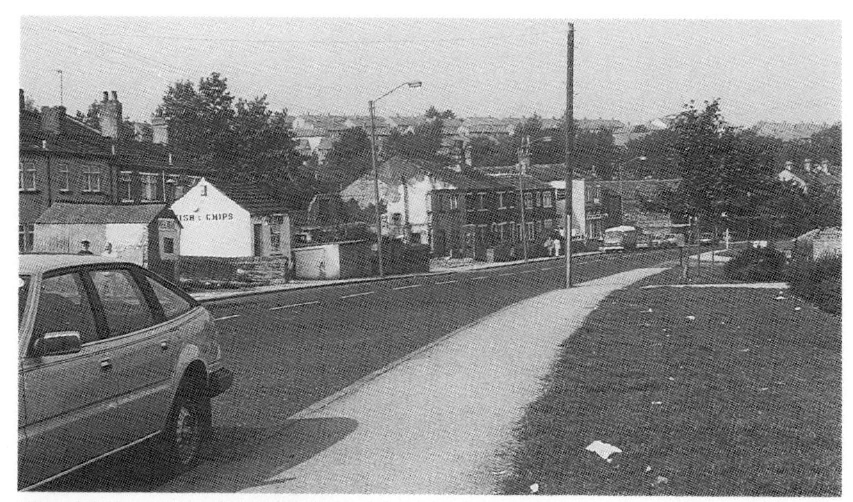

Plate 20. Remains of the left hand side of New Road Side in 1985. The wooden hut housed the leading newsagent business, Hinchliffe's. One of the old fish and chip shops, Greenwood's in our time, was apparently still in business. The right hand side has been demolished and built on again, forming the beginning of the Wycoller Estate.

Plate 21. Nos. 30 (right) and 32 Storr Hill. Through the pylon can be seen the extension to Morton's Mill that Seth worked on alone before the war, on which he was engaged when Plate 12 was taken. (1985)

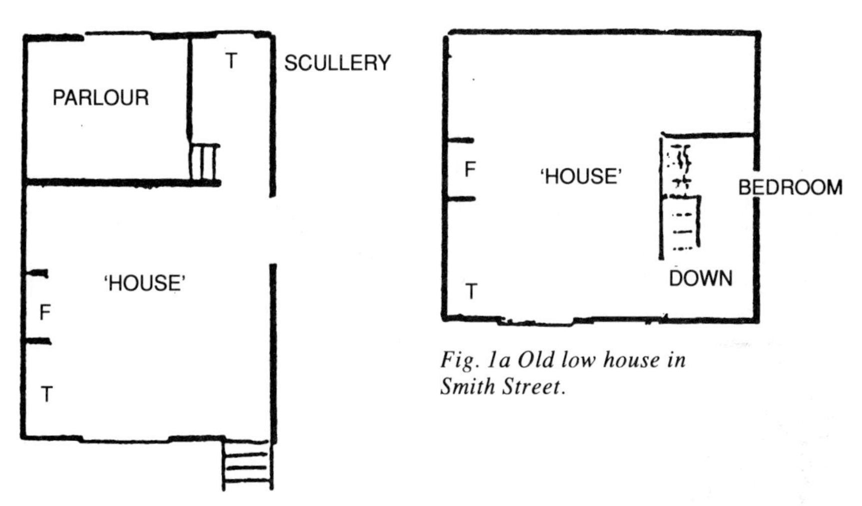

Fig. 1. No. 68 Storr Hill in the nineteen-twenties.

Fig. 1a Old low house in Smith Street.

was rather unusual for these tiny dwellings to have cellars.[2] The view down Main Street, with Vincent Smith's at the bottom on the left, shows such low houses in a better preserved state, still occupied in the 1980s. On John Nicoll's picture, the scale of the respective dwellings is shown by the chimneys, the roofs may well be built of the original cleft stone slabs, and the outside lavatories are the original structures, long since converted to water-closets.

The middens were simply called 'ash-pits' in our day, perhaps because their use was for the most part the disposal of ashes from the open fires, which in turn disposed of most of the garbage, or possibly as a hangover from their previous role as earth privies. The amount and variety of waste and rubbish that was consumed by the domestic fire in the living room of the house would amaze the present generation; practically the only thing that was left to throw away was ashes. Often enough at 17 Elizabeth Street, where there was only the normal, relatively small sitting-room grate, all that was not eaten of a table-fowl, the feathers, fat, head and legs, eventually the carcase also, would be consumed by the fire. It might also be a pair of old trousers, too greasy and tattered to be made into tabs for rugs, that was disposed of in this manner. In either case, the smell produced would be quite intolerable nowadays.

This type of low house, the one-roomed cottage, was not the only form of dwelling built in the first phase of building on Storr Hill Side. The view

Fig. 2. Frank's drawing of interior of 68 Storr Hill. The rectangular large box on the right is a shut-up bed. The only door from outside is done in faintly, and at the back the entrance to the built-on scullery and the steps up to the 'parlour' are shown.

from New Road Side, showing the front of Vincent Smith's New Road Side Post Office (Plate 31), shows also the row of two-storied, 'chaymer-'eight' houses attached to the Babes in the Wood Inn, which were part of the original complex of the Green Market. In all probability, they have been there as long as the low houses higher up the street, and they bear a striking resemblance to the Low Moor Company's earliest housing for their élite workers, of which Hird Road in Low Moor and especially the Short Row, still occupied with very little alteration, are well-known examples.[3] (Plates 18, 19) The Low Moor Company started building houses for its workers in 1801, having previously rented housing for some of them.

Of about the same age as these older houses of New Road Side and the Short Row are Nos. 30 and 32 Storr Hill. (Plate 21) They are clearly included on the 6" OS Map of 1852 and, like all the dwellings so far dealt with in this chapter, were probably built by the Low Moor Company. From No. 30, Annie, my mother, was married in 1920 and Frank was born in No. 32, where he lived for the first twenty-five years of his life. My photographs show them as they were in 1985.

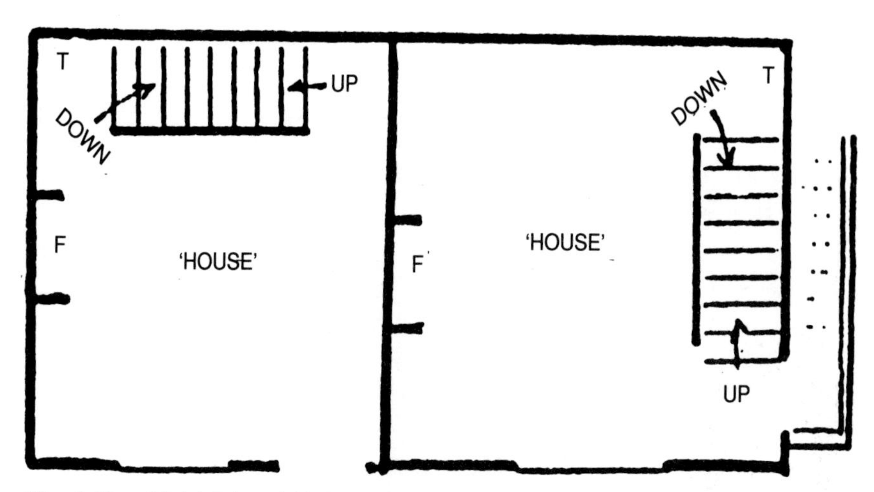

Fig. 3. Nos. 30 (right) and 32 Storr Hill.

Before World War I, the ground plan of these houses (Fig.3) was the ubiquitious single room from which a flight of stone steps led up to the bedroom(s) and, immediately below this, a flight of stone steps led down to a fairly large cellar. Cellars were important for the storage of meat and, at the time these were built, of beer, and these cellars had 'barrel 'oils', stone-built recesses, partly into the walls, into which a barrel would fit without rolling. When they lived at No. 30, Seth used to fancy starting the winter with a side of home-fed bacon hanging in the cellar; he was particular about how it had been fed, too, and tried to make sure when he spoke with a crony for a side of bacon, that it had not been fed on barley. This, he claimed, soon turned the fat yellow and made it go 'foisty'. Annie always had a rather weak and fussy stomach and she never forgot how the sight of this large mass of fat – it consisted of little else – turned her stomach every time she had to go into the cellar.

Upstairs, the area was divided into two bedrooms by flimsy wooden partitions and had a ceiling, i.e. was underdrawn. At the back, a steep slope of red shale came right up to the walls of the houses, and the only window that looked out onto this was a tiny window at the head of the bedroom steps in No. 32. Like the houses in Hird Road, they were, to all intents and purposes, 'blank back' dwellings. Water was piped in to the cellar head, where there was a shallow stone sink, a splash-stone. Heating for all purposes was restricted to a so-called 'Yorkshire range' in each house. The design of this range, which combined most efficiently the

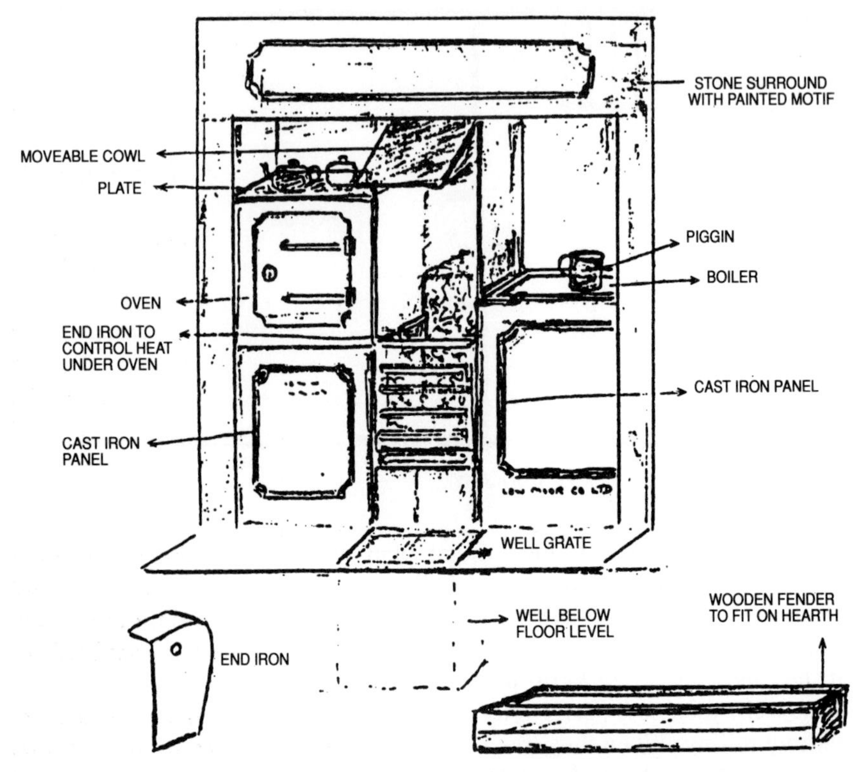

Fig. 4. Frank's drawing of an old fire-range. 'The fire jambs and head-stone (decorated) were painted brown, the rest of the fireplace was black-leaded. Dough was put to rise on the wooden fender – loaves, teacakes, etc. Brass fire-irons replaced the wooden fender at weekends or if company was expected'. – Frank.

heating of the room, cooking and hot water, may be seen in Frank's drawing, Fig.4; also in the excellent description and drawing in *Bowling Tidings*, pp.24-5. The actual fire-basket was thrown forward by a large fire-brick step at the back, which was called simply the fire-back. This was a large ledge on which a whole bucket of coal could be stacked. Accustomed to working in the heat of the pit-bottom, colliers felt the cold of the surface acutely, and were quite prodigal with their large supply of free or very cheap coal. Walter Barker, my grandfather, used to tell Ephraim to fetch up a bucket of coal and throw it on the fire and then fetch another and put it on the fire-back 'to be warming'. Although these houses had cellars, their coal store was in little stone huts at the bottom of the garden or in the tiny yard whence all their fuel had to be carried in a large skep. These coal stores were very often in the same structures as the water closets, which had replaced the old ash-pits. Further up Storr Hill, the houses of Worsnop Buildings, also on the 6" Map of 1852, are typical examples of this early phase of building.

The dwellings so far described, built before 1850, scarcely amounted to a quarter of those to be found on Storr Hill Side by 1900. In the second half of the nineteenth century, the whole of the West Riding underwent an unparalleled industrial expansion that resulted in the population of Bradford increasing from 103,371 in 1851 to 183,032 in 1881, and to 279,767 in 1901.[4] The last figure, however, is misleading for it includes the populations of Idle, Eccleshill, Thornton, North Bierley and Tong which were not incorporated into Bradford until 1899. The population of Wyke grew from 985 in 1801 to 1,918 in 1831, and was about 5,000 in 1875.[5] For the extent of expansion of Storr Hill Side in the second half of the nineteenth century see Map IV.

Two quotations from Cudworth are borne out by the developments on Storr Hill Side between 1850 and 1900. Writing in 1876, he says of Low Moor: 'For some time past more regard has been paid to social and domestic arrangements, brought about, in many instances by the young females of the community, who insist on better homes than sufficed for their mothers and grandmothers. Consequently, a better class of house is springing up, with more sleeping accommodation, and thus the separation of the sexes is better observed.'[6] Another note concerns Storr Hill Side more directly: 'It is about Wyke Common and towards that portion called New Road Side, that the greatest increase has taken place in working-class dwellings.'[7]

Our maps shows clearly the accuracy of the second quotation, and there is plenty of evidence for the first, although it might be difficult for a modern observer to appreciate the relative luxury of Perseverance Street and Daisy Cottages. Roughly speaking, the improvement consisted in replacing the 'chaymer-'eight' houses like the Short Row, Hird Road and the houses adjacent to the Quiet Woman down New Road Side with larger, better built and furbished houses like those just mentioned above, and replacing the old, one-roomed low houses with 'chaymer-'eight' back-to-backs. On Storr Hill Side, it was the age of the back-to-back, in spite of the fact that the Bradford Corporation had tried to get the building of new ones forbidden as early as 1854. They did not succeed until 1865 and even then had to give permission once more five years later, and were not finally successful until 1900.[8] These endeavours would have little effect on Wyke, which, as part of West Bierley, was first incorporated into Bradford in 1889.

There were several rows of back-to-back houses near the top of Storr Hill; we were familiar with those of Elizabeth Street/Barraclough Square, School Place/School Street; and, in fact, the nearest neighbours to 17 and 19 Elizabeth Street lived in the back-to-back combination of Ivy Bank and Rose Bank. The internal plan of almost all of them was virtually a doubling under one roof of 30 and 32 Storr Hill. These were the workers' barracks, erected mostly in rows, that were run up in a hurry to meet a rapidly expanding population. Although the Low Moor Company was still building some houses for its work-force, the back-to-backs were mostly the work of private entrepreneurs, and the names of the streets often testified to their builders: Barraclough Square, Holdsworth Street, Rawson Street, Worsnop Buildings. We suspect that, in some cases, their wives were honoured in the same manner in Elizabeth Street and Mary Street.

The plan of these back-to-back houses (Fig.5) was virtually the same as those in West Vale, Dewsbury.[9] They were two-storey buildings, known in the vernacular as 'one up and downs', and had cellars; stairs went up from just opposite the front door and under these, with access from the other end, stairs went down to the cellar. Both flights of stairs were made of stone. Upstairs originally consisted of one room exactly above and the same size as the living room, but a rough wooden partition, often made of uncovered and untreated floorboards, was added to make a large and a small bedroom. Water was led in at the front, into a sink in a cupboard that filled the space between the chimney-breast and the outer wall. The internal layout was usually very little different from Frank's drawing of the Storr Hill low house interior. Although there was an extra floor, a shut-up bed in the living room still was often necessary, even when there was only a relatively small family for those days. Also, old habits die hard, and an elderly couple living alone might prefer a shut-up bed in the living room, which was heated, and make very little use of the upper storey.

As with all types of housing, certainly in our neighbourhood, there were some good and reliable tenants, who kept their houses clean and tidy, and some who did not. We can remember rows of ten or a dozen such houses looking smart and cared for with scouring-stone corners in white or yellow on the steps and window-sills, while others looked and smelled so unhealthy that one instinctively crossed the street to avoid them.

The first six houses on Elizabeth Street were back-to-back with one side of Barraclough Square and their ground plan conformed to that of the

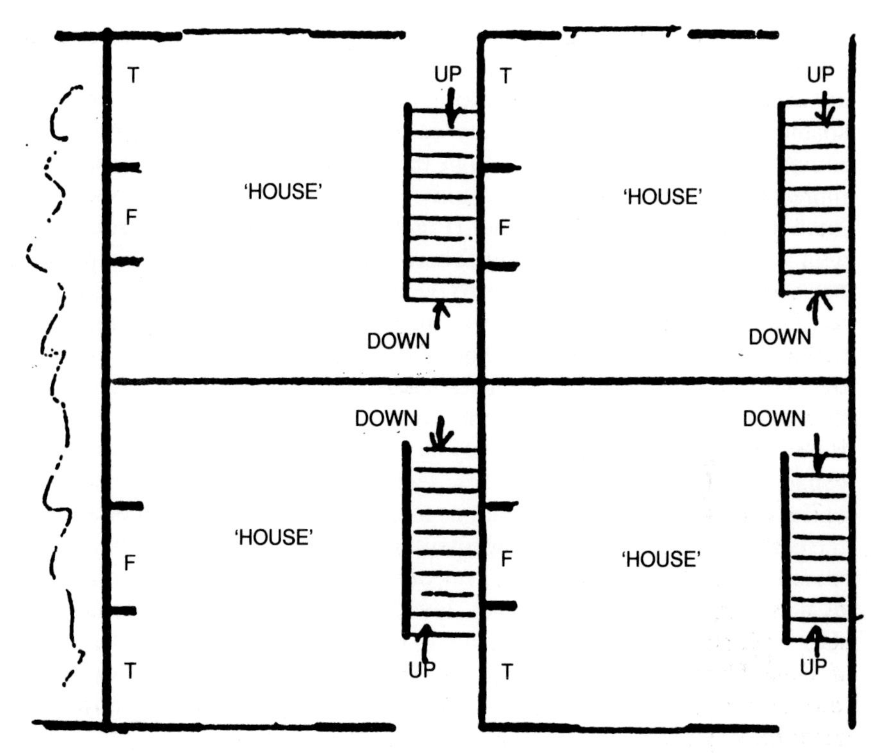

Fig. 5. Nos. 1 and 2 Elizabeth St. and Nos. 1 and 2 Barraclough Square.

prototype, Fig.5. They were occupied until well into the 1950s. There was a common midden for each six houses at the end of the row, and, under the same roof as the midden, one privy for each unit of three houses. Some of these operated on an unusual principle. In the little cabins of brick and stone was a robust, crude wooden seat, quite often fixed, and underneath this an earthenware drain-pipe some 9-10 ins. in diameter descended to about six feet into the ground. At the bottom was a pivoted metal pan, which was flushed by water let out of the sink in the kitchen of the house tilting the pan. It was one of the regular tricks of the inhabitants to flush the device while an uninitiated visitor was sitting on the seat. The effect was often quite dramatic! They were called 'tipplers'.

The short row of six houses (Fig.6), which faced Nos. 17 and 19 Elizabeth St. across our field, were built in the eighteen-seventies, probably at about the same time as the back-to-backs described above. At the time of building they were regarded as dwellings for better-class workers;

even in the nineteen thirties some people designated them as middle-class housing. As a type they are much more comfortable and capacious than anything previously built for working people on Storr Hill Side. They had spacious kitchens, which in many cases served also as living room, as rooms to work and eat in, although the parlour, the big room, was used more than the name 'parlour' would suggest. In addition to the standard kitchen range and a large set-pot (Fig.7)[10], there was a further source of heat in a fire-place in the parlour. There was still no hot water on tap; fire-back boilers appeared at least thirty years later on Storr Hill Side, in fact, we cannot remember any that were installed before 1920. Although each had a small area of garden attached to it, privies were still in one block at the end of the row and some houses had to share. Upstairs, the layout was exactly the same as on the ground floor, one large and one smaller bedroom, the larger one being plenty big enough to partition into two. A capacious 'keeping cellar' with a section partitioned off for coal and barrel-holes, was still considered necessary. The coal was shovelled into the cellar down grates in the pavement outside and an angled chute. There were little fireplaces in the bigger bedrooms of many of the older houses, as at 17 and 19 Elizabeth Street, but these were lit only in the case of illnesses which demanded considerable time in bed. Between the wars, most of these were not occupied by skilled men and their families; there was a clear preponderance of older people and men either retired or unemployed.

When I first knew Laurence he was living at No. 14 Elizabeth Street. He has provided the following plans from memory, some notes and a list of occupiers in the nineteen-twenties and -thirties.

We can just recall seeing a very faded name-plate, 'Daisy Cottages', above the door of No. 10, but we heard this name only from quite elderly people.

The layout upstairs was the same as downstairs in each house. When Frank Metcalfe, who then owned Nos. 13, 14, 15, needed an extra bedroom for an increasing family, he knocked a hole through the wall of the bedroom over his kitchen and occupied William Healey's smaller bedroom.

After this great increase of dwellings on Storr Hill Side between 1850 and 1900, building seems to have completely stopped on Storr Hill Side until the second spate of building after 1950. As far as our collective knowledge goes, only two new buildings were erected between the wars in the inner area of my study: the Gospel Hall in 1922 and Nos. 17 and 19 Elizabeth Street, first occupied about Easter 1925. (Fig.8.)

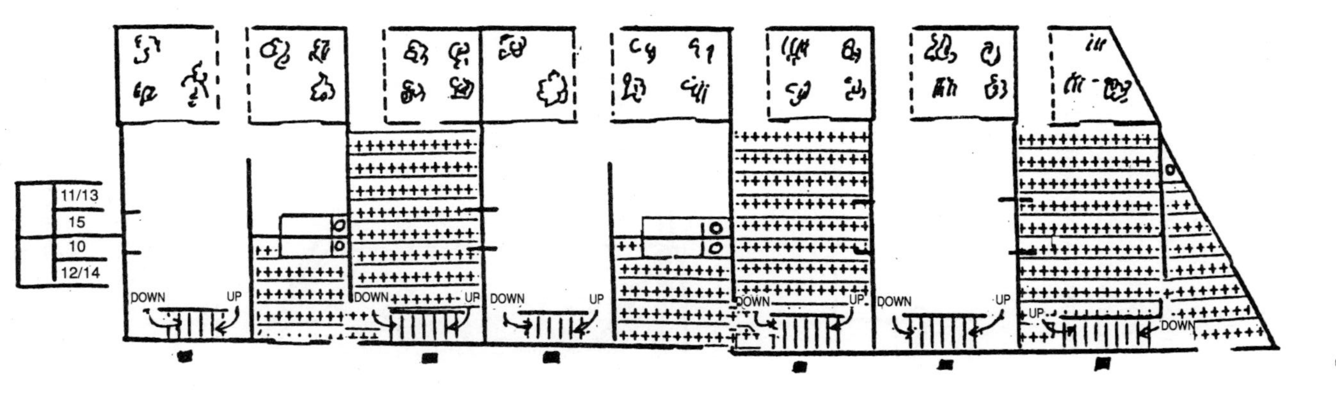

[set-pot symbol] = set-pots. These were the solid fuel type with flues. We think that No. 11 did not have one.

[grate symbol] = coal-cellar grates in pavement. Under each one was an angled chute which led the coal to the coal-cellar under the cellar steps. There was also a small keeping cellar with two barrel holes.

Six families shared the four outside toilets, as numbered, and there was one midden for each side of the row.

Nos. 13 and 15 had a fixture cupboard reaching from chimney breast to outer wall on the right of the fireplace in the lounge; in Nos 10, 11, 12, 14 it was on the left.

Fig. 6. Daisy Cottages in the nineteen-twenties.

When built, these two houses incorporated new design features and techniques, while retaining many that had long been typical of the industrial West Riding. On Storr Hill Side they were unique in that they had fire-back boilers providing hot water from a tap (in Annie's opinion by far their greatest amenity), they had a bathroom inside containing a toilet and a fixture cast-iron bath, and they were very nearly unique in being built of brick. The only brick-built houses other than ours that we can recall made

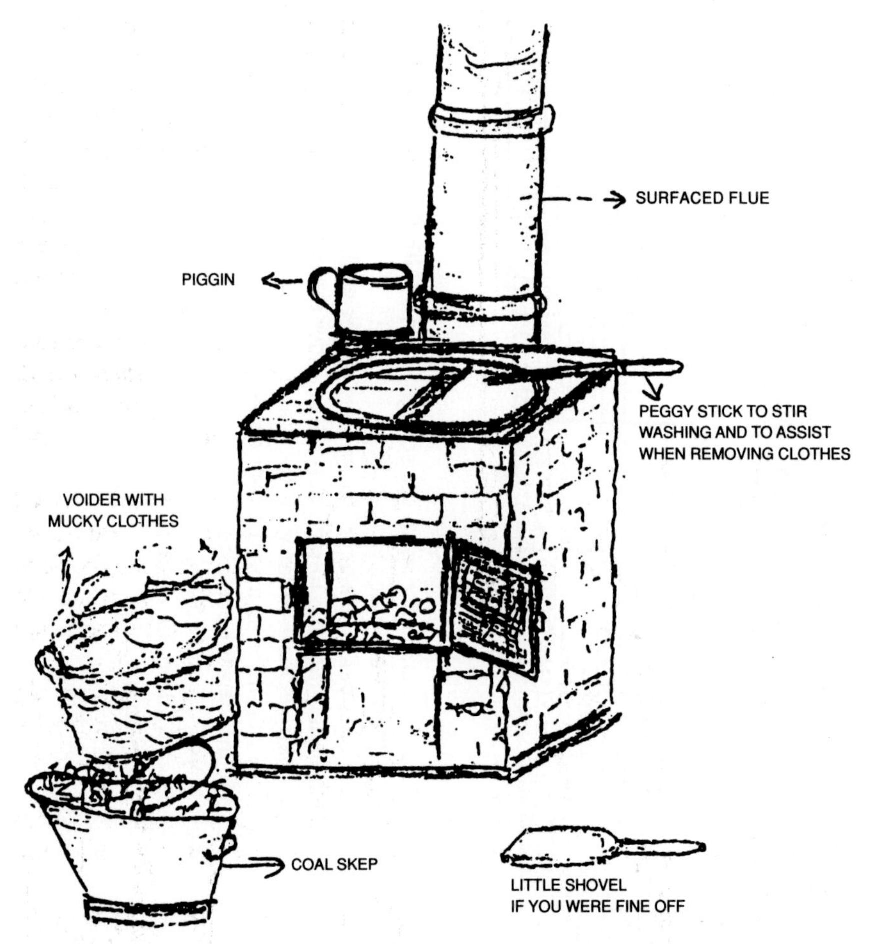

Fig. 7. Frank's drawings of a set-pot. Some of these were built with the flue visible (as above), others were built in to a chimney breast. The surface flue was built with drain-pipes.

up a short row at the end of, and at right-angles to, Rawson Street. World War I seems to have marked the transition from building in stone to building in brick, and this trend has been maintained although many dwellings new in recent years are built in brick coloured and textured to look like stone.

On the other hand, so strong was the tradition of a single room occupying practically the whole of the ground-floor, in which the family ate, warmed themselves, hung their clothes to dry when wet, dried the laundry on wet days on a 'winter-'edge' in front of the fire, read, sang, played cards and, often, the parents slept in a shut-up bed – did their living, in fact – that our house had to conform in this respect. If the family owned a mirror before which both men and women tried on their hats (for, when putting on his best hat, a man, having brushed it with a special brush, took care that it was straight and sat correctly!), it would be in this room, and, on account of the mirror, most men of my older generations shaved there as well. For thirty-five years, Ephraim poured boiling water from the kettle into an earthenware marmalade jar and set it on our deal-topped dining table so that he could shave in front of the sideboard mirror. Small wonder that this room was referred to simply as 'the house', a usage that possibly applied to the whole of the West Riding and much further afield. We also had a good cellar, as in the older houses, with a separate brick-built compartment for coal and a patterned cast-iron coal-grate on the end of the house, through which we shovelled down our coal.

There were two other features in which these houses were very unusual on Storr Hill Side. Seth and Ephraim, as well as Annie and Sarah, no doubt, were insistent upon having the best features of the old and the new, so they employed an architect. He was referred to frequently when the building of the houses was talked about, but I have forgotten his name and have not found any plans or other documentary evidence. The other distinction involved in the building of these houses was that two working men of average income for craftsmen, bought land and built upon it with the aid of a mortgage. By good chance, complete accounts in Ephraim's hand of the building of these houses has survived in an old exercise book. His purpose was merely to show how much money had come in and where it had gone to, so there are several vital questions which it does not answer.

It does not tell us exactly how much, nor from which Building Society, they borrowed. The only mention of a mortgage is 'Interest B.S. £5-13-0'. The term must have been for twenty-five years, as I can remember, just after the war, hearing mention of 7*s*. a month, when Ephraim was arguing

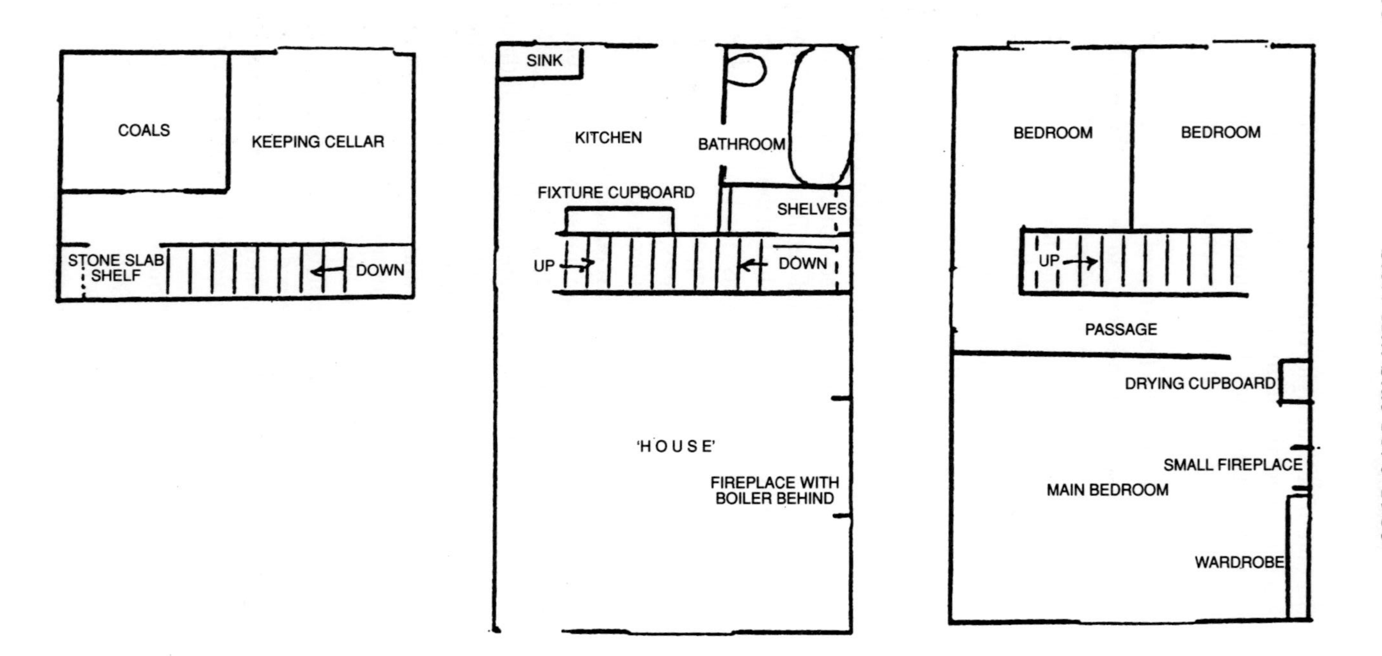

Fig. 8. No. 17 Elizabeth Street as originally built.

Expense

For land in Elizabeth Street Wyke.	L. s. d.
Paid to Uram Jagger on account	10 .. 0 .. 0
1923 May 9th to Harold Stead Solicitor	232 .. 0 . 0
June 29th Wooden Spar's for fencing	2 . 0 . 0
July 6 "	6 .. 16 .. 6
.. 7 .. carting of Wood 2/3. nails 1/6.	.. 3 .. 9
nails 1/11. allowance to carter 1/-. Saw 6/-.	. 8 . 11
.. 2/7. wood 3/6. tar 1/-. wood 4/-. tar 5/-.	16 . 1
.. 2/0. cartage 2/6. wood £5 . 12.	5 . 16 . 6
.. 3/9. wood for gate 12/4.	16 . 1
Tar 4/-. nails 6d. gate hangings 1£	1 .. 4 . 6
Conveying fees £5 .. 7 . 6	5 .. 7 . 6
wood 3/-. saw file 11d. saw sharpening 6d.	.. 4 .. 5
for bricks, 5 £. on account. to A. Chew.	5 .. 0 .. 0
Barrow 24/- sharpening tools 6d.	1 .. 4 . 6
in settlement for bricks, to A. Chew 3£.11/-.	3 . 11 . 0
Comission, per, W. Law 10/-	- .. 10 .. 0
Carting of bricks, etc. to J. Garside £5 .. 1	5 .. 1 . 0
Spars, door, & frame £2 . 9s. Parallel rule 1/7	2 .. 10 . 7
To J. Garside for minion 18/-	.. 18 . 0
	284 .. 9 .. 4

Facsimile from Accounts Book.

Brought forward Expense £ s.. d

per h. 284.. 9.. 4

curbing & channeling. W. B. 14 hrs. 1/3 — ..17.. 6

S. Shaw 13 hrs. at 1/9 — 1.. 2.. 9

To J. Brearley £ 8. 18. 6. for sets & curbstones ..18.. 6

S. Shaw 4 hrs. at 1/9 for grouting channel .. 7.. 0

To J. Garside for cartage of bricks, ashes, mortar, cement, & shovel 3. 7. 6

To J. Garside for lime 39 cwt. £ 2.. 3.. 1 - [illegible] proof 1/6 - 2.. 4. 7

Wages for week ending Ap 15th £ 4 - 14 - 6 4. 14. 6

Lime & cartage 17 - 3. To H. Rhodes for timber £1 13 - 8 2 - 10 .. 11

S. Shaw 24 hrs. 1/9 - £ 2.. 0 10. - A. W. 24 hrs at 1/3 - 2. 0.. 10

- £ 1.. 8. 10. W. A. B. 20 hrs. 1/3. £ 1.. 3. 10. — 2.. 12.. 8

F. Shaw 16 hrs. - £ 1. 0. 0 E. Holdsworth per slate 9/6 1 - 9. 6

W. Barker 20 hrs. £ 1 - 5. 0. A. Wilkinson 44 hrs £ 2 - 13. 10. 3 - 18 - 10

S. Shaw 44 hrs £ 3.. 16. 10. J. Garside £ 5 - 19. 4 9.. 16 - 2

Surveyor's fees & lead. £ 2.. 4. 3. 2.. 4.. 3

Insurance stamps 14/6. M. Jones slating £ 2.. 0. 0) 2.. 14. 6

32 loads of backings, £ 4.. 0.. 0 4.. 0. 0

S. Shaw £ 3 - 8.. 10. A Wilkinson £ 2.. 8 - 10. 5 - 17. 8

£ 2.. 13 - 10 A Wilkinson. S. Shaw 3.. 15 - 10 — 6.. 9.. 8

2. 3 - 10 " " " " " 3 - 1. 10 5.. 5 - 8

Facsimile from Accounts Book.

that he was not going to pay it off earlier than the term, even though he could have done, but whether that was for both houses or only one, I have no idea.

For the land, just short of an acre, they seem to have paid a total of £242 0*s*. 0*d*. as the Expense Account starts as follows: 'For land in Elizabeth Street, Wyke. Paid to Uram Jagger on account £10-0-0'; and, after the date 9th May 1923: 'to Harold Stead Solicitor £232-0-0'. This amounts to exactly 1*s*. a square yard, according to my calculations; Ephraim once said that they could have had land for 3*d*. per sq. yd., but it was so poor that no man in his right mind would have bought it. The next item reads: 'Conveying [sic!] fees £5-7-6.'

The most frustrating feature of the account book is that it gives very few dates and even fewer quantities of materials for the sums paid out. It seems that we can decipher the wages paid for labour only by a small number of chance entries such as: 'S. Shaw 24 hrs 1/9 £2-0-10 – A[rthur] W[ilkinson] 24 hrs at 1/3 £1-8-10. W.A.B. 20 hrs 1/3 £1-3-10.' This pattern of paying craftsmen 1/9 per hour and labourers 1/3 is adhered to all through. Also, the sums paid do not seem to be correct, until one realises that they were deducting 1/2 per week for insurance stamps. It was all casual labour; friends, relatives, workmates and any acquaintance out of work at the time, all seem to have been willing to do an hour or two to earn an honest shilling. Frank's father, Arthur, ex-collier, seems to have been Seth's favourite labourer; they worked together on this and several other jobs and they lived next door to one another down Storr Hill until Seth moved into his new house. There are three or four entries of W.B. or W.A.B. which must refer to Ephraim's father, also an ex-collier, whose presence is surprising as, according to one of Ephraim's oft repeated tales, Walter's reply to his son's statement of his intention to build his own house was: 'Tha'll nivver 'ev enough to build a shit-'oil!'

Seven payments to Irvine Garside are recorded. He lived at No. 9 Elizabeth Street (Plate No. 22) where his daughter, Mary, still lives. Laurence and I were playmates of his son, Stanley. Irvine had stabling and a mistal for about ten cows off Wilson Road. He kept two or three horses and was kept busy on local haulage work, and a typical entry in the account book reads: 'To I. Garside for cartage of bricks, ashes, minion [fine, sieved ash for making mortar] cement & shovel £3-7-6.'

The majority of entries, unfortunately, are of the following pattern: 'M. Jones, slating £2-0-0'; this might have been Mellor Jones or his son, Maurice, and we don't know whether the payment was for labour or materials. Similarly: 'D. Christy [?] £1-10-7½'. David Christie was the local chimney-sweep, who lived in Worsnop Buildings, but at that stage there were no chimneys, and there had certainly been no fires in the houses.

Some relative prices may be assessed, however: 'Barrow 24/-'; 'Parallel rule 1/7; 'Saw file 11*d.*'; 'Gas oven and boiler £7-2-6' – confusing, as there was one of each in each house; 'Gas brackets 12/2'; 'Bricks – 350 – 18/11', i.e. 3 for just under 2*d.* 'Cement 4 cwt. & manhole cover 19/-'. 'I. Garside for lime 39 cwt £2-3-1' – this would be mortar. The cost might well have been 1*s.* per cwt plus carriage.

The present owners of No. 17 have made it more to their liking by bricking up the front door and creating a new one with a little porch where the tiny end window was at the foot of the stairs. Inside, the kitchen has been enlarged by incorporating what was the bathroom and a new bathroom has been installed in the little bedroom at the top of the stairs.

Although Nos. 17 and 19 Elizabeth Street were the only brick houses in the new style to be built on Storr Hill Side before World War II, a considerable number of such houses were erected within the radius of a mile. Bradford City Council built an estate of 'Council Houses' in Lower Wyke, between St. Mary's Church and Whitehall Road (Fig.9). These had

Plate 22. Nos. 8 and 9 Elizabeth Street. A pair of superior back-to-backs, taken from what was Fred Greenwood's hen-pen. Both houses were occupied by families of Garsides, but not related, as far as we knew. To the left of these is the gable-end of No. 17 and on the extreme left the upper parts of Ivy Bank. (1985)

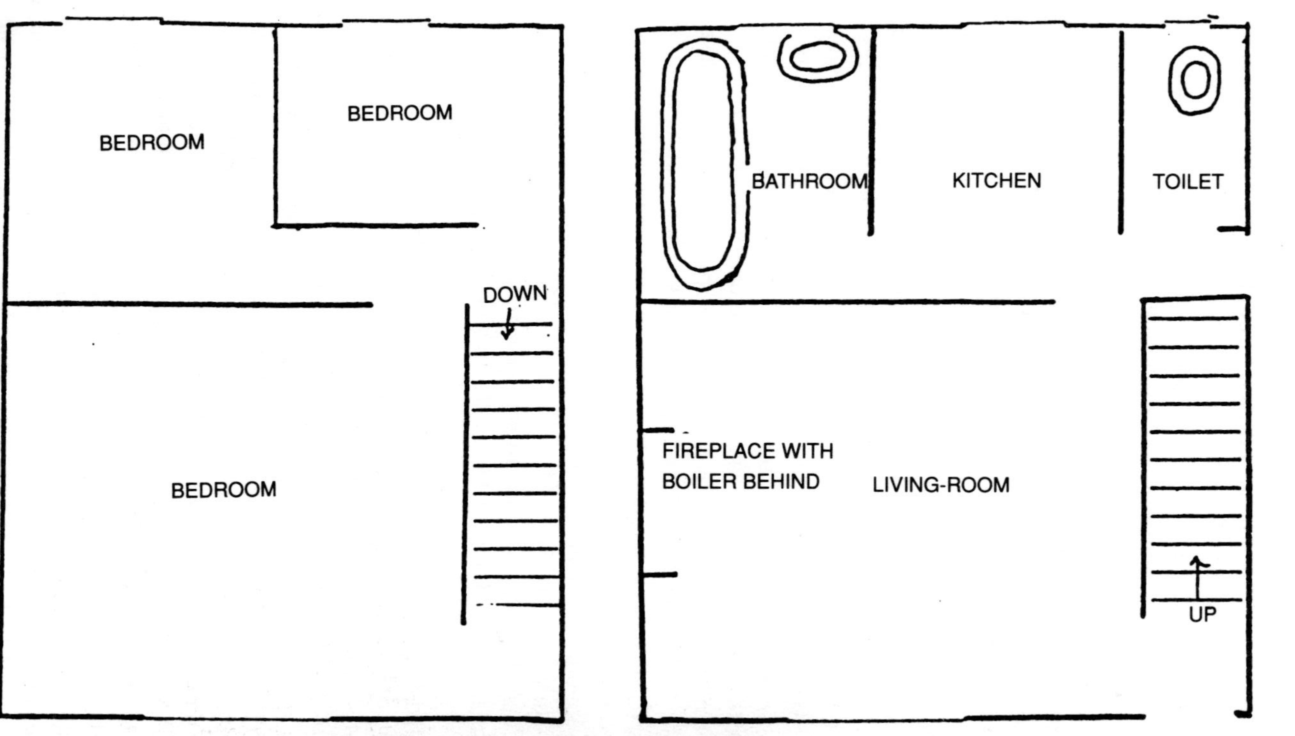

Fig. 9. Typical council house in Lower Wyke in nineteen-thirties.

bathrooms and the toilets were built into the house, but one had to go out of the side door of the house and then through another door to get to the toilet; there was no direct access to it from any room in the house. They had three bedrooms, hot water on tap from fire-back boilers and electric light. Most of these houses shared a common front path.

The attitude of the old, established inhabitants of the area to the people who lived in them was decidedly derogatory, but it is difficult to tell at this distance in time whether they tended to be disparaged by those living in the old-style houses because there was something smacking of charity or the workhouse in the fact that they were subsidised, or whether it was because they constituted an assorted collection of people who had been uprooted and arbitrarily thrown together. They were people who had lost their roots; people did not know anything about their provenances, and were still looking for an identity and equal acceptance in the pubs and shops. What is more important, their parents, grandparents, aunts and uncles were unknown to the old-established inhabitants. They could not be placed in any community, and were therefore to be suspected.

Private entrepreneurs were also building this new type of house not very far away. About 1935, as we secondary-school pupils from Wyke and Low Moor were borne up to Odsal Top on the old trams, we saw a board on the left at the corner of Netherlands Avenue and Huddersfield Road announcing that the new houses being built would cost from £375. They were known as Miss Helliwell's Houses. When I first went to Belle Vue, in 1933, we used to see what remained of the vast stable of draught horses maintained by the Low Moor Company grazing on that land.

A glance at my Map IV, showing a rough picture of the building layers on Storr Hill Side, will suffice to show how much of the surrounding open land of our young days has now been covered by modern housing. Readers will be familiar with the housing of the post-war period, but, to complete my review, Frank has kindly drawn the plan of a bungalow built in 1963 on land that was previously allotments in Perseverance Street (Fig.10). Bungalows seem to have formed the majority of these post-war developments, but latterly 'town houses' such as those which have replaced Barraclough Square have appeared in increasing numbers. These bungalows, constructed of breeze-blocks and brick, were sold new for £2,300 in 1962, and were being offered for sale in 1989 at £50,000.

Frank has been able to recall some house-prices in a historical context for me: in Crowther Row, sometimes called Storr Hill Terrace, the left hand side of New Road Side from the Crown to where the Wesleyan

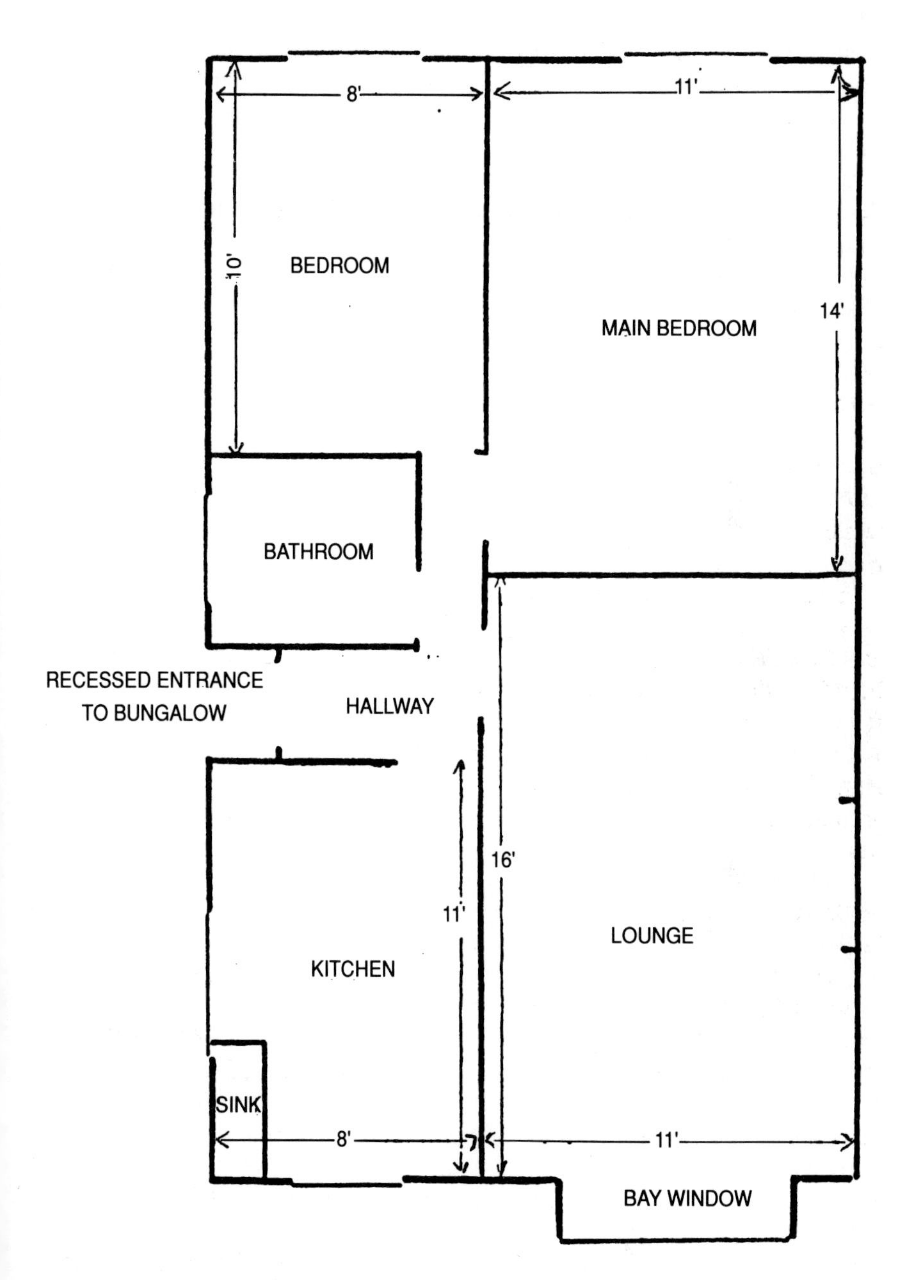

Fig. 10. Plan of bungalow built in Perseverance Street in 1962.

Chapel stood, houses were offered to sitting tenants in the 1960s at £250 per house. One was recently (1989) up for sale at £42,000.

Nos. 16a and 17 Perseverance Street were bought at auction in the Crown Hotel in the 1920s for £450 the pair. 16a was sold in 1989 for £42,000 and No. 17 is now (1990) for sale at £37,000.

St. Mark's Church sold the venerable New Works School to a sitting tenant, Mr Benn, for £1,700.

Map II
Detailed plan-map of New Road Side and Storr Hill, based on the Ordnance Survey 25" : 1 mile map of 1908 enlarged and adapted. The key numbers do not include shops.

KEY
1 Crown Hotel. †
2 Junction Inn. †
3 New Inn. †
4 Babes in the Wood Inn. ‡
5 Quiet Woman Inn.
6 Fleece Inn.
7 Wesleyan Chapel.
8 On map of 1908 'Hall'; in our day swimming baths with municipal library over. Now warehouse. †
9 Gospel Hall, built 1922. †
10 Carr Lane School, now meat-packing warehouse. †
11 New Road Side Working Men's Club. †
12 Conservative Club; known as 'T'Mule'. †
13 House-surgery of Dr. H. Robinson, known as Whittron House.
14 Visiting dentist, Mr. Rushworth, held surgery every Friday evening.
15 'Hannah Taylor Fold'.
16 'Holdsworth Buildings'.
17 John Foster's wheelwright's shop. †
18 Coulson's bottling shed.
19 James Jones, undertaker.

† Standing at time of writing, but possibly derelict.
‡ Demolished but being rebuilt
Further details in text photos.

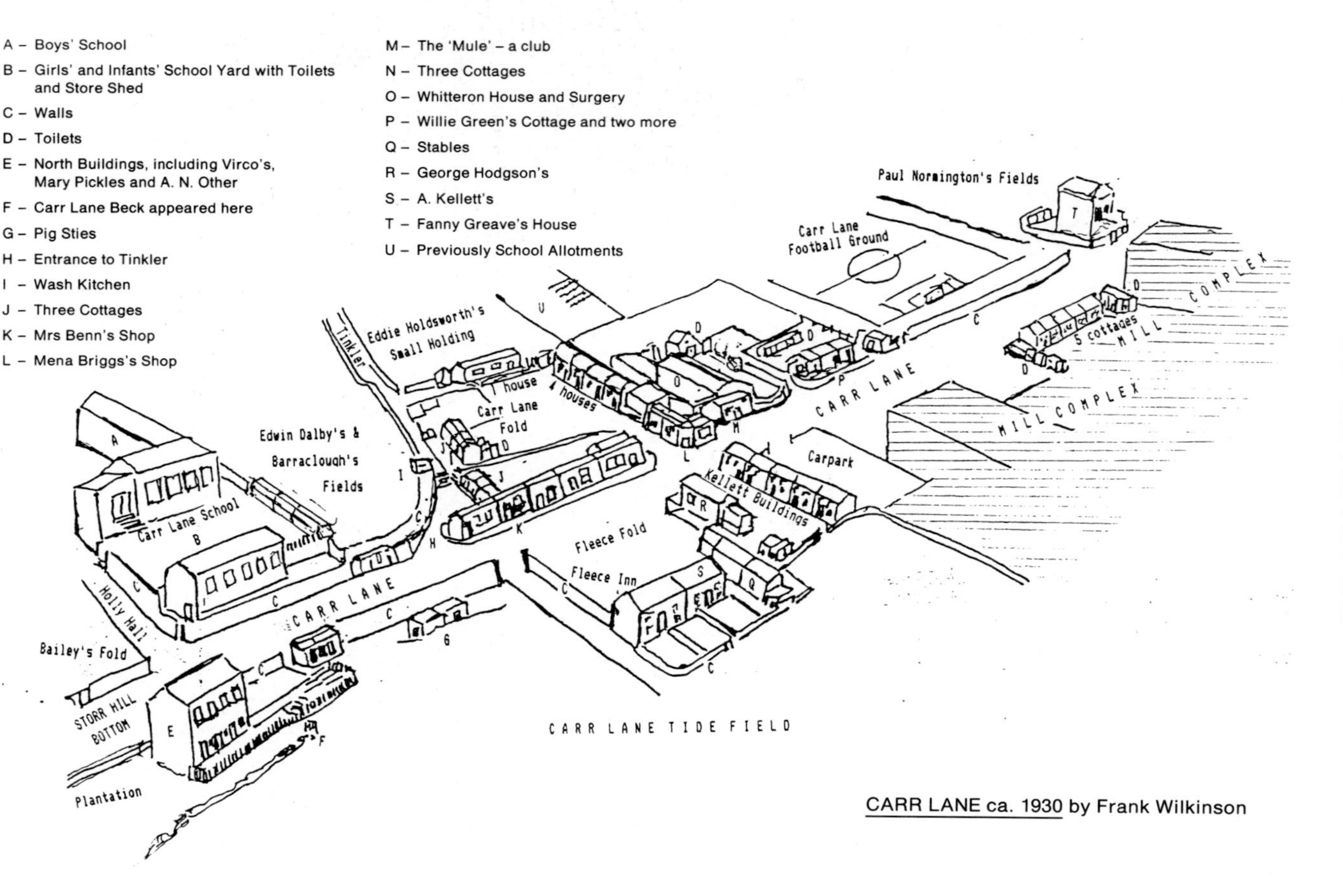
A – Boys' School
B – Girls' and Infants' School Yard with Toilets and Store Shed
C – Walls
D – Toilets
E – North Buildings, including Virco's, Mary Pickles and A. N. Other
F – Carr Lane Beck appeared here
G – Pig Sties
H – Entrance to Tinkler
I – Wash Kitchen
J – Three Cottages
K – Mrs Benn's Shop
L – Mena Briggs's Shop
M – The 'Mule' – a club
N – Three Cottages
O – Whitteron House and Surgery
P – Willie Green's Cottage and two more
Q – Stables
R – George Hodgson's
S – A. Kellett's
T – Fanny Greave's House
U – Previously School Allotments
Paul Normington's Fields
Carr Lane Football Ground
Eddie Holdsworth's Small Holding
Tinkler
1 house
4 houses
Carr Lane Fold
Edwin Dalby's & Barraclough's Fields
Carr Lane School
CARR LANE
5 cottages
MILL COMPLEX
Carpark
Kellett Buildings
Fleece Fold
Fleece Inn
Holly Hall
Bailey's Fold
STORR HILL BOTTOM
Plantation
CARR LANE TIDE FIELD

CARR LANE ca. 1930 by Frank Wilkinson

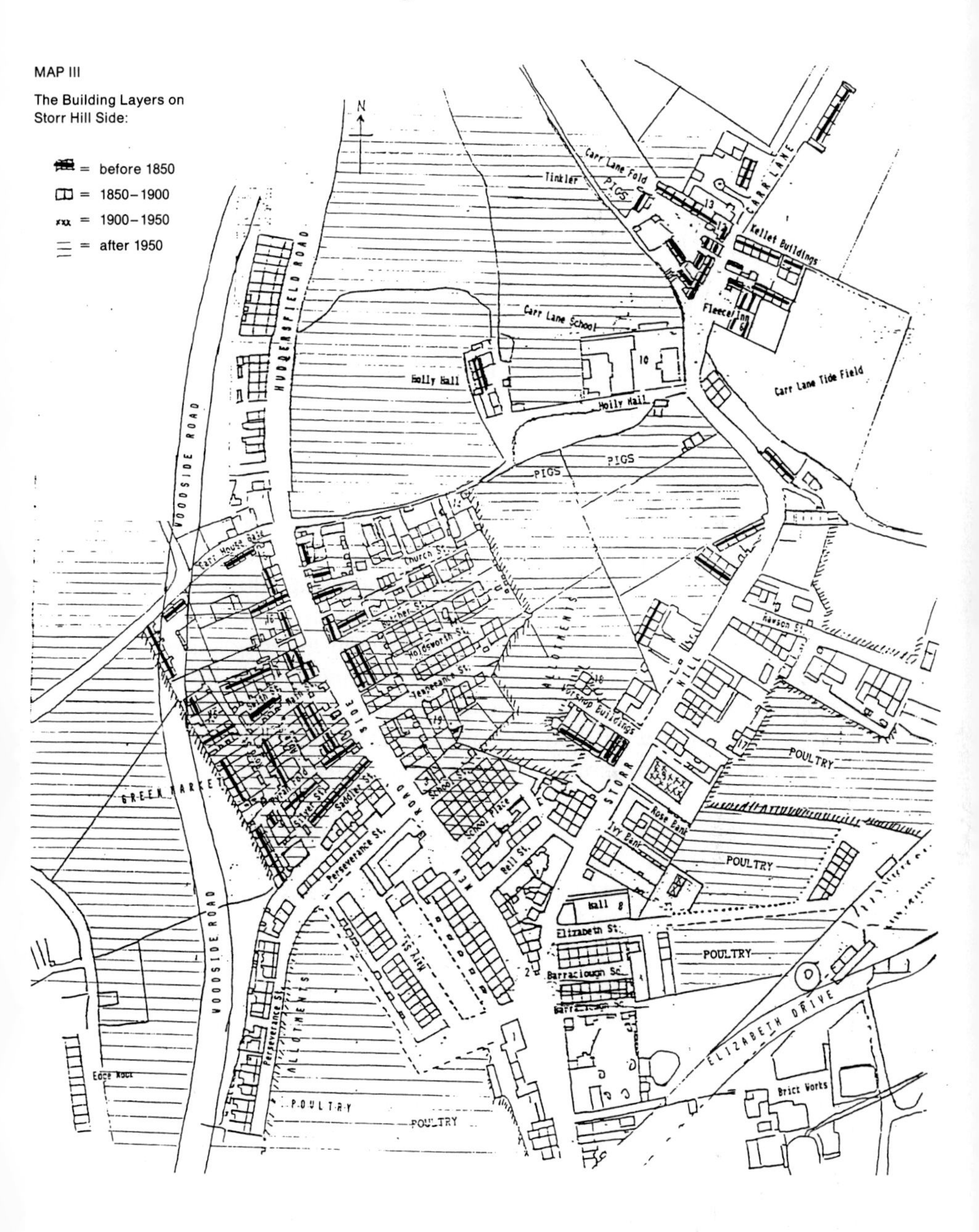
MAP III
The Building Layers on Storr Hill Side:
= before 1850
= 1850–1900
= 1900–1950
= after 1950
N
CARR LANE
Carr Lane Fold
Tinkler
PIGS
Kellet Buildings
Fleece Inn
Carr Lane School
Holly Hall
Holly Hall
Carr Lane Tide Field
HUDDERSFIELD ROAD
WOODSIDE ROAD
Carr House Gate
Church St.
Holdsworth St.
Temperance St.
ALLOTMENTS
Worship Buildings
Rawson St.
HILL
POULTRY
STORR
Rose Bank
Ivy Bank
GREEN MARKET
Silver St.
Saddler St.
Perseverance St.
School St.
School Place
Bell St.
NEW ROAD SIDE
Hall 8
Elizabeth St.
Barraclough St.
ELIZABETH DRIVE
Brick Works
Perseverance St.
POULTRY

Chapter 6

Perseverance Street

Off New Road Side, on the left when facing north, opposite the New Inn, is Perseverance Street (Plate 23). Until after 1960 it was only half a street, consisting of some twenty-seven houses on the north side of the street. On the south corner of the street, fronting on to New Road Side, was a Wesleyan Chapel, built in 1870 and seating about 300 people. Behind this chapel, Perseverance Street is joined by Mary Street, with, on the corner of the two, the New Road Side Branch of the Brighouse Cooperative Society, opened in December 1883. Behind the Co-op were allotments and hen-pens stretching across to High Fernley. In 1961-62, this land was covered with modern bungalows, which have been described above. Our concern here is with the original twenty-six, now twenty-eight, houses.

On the 6" Ordnance Survey map of 1852 there is no Perseverance Street, although the little settlement behind, comprising Saddler Street, High Street, the Green Market, etc. is already there. According to the gaps in the blocks and slight differences in style of these terrace houses, the whole row was not built in one operation. Chiselled into the stone lintel over the door of No. 17, however, is the inscription 'Providence House, 1876'. The name of the street is also witness to the time of its origin, for there can be no doubt that the virtues most esteemed by both rich and poor in our area in the second half of the nineteenth century were Perseverance, Temperance and Providence. According to the latest *A to Z Guide* for Leeds and Bradford, there are still in the area ten street-names based on Perseverance, three based on Temperance and eighteen on Providence. The Temperance Street that was once opposite the bottom of Perseverance Street has now disappeared, but the Temperance Field further down Wyke, where I was born, is still in good condition.

Plate 23. Perseverance Street. (1985)

The Census Returns for the year 1881[1] yield the following statistics on Perseverance Street and its inhabitants: Out of a total of 133 inhabitants, 47 were either at school or below school age; 26 were either widows or married women who did not got out to work, one in each of the houses; the 60 people who did go out to work included 21 textile workers (including dyers and engine tenters, etc.); 13 miners and 10 ironworkers, or 73% of the total work-force; the remaining 16 included a teacher, dressmakers, cloggers, carters, etc. and a joiner, organist and choirmaster! This percentage, 73%, is exactly the same proportion of production workers to the total work-force as were recorded in the same Census Returns in my survey of 293 households on Storr Hill Side.

Four of the infants listed in this Census were known to us personally, as adults, around the year 1930: Willie Thirlwell (the family called itself Thurwell), (Census No. 88), Fred Barraclough (Census No. 90), Luther Wade (Census No. 92) and John Hanson (Census No. 101) were still living in the same houses as heads of families. The first three lived in houses numbered 9, 11 and 13 respectively and the last at No. 22. In each case the gaps between these numbers are the same as those in the

Plate 24. Temperance Street, a typical street off the right of New Road Side. (John Nicoll)

enumeration of the 1881 Census, if one allows for the splitting of No. 16 into two dwellings. It would seem reasonable, therefore, to assume that, in this case, we are able to insert actual house-numbers into the Returns of the Census. (Appendix II).

Although the Parliamentary Papers for 1842[2] list a small pit as 'Messrs Akroyd and Co.'s New Road-Side Pit, depth 150 feet', which the 6" Ordnance Survey Map of 1852 seems to place in what we knew as Church Street, some 150 yards from the bottom of Perseverance Street, most of the miners would work for the Low Moor Company, as would the forge-men and the puddlers.

There were 18 textile workers, including dyers. Some of the former might have worked for John Hind's Wyke Mill Company.[3] The Hind family, after owning textile mills in Tyersal and Low Moor, formed the Wyke Mill Company in 1867 and built the first textile mill in Wyke. This was the only textile mill in Wyke at the time of the 1881 Census. Later, in 1899, the Hind family built the mill on Mayfield Terrace, which we knew as the City Shed, and some ten years later they also built the mill up High Fernley. There were, however, several other mills within a mile radius, a negligible walk for all ages in those days. They could well have gone to Low Moor or Oakenshaw.

The houses of Perseverance Street were regarded as rather superior working-class accommodation in the late nineteenth century. In fact, they were still considered as such by some people in the 1930s. These houses were of a quality that attracted élite workers. Living cheek-by-jowl with the miners and forge-men were a 'joiner, organist and choirmaster', 'a grocer and joiner', a 'brass-moulder', 'a carpenter' and a 'plaisterer'. Apart from one young man who gave himself out to be an unemployed overlooker, every employable person could find a job. Except the married women. All working men of the area until after World War I, and this was especially the case with the miners, considered it a slur on their character as hard-working men if they brought home so little that their wife had to go out to work. It must also be recognised that the lack of household technology and aids to rearing a family made the work of women so much more demanding and precluded their going out to work.

At what we take to be the present No. 5, there was Ruth Kellet, a widow at the age of thirty-three with seven children. Two daughters, aged fifteen and fourteen, were in the spinning, and at that time, the contemporary historian of the worsted trade, W.M. Cudworth,[4] puts the wages of teen-age girls in the spinning at between 4 and 9 shillings a week – 'quite sufficient to feed and clothe them'. Even during the thirties it was not at all unusual to hear older people of both sexes refer to their early and mid teens as: 'When Ah wor i' t' spinnin'.' A son, aged eleven, is registered as an errand boy. The four youngest are at school, 'scholars', although we should regard the status of James, aged 2, as the result of the enumerator's fondness for the abbreviation -do-. There is also the unmarried boarder, Benjamin Seed, aged thirty, a joiner. So there were four sources of income in the house, however small the individual contributions may have been.

A further clerical error shows Martha Bywater as mother-in-law, aged fifty-six, at No. 10 and mother-in-law aged seventy-six at No. 13.

In the family of John Greenwood at No. 19 there appears Manasseh, a son aged nineteen, a joiner by trade. In our day the fish and chip shop a little further down New Road Side (still there in 1986 and still proclaim-ing in large letters on the whitened gable-wall that it sells fish and chips), was Greenwood's and our parents and grandparents sent us to Manasseh's ('Tha mun gooa ter Menasseh's. T'uther 'll be shut') for this staple item of diet of those days. Laurence and I, and many of our playmates, thought therefore that the man behind the counter who served us bore the exotic name, and it was not until I examined the 1881 Census returns and commented to Frank on my discovery of the young Manasseh, and the fact that I would never have taken him to be as old as that when I knew him, that he enlightened me: 'Nou, that worn't Menasseh; i wo deead bi then. That wor 'is son, Hubert.'

In my presentation of the 1881 Census (Appendix II), I have included the returns for Birkby Street. Nobody now living in this area has any knowledge of an adjacent Birkby Street; the only street of this name known to us is half a mile away, down Wilson Road, but the enumerator apparently walked out of the one into the other. The best hypothesis I can offer is that the enumerator, through another clerical error, attached this name to Sadler Street, which is the next street to Perseverance Street as one goes down New Road Side. Sadler Street is not named in the 1881 Census. It is still standing and the number of houses there just about corresponds to the number recorded in 1881. It is also shown on the 6" Ordnance Survey Map of 1852. Like Perseverance Street, Sadler Street was built with houses on one side only; the side nearest to Perseverance Street comprises a clutter of little yards and sheds, many attached to Perseverance Street houses and, notably, the slaughter-house and yard of Mitchell's butcher's shop, which fronted on to New Road Side. I have a vivid memory of lying on top of a wall there, watching Jim Mitchell sticking sheep. Nearly all butchers slaughtered on the premises, often in the yard at the back of the shop, down to World War II. I once saw a bullock pole-axed in an open-fronted, rather dilapidated stable or cart-shed down Wyke Lane; the man wielding the axe looked more like a farm labourer than a competent butcher.

As stated above, these were quality houses in their day. They were (and still are!) constructed of the same hard sandstone as were all the houses of the neighbourhood at that time. There was a stone quarry only some 300 yards away up the lane to Royds Hall, but we cannot be sure that the Perseverance Street stone came from there. Wherever it came from, it was used freely, extending to door and window sills and lintels and the tiny token yards in front of the houses were paved with high quality stone and enclosed with walls with cappings of the same material. Our picture of Perseverance Street shows houses very similar to those sponsored by the Bradford Equitable Building Society.[5]

At various strategic places, usually at the end of each section of development or out at the back, were the 'nessies' ('necessaries'), the outdoor toilets, which were also mostly built of stone, and, even if built of brick, were capped with immense single slabs of cleft stone. On the 24" Ordnance Survey of 1908 they are depicted along some streets in the

Plate 25. Remains of 'nessies' at the end of the Short Row. (1986)

neighbourhood of Perseverance Street like orderly rows of sentry-boxes. By this time new houses were being equipped with a piped water supply (in the case of Perseverance Street it came into the kitchen near the little kitchen window), and, from the beginning, they had gas, but for lighting purposes only. Some houses in Perseverance Street still have appreciable lengths of old gas-pipe embedded in their plaster. In all the houses of the district at that time, hot water depended on the fixture boiler that was part of the fire range which was the sole source of heat for all purposes in the house, except for, perhaps, a tiny fireplace with a cast iron surround in the main bedroom. These ranges were retained in many houses of the district, especially where old people lived alone, down to 1930, although many had disappeared before then and had been replaced by a gas-oven in the kitchen and a more modern fire-place with a fire-back boiler. Some occupants jumped this stage and had a more modern, decorative fire-place installed and relied on a gas-boiler or an 'Ascot' type immersion heater in the kitchen for their hot water supply. The introduction of electricity was spread over at least the decade of the thirties; we can remember its installation in one house in Perseverance Street in 1935 and in another in 1937. The first electrical contractor for quite some distance, 'Wheeler of

Wyke', had his shop almost opposite the bottom of Perseverance Street. Even during the Second World War, houses with a fixture bath with running hot and cold water to it as distinct from the little tin bath on the hearth filled with the 'piggin', were quite rare. Bathrooms and toilets in the house, usually in what had been the little bedroom, were still being installed to supersede the outdoor lavatories in the 1960s.

Hundreds and thousands of houses of this vintage still survive in the West Riding, and the only differences between their outside appearance of today and that which we remember of some fifty to sixty years ago consists of new, white-painted window-frames of modern design, new doors, often of a much brighter colour, and lighter coloured masonry as the result of rendering, painting or sand-blasting. They had originally wooden gutters under the eaves, now replaced with a more modern material – metal, asbestos, plastic – and the iron down-pipes still seem to prevail; not many of them have been replaced with plastic fall-pipes.

The layout was organised around the large, living-room, the focus of the whole dwelling, which could be some 16 ft. square. It contained the old comprehensive fire-range. Every room on the ground-floor, as well as the bedroom steps, housed in a proper stair-well, led off this. In all essentials the houses of Perseverance Street were like those of the Faxfleet Development Scheme of which both plans and impressions of interiors are given in *Workers' Housing*.[6] Only the proper fixture bath in the scullery and the elaborate wooden surround to the fire-range would have been out of place in Perseverance Street as we remember it. It must be remembered that the houses of the Faxfleet Street area were model, planned houses for their time, which was some thirty years after those of Perseverance Street. The Perseverance Street living-room, the 'houses' were more like the inspired drawing of a back-to-back living-room in *East Bowling Reflections* than the Faxfleet Street living-rooms.[7] There were many houses like this in the vicinity of Perseverance Street.

At the rear there was a kitchen, some 8 ft. by 6 ft., from which the cellar steps led down. The other half of the rear of the house might be taken up with a wash-kitchen to which a door led out of the living-room at the bottom of the bedroom steps. Sometimes one such wash-kitchen was shared by two houses. Upstairs, the bedroom steps debouched on to a small landing from which there was access to three bedrooms, two of respectable size and one rather smaller.

Apart from the cellar, which most houses in the neighbourhood possessed and put to good use, there are features which made these distinctly more desirable residences than most in the area at the time they were built. They had proper, separate kitchens of a good size, far better than a mere landing at the top of the cellar steps, the cellar-head, which was all that many quite good houses in the neighbourhood ever had. In addition, they had three bedrooms, separated by masonry walls, not merely by rough, wooden partitions. Amenities like wash-kitchens and the cellar divided into a general area and a coal-cellar with a proper coal-grate were further attractions. Also, they had plastered ceilings, i.e. they were 'underdrawn'. C. Clough Robinson, in his *Dialect of Leeds, etc.*, published in 1862,[8] says that the first question of a couple negotiating the tenancy of a house was, 'Is it underdrawn?' These factors may well be regarded as the reason why these houses are still fully occupied and well maintained. They were solidly built and they were capacious for their time, and so could be modified and adapted to the more essential of modern requirements.

Our collective memory is able to attribute occupants and details of their families for the years around 1930 to each house in Perseverance Street, including the new 1 and 1a which were registered as being on New Road Side in 1881. According to the list on which we all agree, the numbers of inhabitants had decreased from 132 to 92, and children at school or under school age were down from 47 to 23.

The manufacturing basis of the local economy had largely disappeared; there were no miners, forge-men nor puddlers and relatively few people were still employed in the textile trade. One forge-man, son of a forge-man, had fallen back on window-cleaning in his late fifties and was eking out a living in this way when we knew him. Three spinster sisters living together worked at Woodside Mill, and four dyers of various types attested to at least two dye-works still working if not exactly flourishing in the immediate area. Dyeing seems to have been the branch of the textile trade that best survived in our district.

The variety of occupations represented among the inhabitants of Perseverance Street *circa* 1930 attests to the economic instability of the time resulting from the decline of the manufacturing industry, as well as to the wider range of occupation available to working-class people. There was the headmistress of Carr Lane Infants' School and another schoolmaster; a bus-driver whose son later became manager of some famous carpet-mills; and, at that time living with his parents in Perseverance Street, there was a celebrated exponent of crown-green bowling, who became a professional at the game and lived most of his life in Blackpool. In addition to a joiner, a milk roundsman and a painter and decorator, there was (shape of things to come!) one motor mechanic. The occupants of two houses were retired and one lived, as far as we can make out, permanently on the dole. As a further sign of the times, there was a son living with his unmarried mother who had been prevented from marrying the father when the latter was killed in the First World War.

The enormous change in the lives and conditions of those living in Perseverance Street around 1930 was not entirely due to the demise of the Low Moor Company and the slump in the textile trade. Electric trams had linked Bradford with Wyke and Bailiffe Bridge as early as 1902, and well before the outbreak of World War I there was a regular service passing the bottom of Perseverance Street, which, being now integrated into the whole network of municipal transport, was home to men and women who could take up employment ten miles from home, go to Bradford for their more important shopping and send their children to secondary schools five and six miles away. They travelled in relative comfort to sporting events and the palatial cinemas of Bradford were almost as convenient as the little halls in Wyke and Low Moor.

Let us now take a look at the other side of Perseverance Street. On the corner opposite our present No. 1, New Road Side Wesleyan Chapel was built in 1870 and may be considered to have been there from the beginning of New Road Side. Behind where it once stood, Mary Street joins Perseverance Street at right angles. On the corner of Perseverance Street and Mary Street stands the New Road Side Branch of the Brighouse and District Cooperative Society (t' Co-op) (Plate 9). Between the wars, this latter was an important focus of local social life as well as being the predominant shopping institution. Between fifty and sixty years ago, all of us concerned with this chronicle, except our junior partners, John and Colleen, were fetching groceries, bacon, flour, dried goods, treacle, paraffin, firelighters, etc. for mothers, grandmothers, neighbours and other relations from t' Co-op. By the age of eight or ten we could spout out the relevant membership numbers (my mother's was 4150 and my grandmother's 5378), read our lists, often rearranging their order so that the assistant had to walk only once to the same part of the shop, which got us out quicker. We also learned, in a practical situation, to check our change and to speak clearly. To us, looking back, it seems that the greater value lay in the contacts we made and the gossip we heard while queueing. Without either adults of all ages or children being aware of it, the Co-op provided the most complete initiation and socialisation process that the district had to offer. In many families it was normal to have to wait for the 'divi' before the children could have new clothes, which were often second-hand, anyway. As will be seen from the photograph taken in 1985, although the building still stands, it has fallen on hard times and come down in the world, unlike the vintage houses of Perseverance Street, seen in the background, which still perform their original function.

Between the wars and until 1961 the land behind the Co-op and the Mary Street 'nessies' was not built up. It was a stretch of small poultry runs and allotments, stretching across to High Fernley and Woodside Road, which had been newly constructed in 1930 as a by-pass to the old, congested settlements of Wyke and New Road Side. In 1961-62 this land was covered with modern bungalows, which sold at that time for £2,000 to £2,300. An older occupant of one of the original houses recently passed judgement on them as follows: 'They are very good for a small family; ideally for a man, wife and one child. The rooms are very small: lounge approx. 15 ft. x $10\frac{1}{2}$ft., kitchen 10 ft. x 9 ft., bedroom 1 12 ft. x 9 ft., bedroom 2 $8\frac{1}{2}$ ft. x $8\frac{1}{2}$ ft.; bathroom and toilet combined 6 ft. x 6 ft.; there is an L-shaped entrance hall from the front door to these rooms. I wouldn't swap our little terrace house for any of them!' This is a judgement typical of the older generation, most of whom grew up in families of four to six children and demanded housing that would stand up to hard weather and hard wear. On one side of Perseverance Street, the houses are of this kind; on the other, one has more elegant, labour-saving residences, full of the comforts that advanced domestic technology can give, but in comparison decidedly fragile and with room for only one child.

We have not made any assessment of the numbers and occupations of people living in these bungalows. Such details do not differ to any significant extent from those of working people at present living in the older houses. It is the houses themselves which, in a most visible and tangible fashion, implement our account of the intimate history of a street in the industrial West Riding over the past hundred years.

In 1987 the numbering of the original 27 houses remains as it was in 1930. No. 1 is being converted into flats at the time of writing and No. 12 is vacant. Against a total number of residents of 132 in 1881, reduced to 92 in 1930, they now house a total of about 60 people. Children attending school or under school age numbered 47 (32% of the population) in 1881, 23 in 1930 and 11 or 18% in 1987. Six houses have only one occupant, one of whom, aged 93, is now permanently accommodated in hospital. Out of a total of 60 there are 3 widows living alone, and a further 11 people are retired. Two men are still employed in the manufacture of textiles, probably not wool; there is one building contractor and one builder's labourer. While Manasseh's fish and chip shop just round the corner is still in business, a man and wife living in Perseverance Street run a fish and chip shop some seven miles away, which is a clear indication of the change in transport during the history of Perseverance Street. This also brings to mind the acute garaging problem of such streets, probably the biggest disadvantage in their history. There is such a high risk of lock-up garages out of sight of the houses being vandalised that people prefer to leave their cars outside their front door.

A significant proportion of people living in present-day Perseverance Street have occupations which could not exist, even in the imagination, of those named in the Census of 1881. Among the men there are three motor-mechanics, one lorry driver, a laboratory technician and two 'reps' of the kind called 'travelling-salesmen' before the war. Seven wives have either full or part-time work, a high proportion of the women residents when three widows and five retired women are deducted. They include a child-minder, a school-cleaner, a secretary and a shop-assistant. One of the widows is a retired welfare nurse. To the inhabitants of Perseverance Street in 1881 it would also have seemed impossible for one of their children to have gone to university and gained an honours degree, but it has happened in at least one case since World War II. We have deemed it improper to enquire further about 'modern' social phenomena such as one-parent families and cohabitation out of wedlock, which might well be represented in Perseverance Street. There was possibly one case of co-habitation around 1930, but we are not certain of this.

Perhaps the most significant development in living standards in the history of Perseverance Street is the change in ownership. Down to the Second World War most of the occupants would be paying rent for their houses. There were a few owners, some of whom owned a complete block, having perhaps inherited them from the small-scale entrepreneur responsible for building them, while others were owned by the people next door, who had been able to invest in them at a favourable opportunity. Nowadays virtually all the occupants have bought their own houses with the help of a building society, or are in the process of doing so.

While the percentage of Asian people, Pakistanis for the most part, is by no means as high in Wyke and New Road Side as it is in many parts of Bradford, there is nevertheless a noticeable Pakistani presence there. At present there are none living in Perseverance Street, but today's inhabitants are customers of shops run by Pakistanis just round the corner. It may not be long before Perseverance Street enters upon a new phase of its history, and houses some tenants of whom the original dwellers there, the miners, forgemen and mill-hands of 1881, cannot have had the slightest conception.

Finally, the houses of old Perseverance Street may not have been fit for kings but they were capable of housing dynasties of working people. We have seen that four of the infants recorded in the Census of 1881 were still in the same houses as head of the household around 1930. At the time of writing there is one man, now retired, whom we knew as a lad in the same house around 1930. His father, as a schoolboy, and his grandfather as head of the household, are listed in the 1881 Census – all living in the same house!

Chapter 7

Religion and Morality

Long before our day, religious observance on Storr Hill Side had assumed a decidedly 'low profile', to use a modern idiom. All denominations had suffered from the general secularisation of life and the cynicism produced in all working communities by economic slumps, wars and distant, uncaring government. I think that Storr Hill Side may have escaped this cynicism, but the enthusiasm for building places of worship all over the district during the Victorian period seems to have owed more to social motivations and considerations of prestige rather than pious convictions.[1]

The first religious sect to be represented in any part of Wyke was the settlement of the Moravian Brethren in Lower Wyke, founded in 1753. It lies at the other end of Wyke from Storr Hill, and, in fact, I was unaware of its existence before starting on this project. From information received, however, it is still one of the best supported religious institutions in the area and still maintains an active community, being specially noted in the area for its Sunday-school and activities for young children.

The Church of England, in spite of having been the first in the field of the more orthodox sects, and the wealthiest before my period, had suffered more during the first half of the nineteenth century. When Low Moor was still regarded as a less civilised part of Wibsey, and bore the name Wibsey Low Moor, Wibsey Chapel was founded in 1606 and consecrated by the Bishop of Sodor and Man in 1636. This was the church we knew as Holy Trinity.[2] When, in the seventeen nineties, the local population was greatly increased by the presence of the Low Moor Company, less than a quarter of a mile away, the congregation increased so much that a gallery was erected in 1820. But the parish and church were not named Low Moor Holy Trinity until 1964, after the vicar and wardens had petitioned for the name of Wibsey Chapel to be discontinued.[3]

By the time that the other churches and chapels of the district come into our purview, the Church of England seems to have long since lost the battle to various Nonconformist sects.[4] Before going into details, two more Church of England churches should be mentioned. In 1844 Wyke township was made into a church district by the Ecclesiastical Commissioners, but the church, Wyke St. Mary's, was not built until 1847. Its erection was made possible by great exertions on the part of the vicar at the time and 'the partners in the Low Moor Company'.[5]

St. Mark's Church, the Church of England with which the people of Storr Hill Side were most concerned, was consecrated in 1857. Once more, the directors of the Low Moor Company played a major part, and the foundation stone had been laid two years earlier by Mr Charles Hardy. It cost 'about £2,500, chiefly defrayed by the Earl of Cranbrook, who also augmented the endowment bestowed upon it by his late father, Mr John Hardy.' Also: 'A new chancel was erected in 1892 by Lawrence Hardy. Esq., M.P. of Royds Hall and decorated by the parishioners at a further cost of £800.'[6]

In the case of all three churches the main contribution to local life lay in the schools attached to them. From what one can gather, the reason why the directors of the Low Moor Company were so liberal in helping to found churches was their wish to improve the education of their work-force and thus produce a happier, contented and more reasonable breed of worker. Their motives were genuinely paternalistic in the true Victorian tradition, rather than aimed at a docile and cringing work-force. In my chapter on education the schools attached to Holy Trinity and St. Mark's day and Sunday schools at Carr Lane and the same at Newbiggin school have been dealt with, and brief mention has been made of those attached to Wyke Church. At Carr Lane School, a Church of England School, the beliefs and practices of the established church were embedded in the whole curriculum, not only in the morning prayers and hymns, the drilling in the catechism and the life of Jesus; we learned to read from prepared accounts of the life of Jesus and the exploits and martyrdoms of the saints. Nevertheless, the efficiency of the simple curriculum was not impaired by the religious content, and there can be no doubt that these very good schools made a greater impact on the community, and their effect lasted longer, than the churches that inaugurated them.

In 1842-3, James Shaw, baptised 25th March 1787, who married Charity Fletcher 19th April 1808, great grandfather of Seth, sometimes described as a miner, sometimes as a labourer, walked each Sunday for eighteen months from Slack Side to a different church, to hear the morning service. We have been unable to find him in the 1851 Census Returns and must assume that he was dead by then. Seth was the proud possessor of a broad-sheet containing the details of this feat. With very primitive equipment, I made a photographic copy of this broadsheet and later published its contents in detail.[7] After Seth died in 1947 it came into the possession of Annie, my mother, but we could find no trace of it when she left No. 17 Elizabeth Street.

The heading was as follows: 'The following is a list of 78 Different Churches attended by James Shaw in the 56 and 57 Years of his Age. Being a different Church on each Sunday throughout the year 1842 and part of 1843, with the text taken on each occasion in the Morning Service.'

This was a considerable athletic feat, even when it is taken into account that, for such as James Shaw, walking was the only way of getting about. The visit to Ossett on 10th April 1842 involved a round walk of about thirty miles. Two questions suggest themselves: Why were these details published in such detail and with such care? Without this evidence, we should have expected him to be illiterate, but he must have been able to make his own notes about the dates, churches and lessons. Or did he memorise them and get his literate grandson, Shadrach, to keep a written record? Buttershaw St. Paul's was consecrated in 1842, and this would then be the nearest church to where he lived. Was the broadsheet published to help to raise funds for it?

The question as to why he did it is equally difficult. Was he motivated by his own idea of piety? Surely the church belonging to the parish in which he lived would have sufficed for his worship. Was there a social convention or temporary fashion behind this kind of effort? We have been able to discover records of no other similar efforts. Was it the desire to impress people, especially his work-mates and the tap-room, with his athleticism? Strange as it may seem, knowing the breed and its approach to life and society, we lean towards the latter.

Although all the churches visited by James Shaw belonged to the Church of England, the Nonconformist movement was by his time far stronger in the area. As Tony Jowitt puts it: 'In 1851 Bradford had the third highest proportion of Nonconformists in the urban areas of England and the town became a capital of religious Radicalism and one of the centres of the Church-Chapel confrontation.'[8]

John Wesley preached at Low Moor on Monday 27th April 1747, but the seed he sowed that day made no appreciable growth for many years. As was usual with Wesleyan congregations at that time, they were obliged to meet in private houses. Low Moor Chapel was founded in 1809, and a Sunday school was started in 1812. By 1840, the latter had 58 teachers and 180 scholars. In 1854 it was considerably enlarged and an organ gallery added. Prior to this, in 1838, the benevolence of the Low Moor Company, which gave the land, resulted in a 'spacious burial ground'. In 1844 a branch school was built at Oxley Place on land given by Dr Oxley: this was enlarged in 1847 and rebuilt in 1859. Writing in 1876, Cudworth says: 'Until about three years ago, Low Moor was in the Bradford West Circuit. It has now been formed into a separate circuit, including the Wesleyan chapels at Wyke, and New Roadside and Oxley Place School.'[9] On the same page, Cudworth names fourteen 'managers' of the Low Moor Company who were prominent in the Wesleyan movement in Low Moor.

The result of this development as it affected Storr Hill Side was as follows:

> The Wesleyan movement at Wike began fifty years ago, when services were held at Bink's Cottage, Wike Common, and the services were then transferred to Joseph Clark's house, near the present Temperance Hall. A cottage was afterwards taken, and the meetings were held until Mr Appleton, the Photographer, coming to reside at Carr Hall, Wike, greatly helped them to erect the present small Gothic Chapel in Huddersfield Road in 1869.[10]

On the same page, Parker prints the very interesting reminiscences of Mr John Hirst concerning New Road Side Chapel. They had no chapel or school for the Wesleyans in 1858 and were determined to find a place of worship, so they opened a Sunday School in 'the Brick Huts' but took children to worship at Low Moor Chapel. In 1860 they built a school at the cost of £340, which was used as a day and a Sunday school and remained in use until 1870, when they had 250 scholars including 70 over fourteen. The neighbourhood around New Road Side was increasing very fast, and there was need for a place of worship. The result was the substantial school and chapel built at a cost of £1,400 in 1871. Since then (writing in January 1903) they had added a new infants' school and four classrooms and the Bradford School Board had taken over the day school when the city was extended in 1899. They were out of debt at time of writing.

My friends and I found this information in Parker both enlightening and baffling. We had asked one another why the double row of back-to-backs off the other side of the main road were named School Place and School

Plate 26. Sunday School group of unknown date. Annie Shaw is sixth from left on next to the back row. She always did have her head on one side on a photograph.

Street, and now we knew. On the other hand, we must have known lots of people who had attended the school in question, but we had never heard mention of it![11]

Two further developments in the religious life of New Road Side and the vicinity must be recorded. The only public building of any kind to be erected in our neighbourhood between the wars was the Gospel Hall, on land abutting onto ours, with an entrance in Storr Hill. This was the chapel of the 'Brethren' or 'Christian Brethren', a completely independent sect, and it was built in 1922. Its inspiration in this case derived from the visit of an itinerant preacher named George Blackburn who first preached in Wyke in 1906 on the waste land on which Frank's fish and chip shop still stands and which otherwise has never been built on.[12]

Before 1893 there were premises in Wyke designated on the 24" OS Map as 'Salvation Army Barracks'. It was a large hut, opposite the end of Wroe Terrace with access from Huddersfield Road and backing onto the blacksmith's shop which faced into Mayfield Terrace. On the map it seems to have been sited first on the other side of the road, where Amos Petty had his haystacks in our day, but this may be a cartographical error or my misreading of the map. The end house nearest our field on Rose Bank was known as the 'Salvation Army House', and succeeding Captains of the local detachment lived there. They held services in the hut and, of course, they sang on the street-corners and outside public houses. The triangle of cobbles with a gaslamp at the apex outside the Junction was a good stand for them. Their success lay in the fact that they were poor and went to ordinary folk rather than the other way round. It was the turn of the workers in forge and mine to be paternal and generous when the young women sold the *War Cry* in the local pubs; even the coarsest drunks were allowed no liberties with them.

Sixty years ago, however, the predominant opinion in our community accused the adherents of both the Church of England and the Nonconformist (Wesleyans) of hypocrisy, of being non-practising Christians. Of my own circle of friends, the majority came to share this opinion sooner or later. Frank, until quite late in life, spent his spare time in raising money for St. Mark's, through his concert party and through decorating the church when he was a painter and decorator, but he came to the same conclusion during the time that he was the St. Mark's representative on the Synod. The difference was that the Church of England clergy could make no contact with the working man, while the Wesleyan had the reputation of being inclined to material sharp practice, and having to be carefully watched when doing business with him. I had no particular grievance against the clergy at St. Mark's, but, as early as my late teens, I was put off by the benighted autocracy of the leaders of the congregation who attended only when the occasion enhanced their image of themselves as pillars of the local society. They seemed to have made a god in their own image and attended church occasionally to be seen and admired.[13]

Canon Edwin Davis had been appointed in 1894 and was a white-haired, benign, learned old gentleman when we knew him. But he belonged to a different world, and it was always obvious that he was on the outside looking in at the population of Wyke and Low Moor. His successor, Mr Howarth, was equally worthy and made efforts to gain contact with his parishioners and help them, but he too was of a totally different breed and the time was not ripe. He was appointed just before the war, when all kinds of restrictions, the absence of young men of the parish, the blackout, shortages which prevented social events, etc., disrupted the normal life of his parish.

Between the wars, in spite of all this, there were many on Storr Hill Side who were genuine, pious Christians. Most of these were the products of pious families, for whom their religion was an essential part of their life and who allowed Christian principles to dictate the routine and tenor of all their relations with their fellow men and women. In some of them these principles became obtrusive, but many gained the respect of the community by holding them firmly but not as a burden.

In all cases, especially for the women, the social life attached to the church was important. The women cleaned the church, bought and arranged flowers on the altar and embroidered altar-cloths. By this time, fund-raising had become the most urgent business of all churches, and for a majority of regular church-goers the 'dos' of all kinds, the 'concerts' (our generic, blanket, word for plays, sketches, pantomimes, etc), the outings and ham-teas were inseparable from the practice of religion. For them it was the fellowship of law-abiding, honest and well-behaved citizens whom they knew well, the friendly help and comfort from their familiars with whom they had gone to school and grown up, as well as the pleasure they took in singing that held the congregation together. It is this attitude that has survived to this day to a degree that varies from church to church. Wyke St. Mary's took an initiative in 1970, or thereabouts, when Wyke Centre was founded in what had been the school in Green Lane. After initial teething troubles, it now embraces a youth club, Scout and Guide activities, and, since 1974, Wyke Community Council with a full weekly programme of activities is housed there. It is supported by grants from the local Education Authority. There are Darby and Joan clubs attached to the Harold Club and on the premises of the old Oxley Place Methodist Church. There is a Community Association attached to Woodchurch School; and Wyke Veterans still have their clubroom and facilities in Wyke Recreation Ground.[14] All similar efforts made from time to time by St. Mark's seem to have come to nothing.

Societies with a moral content, usually but not always linked to a church, continued to thrive on their social role and what they offered by way of recreation and corporate activity. A well-attended Band of Hope met in the Temperance Hall, and there was a Boys' Brigade attached to St. Mary's Church, Wyke. The example of their hard drinking fathers caused many men of Generation II to renounce alcohol, and the Rechabites flourished. Ephraim was one of them, and, after a debilitating illness that required a long spell in hospital, he convalesced at a Rechabite home at St. Annes. The Scouts did not appeal to the lads of Storr Hill Side, and made little headway there when we were young.

At Carr Lane School we had an extra holiday on Ascension Day, after Canon Davies had put in an appearance and administered a perfunctory examination on the creed and catechism. This aspect was, of course, supported by the Sunday school. All Church of England schools had an allied Sunday school, although the numbers were very much diminished between the wars, and devoted church workers of both sexes made a praiseworthy effort to make them serve a useful Christian purpose. Laurence and I have clear recollections of Gertie Barraclough struggling to keep our attention on a fine Sunday afternoon. When I had to do homework, on going to Belle Vue, my parents decided that I should be excused the Sunday School. Under the auspices of the Sunday school, we were hoisted at Whitsuntide into carts drawn by horses in full-dress harness, and taken for a ride through the neighbourhood, while parents and most of the local residents clapped and waved to us. We felt like royalty for an hour or two, looking down on the cheering crowd! Before going home we were given sandwiches and mineral water to complete the feast. It was not unknown for a little organ to be mounted in the back of the cart, and the children were then expected to show how well they could sing hymns, but I can't remember this happening to us.

Even the Nonconformist Churches, whose ministers and lay preachers moved more easily and effectively among their congregations, gained most of their support from their social efforts, which ensured that these churches remained viable longer than the Church of England, albeit on a much reduced basis. All that I have written here represents a general, comprehensive development, and it cannot be denied that all over Bradford there were, and still are, lots of individuals to whom the Christian faith, of whatever denomination, has remained a source of strength, comfort and inspiration.[15]

But the general decline could not have been otherwise. The education of ordinary people had not been of the kind that enabled them to listen to and analyse arguments, even parables were largely lost on them, and especially sermons in the style approved by the Anglican seminaries, however urbane and sympathetic their delivery, did not stop their minds from wandering or switching off completely. The church had survived so long only because it indoctrinated its members from infancy and because, in the absence of all other kinds of communal entertainment, it provided the weekly Sunday 'soap' opera. This was especially the case for women in the early days. It allowed them to shed the garb of everyday toil, to pass a day of relative rest and at the same time avoid the stigma of sloth and vanity. Their best clothes could be displayed (some kept away because they could not afford clothes that would compete with their fellows) and the solemn dignity of the proceedings, coupled to the chance to sing, was nothing less than a tonic, a break in the routine, to which they looked forward.

When the cinema, professional football (both at first proscribed on Sundays) and later television, to quote but three examples, offered entertainment that the average family of the working class could understand and take pleasure in, the church did not have a chance. Again, at least in the Victorian period, the paternalism of the local worthies made education a corner-stone of its efforts, while the churches of all denominations offered only faith in God as its answer to the growing ability to organise an argument on an intellectual basis. This latter ability may have been only relative, but the preaching of faith lost its power against even the most elementary rationalism.

When it came to morality, however, the church seems to have lost all influence long before our time, as indeed, was the case throughout the land. As the working population saw it, anybody who had wealth and position could safely flout all the moral virtues on which the Christian Church was founded. They observed that no church spoke out against the greed and brutality of landowners and entrepreneurs – nor, in fact, against anybody's greed and brutality. Pride and arrogance, treachery and deceit, were not condemned from the pulpit, unless the church in question suffered from it. The corner-stone of the morality of working people, to give and receive value for money and effort, seemed to them to count for nothing as far as the institutes of religion were concerned.

Only offences against the sacraments of the Christian religion earned the stigma of immorality. A baby had to be baptised, and when grown, confirmed, married and buried through the offices of the church, and the most serious sin of which the poor could be found guilty concerned the marriage vows. Morality became synonymous with sexual attitudes and marital probity. This definition of morality was made more rigid by the position of women in society; it was literally a matter of life and death for a married woman to gain and keep a husband. And so, on Storr Hill Side at least, women tried to push under the carpet sex and all the more intimate features of the relation between man and wife. Sex belonged in the conjugal bedroom, and was allowed only a furtive existence elsewhere. However rough a man might be, he would be very careful about what he said or did in mixed company concerning sex. A flirtatious young woman, any women with pretensions to seduce, real or imagined, was pounced on and her reputation demolished long before she could muster any defence of her character; young men and women who betrayed what was considered to be an immodest interest in sex were reprimanded in the severest terms. Overt reprimands from the pulpit were rare; in most cases that task was left to schoolmasters. Sex was not supposed to enter the mind of a woman teacher, as she had to resign her job on getting married. But it must be admitted that what is said above applies only to the overt attitudes to sex; the covert facts were often quite different. In the modern pattern, there is far more opportunity for a woman to become financially independent and birth control has further freed them from dependence on a husband. The church is no longer the sole arbiter of this problem.

All this has changed. The position of the churches became untenable during two world wars and through the exigencies of a mobile labour force, while commercial interests in the fields of advertising, fashion and pornography among others, exploited the power of the erotic for all that it was worth in the name of progress and freedom of the individual. The societies and movements described above have been replaced by social amenities and charitable efforts, mostly supported by the older generations. One survival of the old days deserves special mention: the gambling on their own efforts which was characteristic of my earlier Generations has given way to earning money for charities by taking on sponsorships when competing in anything. This is a plus point for the young people of today.

For the rest, as far as the morals of Storr Hill Side are concerned, two true examples, in which the same man played a part, shall illustrate the change. Shortly before World War II, when his elder brother had just got married but he was still unmarried, his mother gave a broad hint that it was about time he thought about marriage. To which he replied: 'Nay, bi t'time Ah get wed as'l bi ta owd fer owt like that!'

His mother rounded on him in a flash: 'Less o' that! Ger aht o't'ahs if tha wants ta talk like that. Wi'll 'ev nooan o' that in 'eear!'

About forty-five years later, at about 10.30 p.m. the same man drove his car up one of the old streets off New Road Side to his lock-up garage. When his head-lamps focused on his garage doors, they revealed a couple of fully committed lovers between him and access to his garage. They would be aged about fourteen, certainly no more than fifteen; he knew the girl well and thought he recognised the lad as the son of a neighbour. When he kept his lights on them and gave a blast or two on his horn, the boy shouted. 'Bugger off! We'll go when we've finished!'

Chapter 8

Law and Order

Law and order was not a matter for specially appointed authority and officialdom. One of the most significant developments of the period we are concerned with is the insidious and all-pervading middle class paranoia which makes everybody have recourse to the police and the legal profession on the slightest pretext. People have become accustomed to insisting upon their rights while ignoring their obligations, an outlook they have learned from the national leaders as well as local politicians, who found two world wars and subsequent economic problems too much for them to deal with, while insisting upon retaining their old authority and privileges.

The majority of my Generation I were subjected only to the discipline of the family and the neighbours when young and to their foremen and workmates when adult. There was an ethos attached to each neighbourhood and, one might almost say, to each large place of employment. The neighbourhood might be a very rough one or a less rough one, and this depended largely upon the degree of paternalism and liberalism exercised by the local employer in the later nineteenth century, and, sometimes, the fortuitous presence of families or individuals of bad character at a given time. My chapter on education shows quite clearly that the Low Moor Company had a good record as regards education and the fostering of initiative, however bad the conditions and wages in its pits may have been, and this may well have been the ultimate cause why Storr Hill Side in our young days was rough but law-abiding.[1] It is one of the most serious indictments of the intelligence of the national élite that they have allowed their passion for centralised power to restrict their thinking and debates to overall patterns and systems in education, failing totally to understand that the real factor in the debate is the ethos and outlook of the locality. This is another reason why my Generation II enjoyed the best period in English education. More often than not, their teachers belonged to the locality and automatically shared the same standards as their pupils and their parents. This was a great help to them in their efforts to instil not only the rudiments of the three R's to their pupils but also to improve their manners, general behaviour and cleanliness. Their success in these efforts comes in for special praise by contemporary educationalists. Irrespective of their increased value to their employers in later life, they emerged as law-abiding citizens who settled their differences in their own, relatively harmless, if uncouth, way.

There can be no doubt that the foundations of this reform were laid in school – and continued to be laid in school down to the Second World War. Even in a rough district like Storr Hill Side, teachers commanded respect from the majority of the parents and children. There was an extremely healthy approach to discipline. When men teachers reached the end of their patience with naughty pupils, they would apply any useful weapon that came to hand: proper canes were rare but they used rulers, odd sticks or, even, dug the butt end of a pencil into one's skull. Mr Faulkner at Carr Lane School would tuck a nine- or ten-year-old under his arm and wallop his behind with an old chair leg. It was all part of the game. It hurt, but it happened to every lad and, so long as one didn't cry under the pain, one didn't lose face with the rest of the class.

Besides, there were things which were much more to be feared: being told off by a lady teacher like Miss Blowers, Miss White or Miss Fletcher, any one of whom might slap your face or shake you until your teeth really did rattle, as she verbally reduced you to shreds,; and the other was the threat, the mere threat, of being reported to Mr Russell, the headmaster. Mr Russell was a product of the school in which he became headmaster, many of the parents of his pupils had sat in school with him, and, however much some of these might have scorned him for being a 'goody-goody', a favourite and a swot when they were young,[2] (Sid Smith: '('e went to 't 'eier schooil, an' din't laik wi us') if Mr Russell had cause for complaint, you could be in trouble at home. Mr Russell was not an exception in this. At Belle Vue High School, the threat of reporting an incalcitrant lad to Mr Fisher rarely had to be carried out. When one of the pupils was caught pilfering in Woolworth's, in the centre of Bradford, he immediately put this store out of bounds for all members of the school, and most parents supported him. Mine were among those who couldn't see the sense in my passing the store every day and yet not being allowed to pick something up for them as required. So, when I could not talk my way out of it, I had to sneak into Woolworth's with my school cap in my pocket, trembling with the fear of being expelled from Belle Vue. This respect for authority, so thoroughly imbued, has been another victim of post-war paranoia, particularly in those in authority who nevertheless feel insecure and those who preach democracy with a loud voice and claim their rights, but only so long as their kind of democracy places them firmly on top of the pile.

In addition to the discipline of school, children were brought up under the rule of a despot, normally the father or, in his absence, the mother or grandparents. The rule could be either indulgent or brutal. Beating could be brutal but not sadistic, primitive but not vicious; this was not a demoralised society. It had to be endured, for there was no prospect of open rebellion and, although running away might have saved a child or young person from parental neglect and misuse, he or she would have thereby lost the care and protection that was often provided by the community of neighbours and relatives. There was always somebody among the neighbours who would try to alleviate the lot of a bullied or neglected child. Often the child was protected, taught and disciplined by a number of neighbours, not so much from a sense of moral principle, for they were unable to formulate such things, but simply out of inborn goodness and that dignity which is the feeling for what is right and fitting. In the vast majority of cases, conforming to a rule of discipline in the family presented no problem; it was produced without effort by the natural affection between parent and child.

People lived close together, they walked past one another and beside one another, they did not pass in cases of steel at high speed, looking to neither right nor left. One knew by the greetings and attitudes met with on the streets from other members of the community what one's standing and reputation was with them. No member of the community was left in much doubt as to what was required of him or her. On the other hand, this was as far as their understanding, allegiance and affection really went. The pillars of church and state never have understood that, to the people about whom I am writing, their principles and standards are bound to remain aloof and irrelevant. Quite simply, the people of Storr Hill Side were not aware of having had any help or comfort from them. Help from God was never doubted, nor, perhaps from the local minister or vicar, but the church as an institution with principles and moral teaching could be safely ignored. The same applied to politics at both national and local level. Generation I and the older end of Generation II were their own arbiters and judges as far as the law allowed them to be.

Later on in life, adults maintained a reasonable level of law and order through direct, outspoken criticism, pungent repartee and downright crude abuse and invective. It was no place for the mealy-mouthed and hypocrites did not thrive; one spoke one's mind on the spot, and often people who did not get on well together would keep up their vociferous abuse and nasty, sly digs for years, without resorting to other measures to settle their differences. Men might resort to blows in the street if they were unusually provoked or their pride was injured when drunk. It was nothing very unusual to see grown men, sober, take off their jackets, roll up their shirt-sleeves and fight in the street.[3] These occurrences might arrest the attention of those living nearby or those who happened to be passing, but there was no running to spread the news and certainly no fetching the police. This kind of spectacle was all the more grotesque because the protagonists were totally untrained as fighters and fought like robots or puppets. Such battles were usually a draw, both men stayed on their feet and there was not a lot of blood about. Most incidents of violence were restricted to one swift blow struck in a moment of temper. I once went home after bowling with Seth and others at the Harold Club and told my mother that John — (I really have forgotten his surname!) had pulled out of the game and gone home when his partner challenged Seth and me. Annie said, 'He doesn't like your Grandad. They once met on a trip from the club in a wagonette and when your grandad took his cap round for the driver, John — tipped his pint of beer into it, so Seth hit him with *his* pint glass and broke his nose.'

Law and order was the business of every adult member of the neighbourhood and concern about good behaviour was seen as a mark of maturity. Any of the neighbours would discipline a child of school age that was making a nuisance of him or her self or being downright naughty, provided that he or she knew the parents. Occasionally this was taken too far, and the parents would speak their mind, or even come to blows in defence of their child, but, in the vast majority of cases, the parents approved of disciplinary action by neighbours. It must also be said that the hold of the community was so compelling that very few (we can't remember any) young people ran away from home to avoid trouble or punishment. There was little rebellion against parents, however inadequate the latter were from the modern point of view. As we are dealing with human individuals there were inevitable differences from person to person as to what was right and proper, and people ridiculed one another on account of what were deemed to be eccentricities or even grave faults in the other's scale of priorities. The reproach, 'You ought to know better!' implied, 'At your age you should have better judgement and not act and talk so irresponsibly!' This was a very effective reproach in most cases.

It is true that they were helped in this task by the police, with whom they were on terms that allowed them to let the local constable know what they required of him and did not hesitate to let him know if they thought he was not doing his job properly. In this way, everybody had a hand in deciding what constituted law and order, and thus, in making the kind of community they wanted. The policeman was regarded as an equal member of the community , who participated as an equal in its activities. He might be left a pint outside the back door of a pub to fortify him in the dead hours of the night and to help him to fail to see the after-hours drinking, although there was not a lot of the latter and it was not necessarily a factor. He would frequently be offered tea and invited to take his jacket off on a hot day in somebody's back yard or garden – where the sergeant and malicious neighbours could not see. Unlike today, when many people feel that the surest way to become a suspect is to try to help the police, nobody hesitated to tell the police if they saw something suspicious.

Walter Brook, as well as dressing poultry and fish in the market early in the morning, helped his brother-in-law in his fish and chip shop down Town Gate in the evenings. It would be well after midnight by the time they had counted up, cleaned up and shut up, and then Walter had to walk to Storr Hill. One night, by the Salvation Army hut (called 'Salvation Army Barracks' on the 1894 25" map), a torch was directed into Walter's eyes by somebody who jumped out of cover there. Walter 'let peg', aiming some eighteen inches above the torch, hit some solid flesh, and the torch clattered on the flagstones. From the ground came some fluent expletives in a voice familiar to Walter, so he picked up the torch and helped his victim, the well-known local bobby, to his feet. 'Wot the 'ell did te do that fo'? A dint kno' it wor thee! If tha guz rahnd shinin' thi torch i' fowks' eez baht warning on a dark neet, tha'll get thi bloody 'ied knocked off. Think a wor bahn te wait till t' bloody thief felled me? Daft bugger!'

Nevertheless, the two remained friends as before. They might tease one another about the affair, when in a group of others, each exaggerating the other's stupidity, but they knew exactly how far they could go with one another. They knew the limits of the other's sensitivities better than they knew their own. This kind of relationship with the law also started at an early age. It is beautifully summed up by Sid Smith in a passage of one of his tapes: The local bobby, Sgt. Wood, used to 'claht thi lug-'oil er pauze thi arse if 'i copped the' doin' owt wrong. Sue tha kept aht o' t gate after that.' This, also, is an essential feature of a genuine, well-established, healthy, Little Tradition community, and should be part of the definition of community. Only in the small community is a continuity of relationships to be found, which is based on the fact that most people's parents and grandparents had been known and assessed by the whole community. Knowing a person's pedigree (including the name and the family of the local bobby!) was a sure protection against really vicious quarrels and fights; knowing what to expect of a Terry, or a Bentley or a Lightowler, both good and bad qualities, because that was how their parents and grandparents on one side or the other had reacted. It was as though they were partially excused because the nature of their offence was in their blood. I have said above that it was a rough area rather than a respectable one. There were, in the nineteen-twenties and -thirties, two characters in the neighbourhood to whom all petty crimes, burglaries and such, were instantly attributed. People didn't bother to look for evidence.

Frank's Tale: One evening in the early twenties his father (the Arthur Wilkinson of the Account Book, Appendix III) was leaning over the wall in front of No. 32, Storr Hill when one of these characters came up the hill with his wife. Her face and head were swathed in an old scarf. Arthur, by way of normal politeness, asked him where he was going, and the reply was: 'A 've just 'it t' wife an' brocken 'er jaw, sua a'm tackin' 'er up to t' doctor's.' 'Oh aye,' said Frank's father, and that was all that passed between them. Sid Smith's casual mention of seeing the Low Moor bobby taking in a man who had tried to kill his wife, is entirely in the same vein. Sid is anxious to press on to more interesting things and can't quite understand why John wants further details.

Serious crime, litigation, corruption all existed, of course, however much the inhabitants of Storr Hill Side saw these things as being essentially connected with the 'city slicker' type and increasing in frequency and severity the nearer one got to the city centre! There was no mugging to prevent people going out to places of entertainment of an evening, or even to church; there was no gang-warfare on a semi-professional basis, although the young braves of the tribe would use fists and sticks on one another, particularly in support of their local, amateur football team or when stealing one another's material that was being collected for 'plot' on November 5th. There was no rape and only one or two rare cases of casual prostitution, and I have dealt with the incidence of extreme, but relatively discreet, depravity elsewhere. There was no organised armed robbery of banks and post-offices.

Children were conditioned from their earliest days to understand that misbehaviour, of whatever kind, would be dealt with either by reprimand or punishment. There would be no buying-off or pacifying a naughty child, and if the parents did not see to it, then the community at large did so, exactly as they would try to help a child that was being bullied and neglected at home. If, after being given many precepts and minor punishments when young, a person remained vicious as a youth and adult, there was always flogging and hanging, which served both as a threat and a final solution. According to the psychologists, all members of my three Generations should have been mentally crippled and made miserable for life by such a negative and repressive regime in their young days. We simply cannot understand why so many of us have been able to lead such a happy and productive life!

As was the case throughout the land, the care and support for this scheme of law and order by the community just about survived World War I, albeit in a damaged and weakened force, but it was completely destroyed by the effects of World War II. After 1950, the pattern of behaviour on Storr Hill Side became that of the national pattern.

Although men came back after World War II to their native districts, just as they had done after World War I, a great many of them soon moved away, or to newly developed districts offering modern housing and jobs. They then lived with people assembled from a much wider area whose antecedents they did not know, and they suspected one another from the start. Their children felt the insecurity of their parents and did not trust their new schoolfellows; they learned to beware of being deceived and exploited at an early age.

A man did not live among nor drink with his own workmates because they were so much more dispersed than previously. The place of work no longer imposed certain standards automatically. Some of their wives quickly made friends with their neighbours; others found it more difficult and became discontented. Both man and wife felt at a disadvantage because they could not speak their minds freely and clearly as before.

Authority became more remote. Employers lived at a distance and kept aloof, fearing that the old familiarity might encourage both individual workers and the now powerful trade unions to take advantage of them. The police were not members of the community as they sped about in cars and, in spite of all kinds of technological improvements in their equipment and intensive training, 'seeing less than a dog in a ditch'.

It was not merely that the motor car isolated people from one another, it was, and probably still is, the greatest help to the criminal ever to be introduced. At a stroke it offered him and his accomplices a speedy execution of his plan, relative concealment, especially at night, a speedy escape and removal to a great distance and efficient conveyance of his equipment and his haul. All the new technology at the disposal of the police could not enable them to cope with this! I tell the following anecdote to illustrate the difference between the pressure on the police at the end of the war and nowadays. During the war a surface shelter, a rectangular brick hut with no windows and a concrete slab for a roof, was built in Elizabeth Street near the gate to Uram Garside's hen-pen and in full view of our little end window. It had never been used, being readily assessed as vulnerable to a good catapult, let alone a bomb. But, after the war, Sutcliffe Geenwood at No. 2 was doing a bit of running for a local bookie and earning a few bob a week to eke out his pension. The police, watched by Annie from our little end window, stole into the shelter and took a brick out of that end which looked down the street towards Storr Hill, so that they could watch the comings and goings at No. 2. After two days of this surveillance, they pounced and Sut was eventually fined. No wonder that a soft job, a sinecure or one demanding little or no effort, was called 'a bobby's job' in those days!

All these factors, however, were dependent on and only became effective as a result of the deterioration of the moral content of parental upbringing and education in schools. Parents, themselves demoralised by the aftermath of the war and the furtive, palpably false pretexts of politicians, were all too ready to opt out of this responsibility when authority at all levels, like the teaching profession, repeatedly insisted that it was a job for trained professionals and should be left to such people. Many of the teachers on whom the actual job devolved knew that this was a fallacy, a requirement that could not be met by them, and soon learned to dilute or pass on this responsibility. The resulting friction between parents and teachers, often translated into protest and complaint to the authorities and sometimes taken as far as litigation, destroyed the sound foundations of morality that these two agents, parents and teachers, had once laid so firmly on Storr Hill Side. The final blow was struck when teachers were demoted in the public and official estimation to second-class citizens or even lower, as is reflected clearly by their salaries. There is no future for a society in which a fully qualified and experienced teacher to whom the community had assigned considerable responsibility, earns less than a commercial representative, a bank clerk, or a local government official, all of them without the normal qualifications for a profession.

The large number of dedicated teachers and sensible, loving parents that still existed in the fifties and sixties were powerless to compete with the blandishments of the gutter press and the advertising media, the makers of expensive toys, the sensationalism of the cinema and television and the urge to compete and win in all spheres, cost what may. The macho-idol, childish as it seems to many, is no temporary fashion; it has been there, perhaps under other names, for a generation. All the influences to which young people were exposed were no longer concerned with producing honest and worthy citizens. It is twenty-five years and more since a young lady who had devoted herself with energy and integrity to the Brownies and Girl Guides of her locality told me that she was severing all connections with them: 'The emphasis is now on competition, not on developing character and usefulness; they are even teaching them to cheat when competing with other troops!' This was confirmed by a scout-master from the other side of England to whom I told this story.

This background to vandalism, mugging, the flick-knife, car-thefts, rape and many other components of the endemic criminality of our age has produced the following picture of Wyke and Low Moor, according to the extrapolations from the 1981 Census published by Bradford Metropolitan Council.[4] Crimes reported to the Odsal Police Station in 1981 broke down as follows: Homicide 170 [177.5]; Indecent Assault 32 [31.1]; Burglary 1,391 [1257.5]; Stealing 2,849 [2933.7]; Fraud 84 [123.7]; Other Crimes 393 [462] making a total of 4,919 [4,985]. Both the individual items and the total bear a close relation to the average (in square brackets) for all seven police districts of the Bradford Metropolitan Area. Great discrepancies are observable only in the low figure for burglaries in Bradford Central, 563; and in Shipley 824 against an average of 1,257, presumably accounted for by the small number of inhabited properties in these areas. Bradford Central again stands out by having 262 reported frauds against an average of 123. The cartographic representation of these figures shows the greatest concentration of crime in our area to lie between High Fernley Road, Halifax Road and Abb Scott Lane with the municipal boundary, which follows Judy Woods and the old Royds Hall lands up to Buttershaw, constituting the western limit. Decidedly not the old settled districts of before World War II! At least 90% of this area was farmland or woodland until well after the last war; these are new estates which have not yet developed into anything like old-style communities.

One can only hope that new thinking and a scanty police presence will somehow contrive to revive the cooperation between the law and the public that I have described above. For there is now in Wyke a Neighbourhood Watch Scheme that has attracted a certain amount of attention from national accounts of such things. Has the wheel come full circle since the rule of clog-toe and Sgt. Woods?

Chapter 9

Spare Time and Play

At the beginning of his article in *Victorian Bradford*, David Russell regrets that he is able to produce only a middle class version of recreation in Bradford:

> Street corner 'lounging', women's conversation in corner shops, many children's games, indeed the complete range of 'informal' non-institutionalised recreation can only be glimpsed by the historian. Moreover, much of the material which is available emanated from middle-class sources and, as will be illustrated below, many middle-class observers possessed, for the most part, a highly coloured view of popular recreation.[1]

We, my helpers and I, have two advantages over Dr Russell: we limit our account chronologically to a period for which we may rely on the oral material provided by our elders and our own experiences, and we may take the liberty of restricting the activities to a relatively small sample of people. Dr Russell provides a much wider, formal, context for accounts such as mine, and he is able to start his account at a much earlier date. It is a daunting task from whichever angle it is approached. Education and the economy are relatively simple compared to a subject that stretches in variety from ratting to singing *The Messiah* in a large choir.

Apart from talking, 'callin', or simply resting, the generations of my parents and grandparents, were accustomed to spending their free time in effort and competition. Michael Parkinson, describing his early life in a mining community, has this to say about spare time:

> Recreation was the antidote to a life-time working down the mine and therefore, something to be taken seriously. You didn't play cricket for fun, nor grow parsnips only to eat. These activities were taken up to prove that you were the *best* cricketer in Cudworth or that you could grow the *biggest* parsnip. And if you didn't shape up, that was all the more reason to work harder at your hobby.[2]

Gambling was the true basis, the essential motivation of almost all games and competitions for my Generation I and older members of Generation II, and, because they mostly insisted on betting on their own efforts or their own acumen, their luck as it was called, in sporting matters such as picking the winners, they favoured active participation in relatively small, closed groups. Gambling schools, whose members often came together through a common occupation or place of work, kept alive cock-fighting, whippet and greyhound racing, knurr and spell, quoits, arrow-throwing, crown-green bowls – any sport of skill or strength that might lend itself to betting or a stake of some kind. As Michael Parkinson indicates, exhibiting one's own produce or possessions is part of the same attitude, and it was from this that the fanciers evolved. The amounts involved ranged from playing dominoes in the pubs for Woodbines when these cigarettes could be bought in packets of five for a penny, later twopence, to a fifty-pound wager on one's own whippet or greyhound. There is a widespread story of miners in the canteen (which makes clear that it is a relatively late story, or an adapted one!) betting on which lump of sugar a fly would first alight on.

When we, the Barkers and the Shaws, bought that piece of land on Elizabeth Street, and turned some of it over for a garden, or dug trenches for rough drainage, we found over the years several pennies and halfpennies showing either two tails or two heads. They had been carefully filed to half their normal thickness and then brazed together. Their purpose was to guarantee that one of two conspirators was bound to win when they played a newcomer or an innocent victim at Odd-Man-Out. This game was a pure gamble; the three men each tossed a coin and the one whose coin showed a face different to the coins of the other two took the three coins. In a straight game there were void throws, of course, when all three coins showed the same side. Of the two conspirators, one man had a double-headed coin and the other a double-tailed one, so their coins could not possibly show the same device, and one of them had to be the odd-man-out. No doubt they sometimes surreptitiously swapped coins or introduced intact coins.

Such straight gambling later took the form of dice or cards in the dinner hours of factory and workshop, and especially, in the nineteen-thirties, the football pools. The legal restrictions on betting had become frustrating to the man in the street, and this factor contributed to the immense success of the football pools. Ordinary men and women could then, without let or hindrance and in the comfort of their own homes, exercise their knowledge of form, pit their wits against the odds and dream of winning a fortune. The excitement alone of listening to the results every Saturday afternoon was well worth the stake. At that time, the three Shaw brothers, Fred, Walter and Seth, all in their seventies, convened at Fred's house in Scholes every Thursday to fill in their common coupon. It was a serious business!

A less direct form of gambling, because they were pursuits which demanded some considered and directed effort from the participants, breeding, training, feeding, etc., took the form of cock-fighting or racing dogs, either greyhounds or whippets. Long after cock-fighting had been declared illegal,[3] even as late as the 1920s and 1930s, cock-fighting was sustained by a few devotees. (See the story of Sarannah!) When we were young there were so many Old English Game cocks on local smallholdings and farms, kept for appearance alone or for breeding table-birds, that those kept for fighting went largely unnoticed. As we walked past certain farmyards and hen-pens, Ephraim was at pains to tell me how to recognise those kept for fighting, but I was not sufficiently interested to take in and remember this teaching. On one occasion, I think I happened upon a main taking place two fields away, but I did not wait to confirm this suspicion!

Matches between cocks and between running dogs (we heard nothing about organized dog fights, although one man might urge his dog on to attack another man's dog in a chance encounter) were made in the pubs, the only social centres of those days. The wagers, the conditions, the times and the places were fixed in front of casual witnesses. As I have indicated in my account of Edwin Lightowler, cheating was acknowledged and expected. Apart from the victims of the particular occurrence, most sportsmen admired a bit of clever cheating, surreptitiously breaking or bending the agreed conditions, pulling the wool over the eyes of the judge or referee. But it must be admitted that this was the cause of much of the brawling in pubs and on the street.

Knurr and spell, like bowls, was sometimes played as a team competition and sometimes between individuals. Frank can remember matches in Carr Lane Tide Field, behind the old Fleece Inn, which lasted from about

10 a.m. to 6 p.m. Under the title 'Great Knurr Matches', James Parker[4] gives details of two contests which took place on Wibsey Slack. The first was in 1854 for £50 a side and was won by Wm. Sutcliffe; the second, in 1859, for £25 a side was also won by Wm. Sutcliffe. The distance achieved, measured in scores of yards, averaged 12.2 and 11.33 in the first match and 11.3 and 10.5 in the second, the first being won by 367 to 340 and the second by 339 to 314. They seem to have played six rounds of five strikes each.

There seem to have been several variations on the rules of the sport, based on the length of the 'bat' and the way the knurr was tossed into the air to be hit. According to the information I have been able to glean, when playing with the longer 'bat', about six feet long, the knurr was shot up by a spring device (the spell) released by tapping the structure on a certain point with the 'bat' and then hitting the knurr when it was in the air. With the short 'bat', however, which was perhaps only three feet in length, the contestant tossed the knurr into the air and hit it.

Arrow-throwing, yet another contest that lent itself to wagers and betting, needs some explanation. An arrow, usually 18 ins. to 2 ft. long, was fashioned from some straight-grained wood, shaped a little thicker at the pointed end and flighted with four vanes of paper, at the other end. As lads, we would whittle and smooth for hours to produce one which conformed to our ideas of aerodynamics; sometimes there was only a very little arrow left when we had done! Frank saw serious contests for money carried out with absolutely straight arrows, up to three feet long, little more than ¼in. in thickness and without flights, but we always shaped and flighted them. Both types had in common a cord or piece of string wrapped once around the arrow about a third of the way down from the flight and locked, not tied, with a single knot. This served to rifle the flight of the arrow and extend the leverage of the thrower's arm; it was exactly the same principle and the same method as ancient Greek athletes employed when throwing the javelin: 'The Greeks always threw with the help of a thong wound tightly round the shaft leaving a loop hitched over the fingers of the throwing hand, to increase the leverage of the throwing arm and so add to the speed of projection, and to impart spin so as to keep the javelin steady in flight and carry it much further.'[5] Strangers to whom we demonstrated the technique were always amazed at the distances we could achieve. On a farm in Germany, where I worked for a short time in 1950 to gather material for a thesis, I demonstrated the art to the eldest son of the family, and before the day was out I had been taken to three further farms to show my skill!

Whether provided by private clubs or by the local authority in public parks, crown-green bowling needed more organisation and a bigger outlay of money than any of the above.[6] Land and premises had to be provided and the maintenance of a green required skill and experience. How many bowling greens have disappeared for want of a competent green-keeper since World War II? By the turn of the century the private clubs with bowling greens were augmented by bowling teams using the greens of municipal parks which were often of a very high standard. The top green in Wyke Recreation Ground was usually better kept than the Harold Club greens, although that does not mean that they were more interesting, or more of a challenge, for the bowler. The Harold Club[7] was the prestige bowling club for miles around down to the end of the Second World War, and is still greatly respected among the bowling fraternity. Here, too, betting and wagering played a considerable part, and it was normal for small amounts of money to change hands, or the loser to buy a drink, whether the game was part of a competition, league or cup, or merely social bowling. At the Harold Club a man in employment would team up with an unemployed man to play another similar pair, the earner paying the scot for both if they lost. When the bigger events like the Yorkshire

Plate 27. The Harold Club. The superior working men's club!

Merit and the West Riding Merit were being played, a certain large and red-faced bookie from Scholes, called Birch, was always present, shouting impatiently before play started, 'Ger 'em in t'paddock!' One sunny afternoon during the war, I was challenged by a man aged about seventy to a game for a shilling wager. As I got my woods out of the hut, Seth, sitting nearby and puffing his pipe, said out of the corner of his mouth: 'Tha mun watch 'im, tha knaws. John wor a gruacer, an' i'd nip a curran i' two ta mak' weight!' There seemed to be some kind of link between the game of bowls and pigeon racing, which I have referred to in my account of the Fanciers. It was quite heart-warming to find myself playing bowls in Cheshire around the year 1980 in a team of which three of the members raced pigeons!

There was also competition in leagues and teams well before the turn of the century. Cricket, rugby and soccer, as well as bowls, were established at all levels before the First World War. Young men played these games and older men went to watch them and support them. The local teams, the Sunday School League and the local cricket club were part of the communal identity; schoolboys found their heroes in these small-time teams rather than in the expensive stars of the big league. As Laurie Lee so admirably expresses it, 'Village honours are still severely local.' Without going on the tram to one of the Bradford League cricket grounds, to Valley Parade, or to Park Avenue, which offered not only League football but also county cricket in summer, one could watch and support a local football or cricket team, composed of men whom one might meet any day of the week. One could congratulate or criticise them to their faces – if one was sensible about it – and they, in turn, often offered help or criticism to youngsters playing school football. This advice, however, was usually offered in such a casual, easy-going, manner that no youngster was discouraged, nor sufficiently fired with ambition to become a professional. Nor did school-teachers push children to excel for the sake of their own reputation or that of the school; they merely encouraged them to improve, to be enthusiastic and to enjoy themselves. The exhortations used to fire one of these local teams were quite different in tone, however, and intended to intimidate; I remember the one most frequently shouted to St. Mark's Sunday School team: 'Nah then lads, owt aboon a daisy!' Which was meant to convey: 'Don't be afraid of anything and don't go to sleep. Kick anything that stands higher than a daisy!' For myself, the great bonus of playing football for the school, both at Carr Lane and at Belle Vue, was that I was excused the Saturday morning job of cleaning out hen-huts!

In our experience, cricket was not as popular as the winter ball-games on Storr Hill Side. Perhaps the climate had something to do with it. Suffice it to say that, both at school and in after life, cricket was regarded more as a pleasant diversion for a summer's afternoon, rather than a game to be keenly practised and fought out, although children could get as excited as a man at a cup-final when participating in a game in the street or on a plot of open land, of which there were many. Like so many mansions up and down the country, Royds Hall had its own cricket ground practically over the wall from the manor garden. This was an idyllic place to be on a fine afternoon in summer, with a view across into the Pennines beyond Halifax.[8]

The local nature of this hero-worship of sportsmen gave way to a much wider field of interest as we advanced in our teens. In my case, the most momentous change took place when Bradford Northern came from Birch Lane to Odsal Stadium when I was about thirteen years old. Not until then did I experience a professional spectator sport, the thrill of standing in a noisy crowd watching and supporting a team that was widely reported in the local press, and even, however briefly, in the national press. Going through turnstiles in the company of grown up men, sharing their interest, triumphs and disappointments, is a great boost to the morale of young, people, whether the activity in question be showing bantams or riding in Pony Club gymkhanas. In due course, I diverted my hero-worship from Albert Kellet, the tricky left wing for St. Mark's Sunday School team, to the truly great W.H.T. (Willie) Davis. What other player can boast of having played, when still at school, in a team that beat the All Blacks with No. 10 on his back, and later toured Australasia and won the Lance Todd Trophy with No. 6 on his back? Who else could make opponents move aside and let him through simply by promising a swerve with a little shimmy of the hips while running straight at full speed?

Although it was possible, even for a fourteen-year-old like myself, to get to matches in Halifax, Huddersfield, Leeds, Keighley, Dewsbury, Batley, etc. by using public transport, it was accessibility on foot that decided which sports and which teams flourished in the West Riding. Football, Rugby League (to me Rugby Union scarcely existed before I played it at Belle Vue) and, to a lesser degree, league cricket, catered for large numbers of spectators in relatively little space, and the majority of them could walk there quite comfortably. After a week of hard work, men would rush home for Saturday dinner, have a pint at the local with their friends and fellow supporters and walk at their leisure to the football or cricket ground. They sought and found not only recreation through being supporters, they felt that the team was the standard-bearer and the champion of their areal community and extremely important for their morale.

Standing crushed together, their heavy overcoats steaming with the rain and their feet frozen to the terraces, exercising only their speech organs and their lungs in exhortations and criticism of those who gave them a corporate reputation and identity, and in fervent abuse of unfortunate referees, they ignored the little discomforts and disappointments for a short time. Although spectators were far better behaved than they are now, they could become threatening when provoked by what they saw as an injustice. Bradford Northern had been at Odsal for only one or two seasons, when a referee incurred the wrath of some of the spectators and at the end of the game the police escorted him from the pitch to the pavilion, up the long flight of steps that was made in those days of railway sleepers. I had taken my brother Geoffrey, then aged nine or ten, to that match, but I was separated from him when we got to the level bit at the top, in front of the pavilion, where the crowd was thickest. Two mounted policemen, rock-steady on their horses, were up there surveying the scene, commanding by their very presence. I was getting quite worried until I found Geoff in the safest place that offered itself there – crouched under the belly of a police horse!

The post-mortems at work each Monday morning were also a very important part of their working week. It seems to have been overlooked by sociologists that the recreational outlets of working folk were frequently their only topics of conversation, and without conversation work in the mill, the pit or the puddling shop was very hard indeed. I am convinced that some men chose a bizarre or unusual weekend recreation simply as a means of impressing their work-mates on Monday morning. Talking about football or cricket was much more interesting and capable of variation than the routine Monday morning alternatives that I heard in the factory, such as 'Where did you get to on Saturday?' – 'What and how much did you drink?' 'Was it a good pint?' I have always been surprised at the number of girls and women who, then as now, were regular supporters of football and rugby teams, but, as my memory serves me, they were not so dependent on such things as a source of conversation.

The unchallenged popularity of these sports was helped by the fact that boys could play them in the street with improvised equipment. Any old board that had fallen off a fence could make a youngster into a Herbert Sutcliffe or a Maurice Leyland; a tin can on the cobbles of Elizabeth Street was sufficient to make us see ourselves as Alex James. The latter, inside forward for the great Arsenal team of the thirties, was the epitome of the crafty player of ball-games for us, although we had only heard of him from our elders who themselves had probably never seen him in action. There was even a regular crown-green bowler in Wyke Recreation Ground who styled himself 'the Alex James of bowls'! It didn't seem to do him much good; I can't remember him winning anything, or even playing for the first team.

It is difficult for us today to imagine the attraction for factory, forge and mine workers of time spent at leisure in the open air. They enjoyed such occasions whether they were spent in walking round the neighbourhood visiting friends, walking with the family in one of the many excellent municipal parks, or using public transport to get to Shipley Glen, Ilkley Moor or Hardcastle Crags. The Easter holiday walk on the moors was for young people a celebration of the end of winter almost on a par with the pagan rites of our forefathers. But the regular, habitual walks in the parks were the most important event of the week to many families. Parks were used for occasions[9] like the Low Moor Carnival held annually for charity, of which the procession started at the Robin Hood Inn and finished in Harold Park. The culmination was the crowning of a carnival queen followed by all kinds of entertainments. I remember speed-boat racing on the lake in Harold Park!

Although it would appear that the thinking about municipal parks nearer to the centre of Bradford was prompted by the need for open spaces among the densely built up concentration of mills and back-to-backs,[10] there must have been a different reason when parks were opened in Wyke, Low Moor, Oakenshaw and Wibsey. In these areas there was plenty of land that had been acquired by the Low Moor Company for the mineral rights, and, as the minerals under them were largely worked out by the end of the nineteenth century and the paternal attitude of the Company was as strong as ever, they readily gave this land or sold it cheaply for parks that would benefit their workers.

Oakenshaw and Wibsey parks were taken over by the council when the city was extended in 1899. Wibsey Park had been opened to the public in 1885, and Harold Park in the same year. Oakenshaw Park was opened to the public in 1897 and Wyke Recreation Ground in 1898, and greatly extended in 1900.[11]

Cudworth writes:[12]

> Carr Lane Tide, a famous event in its way, is also fixed about this time [1790s, the time of the founding of Low Moor Company], but this 'tide' seems to have originated with Nan Parish, who has

> the credit, we believe, of starting more than this one. Bull and bear baiting were among the early amusements indulged in at Carr Lane Tide, and the 'roughs' of Low Moor at that time were rough customers indeed.

Writing over a hundred years later, Grace Carter has more information about its foundation, the bear-baiting and what the tide had become in our young days. Our local name for a fair, 'tide', simply means 'time' 'period', as in Whitsuntide, Eastertide, Christmastide. With this word our forefathers indicated a time that was an important landmark in their primitive annual calendar, a time when there was always something going on at a given place, just like the ebb and flow of the sea that is regular and provides a mark of time in the day.[13]

Wyke Tide, on a triangular piece of land opposite the Robin Hood, was a week or so earlier, and usually Geoffrey and I were taken to Horton Tide in November because Aunt Lucy and Grandad Barker lived there, so we got to three tides in a good year. There were certainly noteworthy goings on towards the end of August in Carr Lane from the late eighteenth century to World War II. The glamour and excitement started when the huge steam traction engines came down Carr Lane, sometimes pulling three separate loads each, and had to manoeuvre across the narrow road from a point by Mrs Benn's little 'spice' shop into the narrow gate. The erection of tents, stalls and roundabouts was a thrill to us lads, before the full performance with the music, the movement of the excited crowd, young and old, and the tempting odours of hot pies (Pie Tom was never far from the gate), fried chats, brandy-snap and other delicacies that we only ever saw at a tide. Curiously enough, it is the odours of a tide that have remained with me most clearly, although I cannot describe them now.

The spectacular and gaudy roundabouts remain in the memory of us all. We can all remember Goldthorpe and Marshall's Proud Peacocks and some of us can go back to Church's Cockerills. There was Chapman's hoop-la-stall and the unusual name Kester Brook (I never saw it written, the spelling is mine) sticks in my mind although I can't remember what he offered. What was there varied from year to year, and the thrill of anticipation when one watched the arrival of the fair was almost unbearable. Frank can remember lions and tigers in a menagerie and a bazaar with toys and trinkets in a long tent up against the back garden wall of the Fleece Inn.

It was an institution which, by its very nature, could not keep up with the times. Financially it became unviable, and sometimes one of the bigger owners of attractions would take a lease on the whole event and then let space to his friends and associates only, which limited the variety of attractions. I have heard from two independent sources that the owner of the Proud Peacocks, unable to keep them on the road any longer, burned them to ashes rather than sell them to another owner.

In the clubs there was provision for billiards, snooker, darts, dominoes and cards, games that could be played either casually by men who were there only for the beer or keenly by those who felt that they had something to prove. For the men of Storr Hill Side there were plenty of clubs. The most central was New Road Side Working Men's Club, a poky, dark and dingy building up Main Street, which, however, offered all the essential attractions for working men: drink, games and a convivial atmosphere in which to relax. Also in similar, older buildings were housed a club called 'T'Mule', opposite the end of Kellet Buildings in Carr Lane, whose proper name I can't remember ever hearing, and the Morley Carr Working Men's Club, known as 'T'Neddy 'Oil'.[14] Harold Club was by far the most palatial of such clubs.

Although the people of Storr Hill Side paid little attention to politics, there were the usual Conservative Clubs and Liberal Clubs which gave only nominal support to those parties; their main purpose was the provision of the same amenities as all the other clubs and pubs.

Quite a lot of people were devoted to the swimming baths as a place of recreation and Elizabeth Street resounded every Sunday morning with a lot of joyful excitement echoing from the baths. The slipper baths in these municipal baths were also well attended, as an improvement on the tin bath in front of the fire which was all that there was in the vast majority of households.

Before World War II there was very little interest in any other sports or games on Storr Hill Side, apart from the games of cards and various board games that friends played in one another's houses. The more 'intellectual' games, chess and bridge for instance, were too demanding for the impromptu leisure of working folk, but people spent a lot of time in the family circle and, when friends or neighbours dropped in, playing draughts, whist, rummy, dominoes and other such games. When new, canasta really did become the rage on Storr Hill Side. In the case of the more complicated games, each family was likely to have its own rules! The grown-ups also found time to play snakes and ladders or ludo with the children.

There was very little trace of what is usually called folk-lore left on Storr Hill Side. No trace of maypole dancing, no morris dancers, and, although men and women might 'dress up in silly clothes and blacken their faces and call themselves mummers', all they did was to go round to neighbours, show their costumes and wish them a Happy Christmas before sticking out their hands for some 'laance'. (Frank's description!) Before the last war, celebration of Harvest Home was well observed in all the churches, and on 1st May all the carters decorated their horses with ribbons and rosettes and their best brasses brightly polished.

It took a long time for the attraction of spectator sports to wane as a result first of the motor car and then of television. The spread of the motor car made it possible for working men to become aware of and reach out to many more interests than before. They were no longer restricted to the local, undignified and uncomfortable ritual of the football match. Their contribution to the Monday morning conversation was much more impressive if they had actually gone to the races or the seaside on the spur of the moment, or spent the weekend up the Dales in their caravan. We must also remember that the demands of owning one's house and having to repair and maintain it, the Do-It-Yourself movement, takes up men's time and gives an interest to some, as does driving and maintaining a car.

Looking back over the last century, the two great innovations of domestic technology have everywhere completely changed the aspect of sport. The car has not only made new sports and pastimes such as rambling and climbing possible, it has broken up the corporate nature, whether as a participant or a spectator, of most of the sporting outlets that we knew. Television has put the finishing touch to this trend; one sits at home, warm and comfortable, but alone, in one's family, rather than exert one's self out in the cold and the rain. No longer do men and boys challenge one another, as individuals or groups, casually to a race or to a match; no longer do they back themselves, wager on their own prowess. They are watching an industrial product based on high finance and high wages. At the betting-shop they wager on horses that are running at some distance, even in a foreign country. If they join a club it is likely that it offers organised competition against other clubs and for various trophies and tends to discourage spontaneous competition between friends.

In the above paragraphs, I have deliberately concentrated on the nature of local, popular sport and games, rather than the founding and the successes of the professional sport in the towns around us; that has been amply documented in numerous sources.

Dr Russell's article in *Victorian Bradford*, being more concerned with the fostering of 'social integration' through recreational pursuits, tends to play down sport in favour of cultural activities and interests.[15] On Storr

Hill Side the cultural activities may be summed up as talking, reading, music and dancing, of which the latter two were organised and special provision was made for them. I have accounted for the first two elsewhere in this book.

Not only did the women sing at work and round the piano when they had company, they were devoted singers in choirs, both church and secular, and the most frequent leisure activity that parents provided for their daughters took the form of music lessons, i.e. piano lessons. Sometimes men contributed to domestic music-making with a concertina or a violin, and the brass bands must not be forgotten.[16] Most of the choirs contained both men and women, but there were no women in the St. Mark's choir, unlike Holy Trinity and Buttershaw St. Paul's, for instance, which included women in the 1930s. Martha Heaton's chapter on 'The Religious Side of My Life'[17] and later chapters on her devotion to singing and other cultural activities connected with a Baptist Church, fill part of the gap bemoaned by Dr Russell.[18] 'The majority of leisure *institutions* appear either never to have kept detailed records or to have destroyed or mislaid those they did possess, while whole areas of popular recreation simply went unrecorded.' (my italics). The renowned choirs of the area, such as the Bradford Festival Choral Society, founded in the 1850s, the Bradford Old Choral Society, and the famous Huddersfield Choral Society were supported both with singers and with audiences from Storr Hill Side.

This was serious singing, an art that had to be learned, but popular singing that fulfilled the purpose of keeping up the spirits or maintaining a rhythm while engaged on some wearying, tedious job, or simply to counteract the sense of loneliness and foster daydreams, played a far bigger part in the life of most people. That is probably the greatest difference between popular songs of a generation ago and those of the present: then they had to be singable, they had to have a melody with an easily assimilated and executed rhythm, whereas now the objective is to demand the attention of the hearer either by the sheer volume of noise that seems to be obligatory, or by the complexity of the composition or by the drastic impact of the content of the lyric. They were meant to be sung by groups or individuals without the accompaniment of electronic devices; in the mills and factories they were the often silent comforters of operatives as they sang them in their heads. I have witnessed occasions when one girl who started to sing silently but with lip movements set off three or four other girls to sing the same song in the same manner because they could all lip-read.

My Generation I, as represented by Seth, for instance, had a song in their repertoire for every occasion. Some were purely tap-room ballads, like 'Maggie Malone', 'Aileen Alannah', 'The Baby's Name Was Capetown, Mafeking, French, Kimberley, Ladysmith, Bobs!', 'Nellie Dean', 'She was Poor but She Was Honest'. This style merged comfortably with the hits of the music halls – Harry Lauder's 'I Belong to Glasgow', 'Lily of Laguna' – and Irish folk-songs: 'Danny Boy', 'Bonny Mary of Argyle' and the more sophisticated jigs like 'MacNamara's Band'. The tradition of the music hall was greatly eroded in our day, but, as late as World War II, it was possible to see some of the great acts in the old tradition. I remember Rob Wilton as a comedian and Nat Jackley's sand dance very vividly. From the present-day point of view, it is staggering to think that songs like these were propagated without the aid of the wireless or the film; there were wind-up gramophones and huge thick records, but these were rarely wasted on popular music. We had one at home, but I recall only an old, droning, record of Caruso and another of Gigli singing an aria from *Aida*. But, seeing that everybody sang frequently and in any place, a piece that somebody had heard somewhere and learned from the singer, or, more frequently, one that had appeared as sheet music, or had been used in one of the numerous 'concerts' in aid of church finances, was spread with amazing speed through the community.

Nothing could better illustrate the death of the Storr Hill Side community than the present scene at the bottom of Storr Hill. The tidefield is covered with soulless industrial development; the Fleece Inn is an empty mouldering shell; and the school that once prepared happy children for a happy, productive life is now a meat warehouse full of dead carcases and festooned with barbed wire, more like a prison. Apart from taking care of the essential education of the local children for a hundred years, Carr Lane School buildings accommodated the entertainment and social life of the community, notably the pantomimes.

Around Christmas or Easter, these occasions were staged by a core of supporters of St. Mark's Church. Like pantomimes everywhere, they attached to a well-known theme – Cinderella, Jack and the Beanstalk, Ali Baba, etc. – some acting, a lot of clowning, singing of topical popular songs and dancing. The clowning and singing that for many years revolved round Frank Wilkinson, who in his time played everything from Prince Charming to the Dame, Jack Rhodes and Laurence Harper, was perhaps the central attraction, but we can remember some attractive girls in the appropriate roles and there is no doubt that the greatest amusement, emotion and applause was evoked by the singing and dancing of the younger children.

Even though those involved in a production might number a hundred, and a coach and a dancing-mistress might be imported from as far afield as Bowling, these were occasions which came straight from the heart of Storr Hill Side. They worried about no box-office returns, and they themselves were their only critics. Many will remember the 'Treasure Island' show that Frank wrote – just for a change – with Jack Rhodes as the pirate captain singing 'Dem Bones'.

Songs from the early musicals such as *Maid of the Mountains*, *The Desert Song*, *Rose Marie*, *No, No, Nanette*, *Chu Chin Chow*, and those of Ivor Novello, etc. were popular with many women, Annie included. Films were made of most of these and there were additions to the genre such as *Showboat*. Paul Robeson's performance in this last and the records of his songs were particular favourites of the men of Generations I and II. The people of Storr Hill Side seemed to find Gilbert and Sullivan too complicated and Noel Coward too sophisticated.

It was the cinema that took over all forms of entertainment in the thirties and during the war, and that thenceforward provided the repertoire. The songs that the 'talkie' and the 'crooners' introduced were exactly the kind that the working people of Storr Hill Side wanted, especially the women. They were romantic, escapist and the melodies were catching and easy to sing, and they are still the favourites of most of my early Generation III. In the 1980s, in the big holiday hotels of the Mediterranean, which are kept open out of season by a lot of English pensioners, there will be a small ensemble of musicians in the evening. These cast an experienced eye round the lounge and for the rest of the evening will render 'Deep Purple', 'Jealousy', 'Stardust', 'Wish Upon a Star', 'Two Sleepy People', 'Begin the Beguine', 'Just the Way You Look Tonight', 'Home on the Range', 'Smoke Gets in Your Eyes', 'Last Roundup', 'These Foolish Things', 'The More We Are Together', 'Over the Rainbow' – and many others.

The songs of Irvine Berlin, Cole Porter, Jerome Kern, George Gershwin and their contemporary colleagues beguile people old enough to have heard them when new, in their original setting, just as much today as they did fifty years ago. The above have perhaps retained their popularity by virtue of their melodies, but many others are remembered for their words, such as the songs from the 'Road' films, those of Al Jolson, the ditties of the child prodigy Shirley Temple, such as 'Animal Crackers in My Soup' and 'The Good Ship Lollipop', and later, the wartime songs of Vera Lynn which had the additional advantage of sentimental melodies.

The successors of these were the songs from the musicals like *South Pacific*, *Oklahoma*, *Annie Get Your Gun*; and after these some of the songs of the Beatles, but after that the pop-group numbers tended to become unsingable shrieks, suitable only for the pandemonium that accompanies formless, hysterical modern dancing. What would the Victorian moralist have said, who was so disgusted with the goings on in an early dance hall in Bradford?[18]

The tunes from the pre-war films were also good for dancing, which further cemented their popularity with my generation. For the young people of the mills and factories of Bradford in the first half of the twentieth century, the dance hall, often named dancing school or dancing academy because instruction was offered as well as entertainment, was a most important outlet at the weekend.[19] It was the only institution that offered a relaxed situation in which young people of both sexes could be together and enjoy themselves. There were dances in most localities, in clubs and village halls, and they were often sponsored by the church. In the Harold Club, for instance, the dancing and the drinking were carefully separated on different floors. To this day, in village halls, clubs and cafés, there are regular, quite well supported, opportunities for members of my Generation III to dance as they danced when young.

The first time I was taken to 'the pictures', was in 1927, when the silent version of Remarque's *All Quiet on the Western Front* was shown at Wyke Hippodrome.[20] The other local cinema which shared in the great boom of the cinema in the thirties as it affected Storr Hill Side, was Low Moor, about three-quarters of a mile away. The latter was smaller and more intimate and both of them had double seats down the wings of the ninepennies.

We saw all the classic comedies of Charlie Chaplin, Laurel and Hardy, Harold Lloyd, Eddie Cantor; we remember great films like *The Good Earth*, with Luise Rainer sieving the parched and barren soil through delicate and perfectly manicured hands! As lads we often enjoyed the supporting cowboy film with Tom Mix better than the main film like Greta Garbo in *Camille*. I have spoken recently to representatives of both sexes of my own age for whom the films of Deanna Durbin are their most abiding memory. When on night shift during the war, I sacrificed half of my daily sleep to go down to the Odeon Cinema in the afternoon to see my first colour film: Laurence Olivier in *Henry V*.

The BBC was founded the year I was born, 1922, and when I was quite tiny there were people on Storr Hill Side sitting very close to their crystal sets completely absorbed in the new miracle. Older playmates felt quite important when they had to take their parents' wet batteries to Reggie Bennett's Crown Garage to be charged. My earliest memory of the radio is of being in Scholes with Walter Thornton, who was shortly afterwards to marry my Aunt Eva, in a packed front room on a street just about opposite the Rising Sun, where I sat on the floor in front of a huge, primitive radio set to listen to Arsenal beat Huddersfield Town 2-0 on 26th April 1930. Another early memory is of crouching with Seth before their huge, carved and polished set (we didn't get one for at least another year) to listen to the fight between Benny Lynch and Small Montana for the Flyweight Championship of the World on 19th January 1937. Small Montana won.

I found radio and television so compelling, such new miracles, that I was never able to do anything, not even read the newspaper, within sight or earshot of radio and television. It took charge of me and still does, to the extent that I have never become a devotee for fear of never getting anything done. Although I still watch a lot of sport, news, feature films and one or two comedies, I can easily forget my intention to watch a given programme. I never did buy a radio set until it was demanded by my wife and children, and I first acquired a black and white television set about 1961 and a colour television set in 1982.

The idea of sitting alongside a reincarnated Shakespeare to watch a production of one of his plays in a present day sitting-room, with handset control of the television, or with Goethe watching and hearing Gounod's *Faust*, really does appeal to me!

Chapter 10

Children at Play

As I have indicated in my chapter on Education, children used to be spared the pressure to succeed that is prevalent in the middle-class outlook of today. The pharmacist I normally use has bottles on his counter labelled 'Eleven-Plus Tonic'! There were still men and women around who could remember little boy chimney-sweeps, stunted and half-fed, and my Appendix I presents further evidence of what the poor had to put up with to be accepted as 'deserving poor'. But in the little time that they were free, they could sleep and play; they were not continually pressurised, both in the home and out of it, to excel, to do better. Nor was the outside world, as far as they were aware of it, so complicated, presenting so many puzzles to young minds. It used to be limbs that needed rest, now it is minds and nerves that are subjected to the same kind of strain. My period begins just as the reforms concerning child-labour and education, which were the great achievements of the late Victorian age, were beginning to have effect, although there were still a great many employers and parents who succeeded in ignoring and side-stepping this legislation.[1]

It is my opinion that the children who grew up on Storr Hill Side between 1890 and 1940 had the best upbringing and education that has ever been provided in this country. I have tried to explain this opinion in several places in this book. Here I am concerned with how they exercised their minds and bodies, when it was left completely to them.

From an early age, girls had less free time and more domestic duties than boys, but most of them did manage to make plenty of time for play. They spun tops, skipped, and played with dolls, dolls' houses and dolls' prams; they had a great variety of ball games, often of an eliminating kind, which were played in a highly competitive spirit, with great excitement. Skipping was the standby amusement; there was individual skipping with a lot of fancy steps and there was 'long-rope' skipping in which a rope up to ten feet long would be 'twined' either by two girls, one at each end or by one girl with the other end tied to a fence or a lamp-post, and one or more girls skipping. With the cry 'Pepper!' the rope was turned as fast as possible, tapping the ground with machine-gun rapidity and making those skipping jump up and down with the same tempo. They dressed up in rags and cast-offs, performed their own little impromptu 'concerts', uttered magic formulae in chorus under the direction of a leader and sang songs that had been handed down for generations. In some ways they were more inventive in their play than the boys and had a greater variety of games. One such game. as far as I have been able to discover a very local one, was called Prick in Book, a kind of lottery, and consisted of various objects like silver paper, old picture postcards and Christmas cards, little drawings, etc. being secreted in the pages of a substantial book. Each girl took it in turn to prick a needle into the end of the pages of the tightly closed book and 'win' the 'prize' hidden at that point in the book. There were many such invented games played by both sexes, many of which are unknown today.[2] Rounders was their most popular ball game when they could find an open space for it. Like the boys, they would play marbles, hide and seek, piggy in the middle and bowl hoops, of which a great many must have been made as 'foreigners' on the Low Moor Company premises.

Girls read a wide range of comics and periodicals. For the very young there was *Chicks' Own*, and they could then proceed to the *Rainbow*, *Comic Cuts*, *Tiger Tim* and the *Wizard*, among others, this latter group being popular with boys also. For young ladies there was the well-known *Peg's Paper*. Piano lessons, dancing lessons and sometimes membership of a choir were also possibilities for older girls.

To the age of eleven or twelve their play was in marked contrast to that of today, when adult-organised activities, music lessons, dancing classes and swimming clubs, for example, take the place of the above games. There was no equivalent of 'Blue Peter' and the activities generated by this and similar programmes, nor was there 'Top of the Pops' to hypnotise them from the age of about ten. Parents of between the wars would be horrified to see children of both sexes having birthday parties in the form of a hired disco. There would have been something decidedly wrong with a boy of ten or twelve who wanted to celebrate his birthday, or anything else, in that way! Such 'showing-off' by the parents was very much frowned upon on Storr Hill Side and contravened the practical outlook of the community. Moreover, a considerable residue of propriety and decorum on Victorian lines was observed in the upbringing of girls.

On the whole, boys did not read as much as girls, but they read all the comics they could lay hands on and the library's stock of adventure stories for boys was well used. The improvement in the quality of books for young children since World War II is one of the most heartening achievements of the period. In the house, if they were lucky, they might have bits of Meccano and a few model farmyard animals, a humming top to spin on the table or on a plate, or a toy train. Both boys and girls – and their parents – played draughts, ludo, snakes and ladders, snap and other simple card-games.

A lad might have his own junior size football (even these were made of leather panels sewn together!) or his own cricket bat. These were luxuries indeed, and most lads had to make do for most of the time with the bits of wire, nuts and bolts picked up in the street, balls from bearings, marbles and conkers and bits of string – things that have always formed the traditional contents of a boy's pockets. There could be no better training for the imagination of a future craftsman!

Outside it was a different story! Football and cricket were played to rules dictated by the surface and restrictions of the street and with the available equipment, which might be primitive in the extreme. All of us learned to use our feet at football with balls no bigger than a tennis ball, and the adjustment to a proper football when the opportunity arose was quite difficult. If the street was the pitch, as often as not the goals were as wide as the pitch, unless it was a very serious game when jackets, jerseys or other objects might be laid down as goal-posts. If you are used to wearing clogs, even a kind of football with a tin can is possible. We played cricket with the same ball as we played football, the bat being any bit of board that would serve; it might stop at your knees or reach to your shoulder! Again, there was little resemblance to the real game, and adjustment was difficult, but the cunning, the agility and the correlation of hand and eye that our games produced, stood us in good stead when competing against boys from a background where they had the proper equipment and conditions from an early age. We threw arrows, made catapults and bows and arrows (which never worked!) and in winter we snowballed one another and sledged down Storr Hill on contraptions that were little more than boards nailed crudely together; some had iron runners, many did not. By our standards, of course, Storr Hill was the best road for sledging for miles around, as good as the Cresta any day, and we had no need to be worried about motor traffic, as the vast majority of vehicles that tackled the hill in those days gave plenty of warning of their slow ascent with their motors alone.

The girls had more formalised games than we had. Not the rules but the excitement and the hunter instinct governed our versions of hide and seek, relievo, and such games. It was from these factors, not winning at games played according to rules, that we gained our thrills and excitement. We played marbles, for instance, according to rules entirely of our own making, which bore no resemblance to the firmly entrenched rules which our fathers and grandfathers observed.

Our version of tip-cat was played on the unmade parts of Elizabeth Street as follows: the equipment was a fairly stout stick, some 2-2½ ft. long, and a piece of round wood, the 'piggy', 3-4 inches long and ¾-1 inch thick, either turned, like an old chair-rail, or as off the tree, if straight enough, and pointed at both ends. The game started and finished in a circle scribed in the dirt or ash of the street, usually about 2 ft. in diameter. By tapping one of the pointed ends, the 'piggy' was made to spring into the air so that it could be struck as far as possible by the striker with the stick. The other players then endeavoured to throw the piggy back so that it came to rest in the circle. If it landed short the striker tried to hit it even further away. A throw which threatened to land in the circle, could be prevented by striking the 'piggy' while it was still in mid-air. The thrower who succeeded in landing the 'piggy' in the circle then took the place of the striker. If a strike landed near enough to the circle for the thrower to leap from 'piggy' to circle, he took the stick from the striker as though it had landed in the circle.

Tom cats are supposed to wander further from home, to cover more ground in their curiosity, looking for prey, adventure and pussies, than the female of the species. Although these objectives did not quite apply to us as lads, we roamed far afield in twos and threes, spontaneously, without arrangements, just working off surplus energy and trying to satisfy our curiosity, but never succeeding. There was scarcely a square inch of ground between the Guide Post and Norwood Green, between High Bentley and Oakenshaw Cross, that we did not know – and, in those days, we could find our way over all of this area quite safely in the dark.

There is no doubt in my mind that helping the grown-ups perform grown-up jobs was the most satisfying pastime of all, provided that they did not shout at you or leave you standing about for too long just watching them. With these reservations, the introduction they were given to adult activities while still at school and quite young was the best pastime for all for both boys and girls. They were made to feel that they had some value to their elders; they were admitted to the sphere of work. How the cleverer boys and girls from middle-class suburban backgrounds manage to put up with being deprived of this satisfaction until they reach the age of 21-22, without rebelling and opting out, has always baffled me. Through nothing more than running errands and learning housekeeping lore at an early age, many girls from the homes of factory-workers and miners later ran successful small businesses.

Chapter 11

Women's Activities

If one looks at Victorian society of all levels, the contrast between the privileged position of men and the relegation of women to being a second-class variety of the human race is very striking. It is obvious enough in the fields of politics, education, employment and religion, and it extended equally clearly to their spare time pursuits. Apart from house-work and shopping, it was the church and its social activities that had first claim on women's time and effort. Sunday school work in all its aspects, charity work, entertainments to raise funds for the church, children's or old folks' treats and outings, and perhaps the Girl Guides or the St. John's Ambulance Brigade were approved and had no stigma attached to them. Apart from these and genteel, orthodox interests in art or music, everything else that women might indulge in might incur accusations of impropriety.

Above all, there was no public life, no careers of prestige and responsibility, no politics, not even at local level and they did not have the vote; for them there was no commerce beyond the little corner shop, no newspaper work, no designing, and no teaching for married women. Women in public life who extol and long for the Victorian values in life, don't know what they are talking about. Unmarried women, although as servants at all levels, as mill-girls, nannies and office workers, they made an essential contribution to national life, had no freedom to choose for themselves or make any decisions on family matters. They were not allowed in pubs or clubs, going alone to the theatre or music hall was to risk grave criticism and abuse. They were not allowed to wear trousers or go hiking in shorts.

Such general, national, mostly middle-class, features of women's position in society were less rigidly observed by the working-class women of Storr Hill Side. Or, more precisely, they made their own choice of these features. Outside things didn't matter.

The domestic duties of women on Storr Hill Side, as in most parts of the land, were clearly defined and are easy to describe. On Monday, they washed and sometimes they ironed, sometimes they left it until Tuesday, when they did part of the cleaning, perhaps just the bedrooms. Wednesday was baking day almost everywhere, and was the day most people remember from before the war. As far as the women-folk were concerned, it was on Wednesday that their reputation as a housewife was at stake, the day when they tried to impress both their own men-folk and the neighbours. Flour was fetched from the Co-op in stones and half-stones and, after much elbow-grease and puffing and panting in the kneading of it, a huge quantity of bread would be baked in the cunningly managed oven in the fire-range or, by our day, in the gas oven. But, with the voracious appetite for confectionery that prevailed, the bread-baking was only half of the task or less.

I don't think that we were a great exception in this respect, but the amount of sweet confectionery that we got through would ruin both the health and the finances of the average family of today. Perhaps the poultry made Annie extravagant; I can remember a time when, in spring when eggs were plentiful, she would start baking-day with three dozen and, on at least one occasion, she sent me to get more from the nests. When Irene Garside who then lived on Rose Bank was going to get married, early on in the war, we were able to give her a dozen eggs for the cake, as a much appreciated wedding present.

On Thursday they did some more cleaning and on Friday they shopped, if they had any money. If they had to wait until Friday evening for their husbands' wages, they shopped on Saturday morning. This pattern, although there were small differences from individual to individual, persisted from the beginning of my period to after World War II, until it became frequent for wives and mothers to go out to work.

Having written the above paragraphs, it struck me that it is nothing less than a gross impertinence on the part of a man to undertake to describe the daily life and work of women in the Bradford area. Among the recent spate of works on local history written by women who lived and worked in the traditional routine, there are several works which offer vivid, detailed pictures of this important aspect of society. It has all been done so thoroughly, so extensively and so ably by Bradford women themselves, that I shall merely draw the attention of the reader to five publications by the City of Bradford Metropolitan Council Libraries Division. The two earliest, both published in 1980, are *Reminiscences of a Bradford Mill Girl* by Maggie Newberry (reprinted 1981) and *East Bowling Reflections* by the East Bowling History Workshop. I hope that the male members of the Workshop will not be too offended if I include this as a book by women; the list of those responsible contains twenty-four women and ten men. These were followed in 1983 by *A Tale That is Told* by Martha Heaton, and in 1988 by *A Family Affair. My Bradford Childhood, 1900-1911* by Kathleen Binns. The most recent, and to me the most inspiring work of its kind that I have read, is *All Muck and Nettles. The Early Life of Burler and Mender No. 57* by Vera Smith, which has just appeared at the time of writing, 1990.[1] Between them these ladies have covered the daily life of the women of Bradford in the first half of the twentieth century in greater detail and with more authority than any man could ever attempt. Apart from *A Family Affair*, they all feature life in city streets and in back-to-backs and all against a background of work in the mill. *A Family Affair* gives a very good insight into the family life of a stuff merchant who was in partnership with his father. Kathleen Binns' portrait of her father, the Quaker business man, is a unique picture of such a man at home and his relationships with his family. Altogether, it is a valuable account of what I like to call The Great Tradition. It supports my argument that one of the great factors in the Bradford success story was the fact that those with the authority and the initiative in business were fully in touch with and shared many features of the daily life of working people.

The spare time pursuits of women of my Generation I arose from and merged with their domestic duties and were often indistinguishable from them. When they had to vindicate their value to the community, either in earnest or light-heartedly in fun, they claimed that 'Women's work is never done'. And indeed, it did seem that they were always making some contribution to the well-being of the family and often worked until late in the evening when everybody else had finished work. But the idea that this constituted a penitential life not far removed from slavery is an invention of modern sociology operating from a modern middle-class point of view. They had their work to do, and they did it; but, partly through the teaching of their mothers and grandmothers and partly through their own initiative and common sense, all except the most deprived and unintelligent were able to develop ways and means of amusing themselves and relaxing *while they worked*. Unless it was an emergency, they made shopping into a brief but regular social occasion. There were no foremen and no piece-work or bonuses in their job, and once the day's work was on its way, they sat down with their knitting and looked out of the window to see what their neighbours were up to or they went round and drank a cup of tea with a crony. They could relax even at work, and while shaking the tab rugs or scrubbing and colouring the front-door steps with scouring-stone, they talked and joked or just complained.

Needlework of one kind or another was by far the most frequent activity. Apart from those who were sickly, disabled or slovenly and unintelligent by nature, they knitted, sewed, crocheted, embroidered, tatted, darned and talked while they rested and relaxed. They enthused over patterns and lost no time in asking their friends and neighbours for their approval when they had a new piece of work to show. This activity, even when it was applied to a considerable pile of mending and darning, as was necessary in some families on most evenings, was restful and convivial. One of the great improvements in the lot of women was effected by the spread of man-made fibres as opposed to the healthy and comfortable natural fibres which needed so much more mending. Even in the young days of my Generation I, however, there was no great practical need for the products of their needles; on Storr Hill Side, at least, textiles were cheap enough to be within the reach of all except, perhaps, when there was a young family and the man was out of work. This changed in the years after World War I, a slump time for Storr Hill Side, and at Carr Lane School we were contemporaries of lads who, year in year out, were dressed in the distinctive garb of the Cinderella Club charity.

Perhaps their greatest pleasure and comfort was in singing. They sang at home over their domestic duties and at work, even though the noise of the machinery made them inaudible. The text and the tune filled their hearts and minds, and they had no need of an audience. A good singer was a valued asset to any workshop that was not too noisy.[2] There were also the choirs, popular with both men and women, and not only the churches and chapels but the choral equivalents of the brass bands. A lot of singing round the piano at home took place. Seth and Sarah had one and Aunt Eva had piano lessons at a time when Seth sometimes had to borrow 3*d.* from Annie to go looking for work. Perhaps Aunt Eva married Walter Thornton because he was a good singer?

Between the wars some improvements were made in the range and nature of spare-time opportunities of women. Once more, public transport played a leading part: 'Tramways provided access to shopping centres any day of the week and many village mothers and daughters followed a regular pattern of going to Bradford every Saturday afternoon whilst the menfolk went to the match, football in winter, cricket in summer.'[3] It was surprising how many women went with their menfolk to the match; women approaching seventy, and even eighty, years of age can still remember the stars of the Bradford football and rugby teams, whom they watched from the terraces between the wars.

The cinema constituted the greatest contribution to the recreation of women in my lifetime. Here was the great substitute for the pub where man and wife could go together without incurring any stigma and be entertained and enthralled for less money. For the first time in history, ordinary men and women could be introduced en masse to another world, however unreal and however escapist the content of most of it was. Not all of it was the bread and butter romance and glitter of Hollywood; the first time I was taken to a cinema, I saw the silent film of Remarque's *All Quite on the Western Front* at Wyke Hippodrome. There was a horror film as supporting programme; the audience shrank away from gap-toothed ghostly faces rushing out at them and filling the screen. I was only five years old at the time and didn't sleep very well for a night or two, but I threw a tantrum when Annie and Ephraim were determined to stay at home on the following Saturday evening! Once 'talkies' came in, they produced not only comedies, musicals and romances against a lush American background, there were frequent attempts at really serious works.

At the local cinemas there were two different programmes each week, and lots of people went to the cinema twice a week. Michael Parkinson, brought up in a mining community like Storr Hill Side had once been, admits to going to the cinema twice a week in his teens. Women in particular perused the local paper for the forthcoming programme, talked to their cronies about the offerings both before and after, and found that they had less to talk about for a few days if they had to forego a programme. A visit to one of the big cinemas in Bradford which offered all the trappings of the latest entertainment as well as the aura of luxury, was always a treat. It was as though the opulence of a metropolitan opera house – London or Paris – had been made available to everybody.

Almost immediately after the war, the scope of employment and leisure time pursuits for women was enormously extended. Women as secretaries and administrators assumed a hitherto unheard-of importance. With a little parental support, sometimes without any at all, any girl could obtain a degree and make a career. Women as medical consultants, as solicitors and barristers, as political figures, heads of big schools and leading reporters and journalists, became commonplace, although they rarely were promoted to the very top of these professions. Working women improved their prospects by taking night-school courses and gaining degrees through the Open University. I had taken an introductory course in

Russian in my first year at the university, and, when I took a job in a G.E.C. machine-shop, expecting to be called up before I could complete another year at the university, Annie promptly and independently registered me for a course in Russian at an evening institute – I forget which. But she forgot that I had to work alternate fortnights day-shift and night-shift, and in any case, day-shift did not finish until 7 p.m. So she had the registration changed to an afternoon course in Russian at the Margaret Macmillan Institute on Manningham Lane which she attended herself with great diligence for about two years until her teacher, a native Russian lady, died, and Annie could not get on to the same wavelength as her successor. She chanted Russian declensions while waiting for the kettle to boil, but she dared not do it when hanging out the clothes 'in case they took her to Menston'!

I was always surprised at the number of women who got together in informal groups in support of the Independent Labour Party. Annie was a member of such a group, and, although they never seemed to do much except make a token subscription to the Party whenever they had afternoon tea or morning coffee together, or do the catering for a meeting of the Party, much as they had always done for the church bazaars or the local cricket club, they were in touch with politics and had an opinion in common.

The spread of opportunities for women wishing to participate in sport and other leisure pastimes has continued to increase to this day. As in other aspects of life, there is now nothing unique about the developments on Storr Hill Side. Throughout the country, nobody takes any special notice of a woman in trousers; they go into the pubs and join clubs; they support their own organisations such as the Women's Institute, the Embroiderer's Guilds, the W.R.V.S. the Townswomen's Guild and many others. There were women's football teams and swimming clubs before the beginning of my Generation III.[4] Now only lack of means and time can prevent a woman from owning and driving a car, or an aeroplane, or training race-horses, and she can do shot-putting, scuba-diving or own racing greyhounds in her spare time.

Chapter 12

The Fanciers

On Storr Hill Side people had room about them in which either to relax or to pursue some creative or rewarding interest. Even the tiny frontal areas to the terrace back-to-backs, which were regarded as either gardens or yards according to the attitudes of the occupants, allowed them to exercise a little talent and inclination to create. Talking to the neighbours over the low walls separating these areas was an essential part of their social life; and, if they fell out with their neighbours, at least they did not have to use the same paths to the door, nor the same door and staircase as was often the case in the urban slums.

There was room for rabbit-hutches, bike sheds, clothes posts, hurry-carts and, in the absence of a cellar with a coal-grate, a little structure, often of brick with a stone-slab roof, attached to the inevitable outdoor toilet. A clothes-post in this area, paired with another across the street or with a hook in the wall of the house or building opposite, gave each housewife an undisputed place to hang out her washing and to a great extent obviated 'Battles of the Clothes-Line' as recounted (in phonetic script) in Joseph Wright's *Windhill.* On occasion, I have seen three clothes-lines hurriedly detached from hooks in the wall of the swimming baths and folded up with the clothes still on the line to allow a loaded lorry to proceed down Elizabeth Street. But I can't remember ever being there to hear the comments when, because Elizabeth Street was a cul-de-sac, the operation had to be repeated to allow the lorry to come back!

The 25" map of 1908 shows not only several open spaces of an acre or more on the periphery of the small built-up areas, it shows many gaps of 100-200 square yards interposed between the streets and houses. Most of the larger green spaces were split up into smaller parcels as allotments and hen-runs, and were rented on a private basis. The small triangle of land on the map of 1908 in the south-west corner of our land on Elizabeth Street, abutting on to the wall of the coke-yard of the swimming baths, was rented by Dick Greenwood as a hen-run. There were three dilapidated, pent-house roofed huts huddled against the wall of the baths yard, one of which was reputed to have housed a pony and trap before we bought the land. I can just remember Dick keeping a few aged and neglected hens in them. In the Account Book for the building of our houses (Appendix III), a rent payment of 15*s*. received from Dick, presumably an annual rent, is recorded for 13th June 1924.

This was the typical holding of a fancier. These were men (it was still very much a man's world) who had developed an enthusiasm for some creative pursuit, usually outdoor, in their spare time. Not all fanciers were intent upon showing and competing; many were satisfied to implement their family budget with eggs, table-birds, the annual side of bacon, vegetables or plants, but all of those worthy of the name 'fancier' took a pride in the well-being and quality of breeding of their stock, and their activities and standards were of great importance to the quality of life on Storr Hill Side. Whatever their approach may have been, their activities demanded some degree of initiative, planning ahead and responsible care.

Sometimes before his tea, sometimes immediately after it, a man would see to his poultry, check to see if his plants needed watering or tying up, or dose an ailing dog. Inevitably, willingly or unwillingly, sons were drawn into these activities, and most of them acquired a degree of initiative, a sense of responsibility and often what we might nowadays call managerial skills. They learned at an early age that what one gets out of an enterprise depends on how much one puts into it, and they also had a good idea of what was a fair price for the objects of their fancy, which gave them an initial training for pursuing off their own bat not only the same interests but any similar pursuit in later life. Simply because they grew up in families in which the menfolk followed such interests and their mothers could make ends meet, many women were able to run successful small businesses in later life. They learned to recognise when they were out of their depth in their endeavours and to accept guidance; it taught them to co-operate to a reasonable extent with those in authority. No *system* of formal education has ever done quite so much!

The fancier most intimately known to me was Ephraim, my father. On the small acre of land that had been bought in 1924 on which to build a pair of semi-detached houses for us and my grandparents, he and Seth kept poultry. Earlier, before I was born, they had both been competitors; Ephraim had shown dogs, both his own and other people's, while Seth had been secretary of a local homing pigeon society. Ephraim still liked to have a dog about the place, and Seth had to have a few pigeons in a loft over a hen hut. But the poultry was there to provide interest and pay the rates, not for exhibition. Ephraim rarely exhibited; perhaps a dish of eggs at the Thornbury Tramshed Employees' Show now and then, but no more than that. He was nevertheless a true fancier, who insisted on a pedigree laying flock of White Wyandottes; he subscribed to and learned from *Eggs*, the weekly organ of the Scientific Poultry Breeder's Association, and spent most of his Sunday mornings walking round the district looking at, praising, criticising, learning from the stock and methods of other poultry fanciers.

When we were in full production, in late spring and early summer, he took twelve to fourteen dozen eggs a week in a pigeon basket to his workmates at Thornbury. The prices charged were based partly on the market prices in the *Telegraph and Argus* and partly on the prices given in *Eggs*. We had a Gloucester Glevum 160 egg incubator in the spare bedroom, whose functioning each year was timed to produce two hatches in March, so that by May we had at least 200 chickens to look after. As half of them would be cocks, we had plenty of chicken meat for ourselves and friends from July to Christmas.

Hundreds of hens were kept all around us, in numbers varying from six to sixty, but I don't think that any of them took it as seriously as Ephraim. I had to take an interest. At the age of eleven to thirteen, or thereabouts, I was encouraged to keep bantams, which, in lieu of pocket-money, were fed and housed for me among the rest of the poultry. I had to make my own pocket-money from selling eggs and trading in birds, and I was usually better off than my playmates. One could start as a fancier at an early age, and when, after being taken to several livestock shows, I got the idea of showing my bantams, at least six men bombarded me with advice. I had a lovely little Black Wyandotte cock, proud-eyed and broad-chested, who would have a go at cocks weighing four times as much as he, and I thought he would be invincible in a show-cage. Among the many bits of advice I got, I was told to first wash him thoroughly, then rub his legs with paraffin to get rid of the bits of scale, for he was no longer a young bird; to bring up the rich red of his comb and wattles with camphorated oil; and to get him tame by frequent handling, during which he could be stroked with a rag bearing a tiny amount of wax furniture polish. It was a serious business! They all insisted that, when showing bantams, the good little one always beat the good big one, being more genuine, not crossed with full sized birds. But they were considerably out of date! When I showed, both at Bingley and at Brighouse, I was beaten by two Golden Wyandottes and a Black Breasted Red English Game cock, all of which were twice as big as mine. There was a new thinking on the part of the judges! Brighouse Show, in particular, was a regular appointment for us. At that time Mr Masarella, now *chef d'équipe* of the British show-jumping team, and his sister, then in their late teens, competed every year in the show-jumping ring.

Not all poultry keeping was as extensive and well-organised as ours. Many people knocked up a pen out of any old wood they could lay their hands on, barely big enough for a dozen hens, and paid a token rent for it. Where there was a bit of waste land, or the green fringe to an unmade street, as there was on half of Elizabeth Street, people simply let their hens run out on to this. They fed them mainly on scraps and were satisfied with low yields.

But some of these makeshift pens and huts housed birds of high pedigree, whose owners were true fanciers. I remember a hut containing half a dozen Yokohamas with five-foot long tail feathers. The floor of the hut was covered with a deep layer of clean shavings to keep this exotic plumage clean for exhibition. The accommodation of three Light Brahma bantams and a cock to match was a little loft of no more than two square yards and likewise deep in shavings, this time to keep clean the delicately feathered feet. From both these tiny establishments the eggs and chickens fetched good prices from enthusiastic exhibitors. There is still a lot to say about poultry on Storr Hill Side, enough to warrant a more extensive account.

Mainly heavy breeds of poultry were kept in the hen-pens of Storr Hill Side before they were all built on. They all had to run out in the open and heavy breeds seemed to stand our raw climate better than the light breeds. We specialised in nothing but White Wyandottes, and the two other most popular pure breeds were Rhode Island Reds and Light Sussex. In addition, however, there were still some pure Plymouth Rocks, Buff Rocks, and even White Leghorns. This latter breed was a favourite crossing subject with Rhode Island Reds. Looking back, I am surprised that there was such a high proportion of pure breeds, although, of course, there was a great variety of random cross-bred birds. True fanciers were able to indulge in less well known and new breeds: our hen-pen sported at various times Welsummers and Lord Greenway's Cuckoo Marans when they were new; and we hatched and matured some Blue Andalusians from a casual sitting brought home by Ephraim. They were so neurotic and flighty, rising like a flock of pigeons whenever anybody went into the pen, that

Seth insisted that they had a lot of wild pigeon in their breeding, and that was where their colour came from! By searching the neighbourhood, one could find at least a dozen varieties of pure-bred poultry and a great many cross-bred birds.

There was the same kind of endeavour when it came to gardening, but with less success, due no doubt to our climate and soil. Many planted indestructible perennials in the tiny plots before or behind their dwellings and let them live or die. If they died, somebody handed over a replacement, often one that had happened by chance in their own tiny plot. The amount of London Pride and Primula 'Wanda' to be seen was indicative of this attitude; likewise the ubiquitous privet, which appeared as little specimen bushes, hedges or untrimmed thickets wherever one looked.

Each spring, some would turn over a bit of their back garden or a so-called allotment, or a disused hen-pen and plant a few potatoes, a score of cabbages (young brassica plants were always sold by the score) and cauliflowers bought for a few pence from a friend or neighbour whose gardening interests were a little more active. These had to take pot luck once they were planted, for, although many people weeded and manured fairly well, they did little else. Alfred Snarey, who had one of the allotments approached from Worsnop Buildings, was a dedicated gardener who took pains with both flowers and vegetables without being a keen exhibitor. By contrast, there were quite a few men with small gardens who liked to exhibit at all the local shows without ever learning how to do the job properly, or taking anything like the necessary care. There were, however, some true horticultural fanciers on Storr Hill Side. I have written elsewhere of Harry Dalby and his cabbages and about Walter Brook and his chrysanthemums. On the subject of chrysanthemums: we fancied the following in the 1930s, 1940s and early 1950s: Una and sports, Bronze Early Buttercup, Chatsworth, Westfield Bronze, Hope Valley, George McLeod, Sylvia Riley, Susan Alesworth, Blanche de Poitou, Elizabeth Vallance, Winn Quinn, Fred Shoesmith, Duke of Kent, Yellow Duke, James Bryant, Shirley Primrose, Annie Curry and sports, Swardeston White, Monument, Progress, Marie Morin, Balcombe Perfection, Ada Stevens, Enton Beauty, Mayford Supreme, Rayonnante and sports, Friendly Rival – and many more.

William Parrish, who lived at 10 Elizabeth Street, should be added to the florist fanciers, for his life seemed to revolve around the border carnations which he grew on the exposed hill-side between Elizabeth Street and Rawson Street. To look at the soil, one would have said that it was one hundred per cent clay, but he must somehow have ensured drainage and alkalinity for his plants grew and proliferated. As far as we can remember, he did not exhibit, but he bought in the latest hybrids from The House of Douglas, and so impressed some neighbours and some keen exhibitors with their beauty and quality that he had no difficulty in selling most of the young plants he raised. I remember his greenhouse, which consisted of about six courses of bricks above ground and eight courses below, capped with a steep-pitched roof of old, second-hand glazing bars that shook in the wind in spite of being so near the ground. There were stone steps down to the door; it was rather like an old vine-house. William was not a popular character on Storr Hill Side; he had the reputation of never giving anything away, neither help, nor plants nor charity and of charging old ladies 3*d*. for a handful of sand with which to re-pot their aspidistras.

Another such was Oliver Bentley, whose house and garden were approached by going down the little lane off the end of the Crown Garage. Oliver was another chrysanthemum man, but he kept a much lower profile than Walter Brook. He was a proud man, easily offended but not mean. I remember him taking umbrage when I said that his rooted chrysanthemum cuttings were worth more than the 3*d*. he was asking. This was well after the war.

There were shows for garden produce everywhere, in pubs and clubs, schools and village halls. The classes were designed to allow people with a dozen or a score of plants on a few square yards to win: classes for six cut viola blooms on cards, for three chrysanthemums or carnations, for one cabbage or one marrow. Vegetable marrows were especially popular for this purpose and were grown with as much devotion and mystique as are leeks today in some parts of the country. I have known old ladies carefully slit the stem of a half-grown marrow and insert a thread of wool as a wick the other end of which was in a jar of sugar and water. When growing, marrows were largely concealed by foliage, so the lads of Carr Lane School seized their opportunity to get their own back on a keen lady exhibitor who was always complaining to Mr Russell about their behaviour. They slipped over her wall in the dark and simply cut through the stems and left her show marrows lying there apparently untouched. But, of course, they were just as big a month later, when she examined them!

One fanciers' activity that was equally popular with Generation I and Generation II was pigeon-racing. There were lofts, usually painted white and therefore conspicuous, all over the district. Fred Greenwood, a collier, lived at 7 Elizabeth Street with his wife and four children. His hen-pen was bounded by a high wall that marked the end of Barraclough Square, and the ash-pit and outside toilets near the house were crowned with a fairly large pigeon loft. Fred and his eldest son, Willie, were keen and active members of the local homing society. The birds were released usually on Saturday morning (from longer distances, on Friday evening) and were expected home on Saturday afternoon. That was when we youngsters who normally wore clogs, had to tiptoe on the stone setts of Elizabeth Street, or risk having a clog applied to our persons. Fred was the only collier on our street in the thirties, as far as I can recall, who sometimes had his monthly ton of coal delivered. It was tipped loose on to the pavement and then shovelled into a tiny brick structure, not much bigger than a large domestic fuel bunker of today, but stood in the corner of their yard.

Another pigeon fancier quite close to us was John Foster, who maintained a fairly large loft above his wheelwright's shop. The loft was what remained of a second storey that had housed a commission burling and mending undertaking before John had taken the premises. John did not belong to a homing society nor enter any races, as far as I know, but he was very fond of his birds and proud of them.

Seth, also, was attached to pigeons, and we always kept a few in a loft over part of the nearest hen-hut to the houses. In this loft Seth kept a few 'homers' and I had a mixture of birds, tumblers, rollers, fan-tails, etc., most of them having been brought home by Dad from the Harold Club or, in his egg basket, from his workmates at Thornbury. Seth taught me how to 'settle' them, so that they always came back to our loft, and how to manage them. When I was about fourteen to sixteen years old, and could travel by myself to Rugby League matches as far afield as Halifax, Huddersfield, Keighley, or Dewsbury, I often took with me Seth's favourite pigeon, 't'owd cock' as he was called, in a carrier bag. On occasion, he travelled in the capacious pocket of my old, loose-fitting raincoat. At half time I attached to the leg of the pigeon with an elastic band a small piece of paper with scores and scorers on it, and threw him up. There was rarely any comment about this from nearby spectators. I think that I acquired my first cheap watch as a present from Seth for timing those pigeons. We solemnly synchronised our watches before I set out! Long before there was a detailed radio reporting of such things, Seth would have the half-time details of the relevant match, and he would walk along to the Junction Inn, where there were always a few men standing talking on the heavy door in the angle of the porch through which the barrels were rolled into the cellar. They soon learned not to scoff at his advance information as an impossibility when his information was repeatedly borne out about three hours later by the pink *Telegraph and Argus*. They hadn't got too many 'tanners' to lose in those days!

I have named and described only three of the many pigeon fanciers in the neighbourhood. As a young man, it seemed to me that a fine Sunday morning was not complete without a flock of silver-winged pigeons clattering and swishing around in the sky.

Dogs were very numerous, but, in our immediate vicinity, people did not insist on pedigree, nor even pure-bred animals. Most of those seen on Storr Hill Side were the result of chance encounters. As far as I can remember only Mrs Dawson on Rawson Street bred dogs for sale, but I can't remember what kind they were. I remember that Dick Greenwood had two planned litters from his fine bulldog bitch. For the rest, chance puppies were passed on between friends and neighbours, and their owners got as much pleasure and interest out of them as if they had pedigrees reaching back to champions at Cruft's.

Before his marriage, Dad had been an enthusiastic breeder and exhibitor of Airedales. He showed not only his own dogs all over the West Riding and as far afield as Manchester, he was often asked to show somebody else's dog, because he knew how to groom one and handle it in the show ring. He taught me how to recognise a good terrier and how they were groomed to show off to the best advantage. He became known on Storr Hill Side for this talent with dogs, and eventually it caused him considerable anguish. All the old folks, often widows, would ask him to take their dear little pets to be put down when they were suffering from age or disease. He did this so often in retirement and came home so distressed that he finally refused.

Walking round on a Sunday morning with him made my legs and feet ache as they have never done since, but scarcely a walk failed to yield something of such interest that many memories are with me still. He once pointed out to me the man reputed to have run the fastest hundred yards in Britain in his day; he also pointed out a man who, with his partner, had bred a Fox Terrier that had grown too big and too strong in the jaw for its breed, so they dyed it chestnut-brown and showed it as an Irish Terrier! And they won two challenge certificates with it before they quarrelled and betrayed each other.

One Sunday, Dad took me further afield, to the other side of Bradford, to visit an old friend whom he had met through showing dogs. This was a delver, who had worked most of his life swinging a short-handled eight-pound hammer all day, chiselling away at stone, in the quarries at Cutler Heights. He was credited with having dressed much of the chiselled stone of the façade of Cartwright Hall.

Off one end of his ordinary, semi-detached house, possibly a council house, he had a plot of land of about 150 sq. yards. We admired his poultry, some really classy Brown Leghorns, if I remember aright, and his chrysanthemums, strong healthy plants just coming into bud. Dad spent some time looking at and handling his Irish Terrier dog which, although it had never been exhibited, conformed pretty well to the standard of the breed. It was agreed that our Irish Terrier bitch, Peggy – we always had bitches called Peggy! – should be put to this dog when next on heat. Dad told me that this arrangement was the reason for the visit. Only after this did we go into the house for a cup of tea.

The conversation went round to exhibiting poultry and Dad said, 'Show 'im t' feathers, Holmes.' A large round hat-box of the old type was produced, opened and unpacked with something approaching reverence. In it, between layers of tissue paper, lay a magnificent set of jet-black sickle feathers from the tail of a Black Hamburg cock. Holmes, it appeared, had once bred a Black Hamburg cock with the best tail of its breed ever seen. He had won a class with it at the 'Fur and Feather' show at Crystal Palace. When he got it home, he plucked out the wonderful tail feathers (I never knew whether the cock was dead or not when this happened) and stored them in the hat-box. He claimed that those feathers had subsequently been to Crystal Palace and other major shows in *nine* different cocks! Whether they won or not was never mentioned. I later found out that the story was widely known and believed. There is no doubt that the feathers were preserved and revered. How he did it with his delver's hands must have involved an extraordinary feat of dexterity.

Now there was a real fancier! He produced everything to exhibition standard and was well known locally as an authority on poultry, chrysanthemums, violas and dogs, especially the last. To those who knew him, it was no surprise that both his daughters became well-qualified teachers and his son gained a first-class honours degree. The choice of a high school for my secondary education was decided by the latter's success.

The fact that I am able to call so often on personal experiences in this account will make it clear that the fanciers survived in strength at least until the end of the last great war. They were certainly well represented in both Generation I and Generation II, and, even today, Generations III and IV can boast a few fanciers. Were they, as is sometimes maintained, survivals in the subconscious of the rural life that had preceded the industrial age? As a representative section of the community, they declined rapidly when the whole aspect of spare time pursuits changed with the spread of spectator sports like football and Rugby League, with the cinema, car ownership for the many, radio, television and, perhaps most effective of all, house ownership for nearly everybody.

Chapter 13

Talking, Kidding, Sayings

Talking

Before there was talking there was sitting, just sitting. The account of the Bramleys in James Herriot's *It Shouldn't Happen to a Vet*, is neither exaggerated nor improbable, not even quaint. James Herriot, obviously fascinated, describes the scene in detail:

> They weren't grouped round the fire but were jammed tightly on a long, high-backed wooden settle which stood against the far wall. The strange thing was the almost exact similarity of their attitudes; all four had their arms folded, chins resting on their chests, feet stretched out in front of them. The men had removed their heavy boots and were stocking footed, but Miss Bramley wore an old pair of carpet slippers . . . They were not asleep, not talking or reading or listening to the radio – in fact they didn't have one – they were just sitting . . . It occurred to me that this was probably a typical evening; they worked hard all day, had their meal, then they just sat till bedtime.[1]

The older folk, my Generation I, on Storr Hill Side were quite content to take their weight off their feet and simply sit, not doing anything, to all intents and purposes neither thinking nor reflecting. It was sufficient for them to be in a resting position; if this was all that offered itself, they did not demand anything better and they could make themselves comfortable almost anywhere. People like Edwin Lightowler, who worked long shifts on the pit bottom at the age of eleven, could be comfortable on a haphazard pile of undressed stones, as in my picture (Plate 8). It was normal to find Walter Armitage Barker just sitting; my grandmother, Sarah, and her sister, Clarissa, remain in my memory as rarely doing anything else, unless it were knitting. And, when one thinks about it, without the ability to read, certainly unable to read without effort, no radio, no handicraft outlets, and little that remained to be said after a lifetime in the same company, what else was there to do?

The real, basic recreation of the older members of the Storr Hill Side community, however, was simply talking to one another. This was the way they had been brought up and it remained their way of life. For most of them it was the one way in which they could relieve the tedium of long shifts in the mill or machine-shop, for there was always lip-reading. For the miners who simply could not communicate on a social level when at work, talking was even more important, and the talking in the pub was as important as the beer. Even the silent and taciturn characters lost no opportunity of being in the group and listening to their more voluble neighbours and workmates. In Generation II, when there was more popular reading matter, more radio and cinema, there was a large proportion of folks who preferred to talk and who went to the pictures largely in order to be able to talk about the film to their particular group. All their real talking had to be in their group; only among their 'familiars' were they able to communicate freely. Students and researchers in the field of sociology, historians, teachers and politicians do not seem to realise that they can never get past this barrier.

On any day of the week when I was young, in all quarters of the neighbourhood, there would be old men, or unemployed men, sitting on low walls or on seats in the park, round the bowling-green, standing in shop doorways in bad weather – all talking. Down in Judy Woods, the rough seats made by Harry Dalby were fully occupied on fine days by old men, many of them with faithful and clever little dogs. The picture I have included of Harry Dalby was taken in exactly such circumstances. The big plank cover over the hole down which the barrels were rolled into the Junction Inn's beer cellar was also a favourite place, because it was sheltered in the angle of the porch and the pub itself. My Generation I never really took to entertainment outside their own home that did not allow them to talk at the same time. If this condition were met, they would endure, often for lengthy periods, the most inclement weather and the most uncomfortable positions. In the pub, playing dominoes, ratting, racing whippets, indeed, engaged in anything that allowed them to pick their company and talk, they were happy. Especially the colliers, if my recollections are accurate, tended to support cricket rather than football for this reason. Crown green bowls also fulfilled their requirements. For quite understandable reasons they favoured rest and conviviality to professionally engendered, mass tension and excitement. It seems to me that football, Rugby League, the music halls, although they were there and patronised by people living nearer the centre of town, did not really take off in our district until the first decade of the twentieth century, and the dance halls and cinemas had to wait until after the first war for their heyday. Seth, and many of his contemporaries in our area, had never seen either a professional football match (nor stood through an amateur one), or a rugby match, and although there was very frequently a music-hall song on their lips, they had got them at second hand, without ever being in the audience. Dance-halls did not really flourish until my Generation II were grown up and the older end of my Generation I, apart from a small number who became really addicted, never did become familiar with the cinema.

It was about the end of World War II when my grandmother, Sarah, persuaded Seth to go to the New Victoria with her one afternoon. She succeeded in this only by promising him that it was all about a dog called Lassie, who was the heroine of the film. She dressed in her best and made him do likewise; they were going to what the majority of friends and neighbours held to be the most luxurious place of entertainment in the city. Once they got past the pay-box and into the dark, Seth was lost and bewildered, and the young lady with the torch had to be patient in getting them into a seat. After a couple of minutes, during which Seth stared in amazement and Sarah tried to get into the story, she became aware that the man on her right was so tall that it couldn't possibly be Seth. A surreptitious examination showed her that he had not known to put his seat down, and was sitting on the edge! No other cinema had such deep and well-padded seats as the New Vic. Her despairing cry of 'Seth! Seth! Put thi seeat dahn!' must have been heard by everybody in the ninepennies. True!

They even installed chapels of the gossip cult, known in the vernacular as 'call-'oils'. A workshop, or corner of it, a cellar or a hen-hut, usually with some form of heating such as an old iron stove, of which there were a great many around, or a paraffin stove, even a little fireplace with a brick chimney, could, by general consent and usage, acquire the necessary recognition. It could be the kitchen of a popular character whose wife was not too pernickety. The establishment of a 'call 'oil' depended largely on the personality of the owner and the company he attracted. Mostly the host was a Generation I man, but the institution was kept up by quite a lot of Generation II. As far as the 'call 'oil' is concerned, only the men come into question, as it was essentially a bastion of male freedom, where they had no need to moderate their language, remove muddy boots at the door or spread newspaper before they were allowed to sit down in their working clothes.

A typical workshop development of this kind was the clogger's shop of Tom Hoyle down New Road Side (Plate 29). Nearly all of the men and many of the women of our neighbourhood wore clogs for everyday wear or for jobs which made them suitable footwear. I wore them to play out in and on rare occasions wore them at Carr Lane School. So Tom's shop, in one of the more decrepit houses fronting on to New Road Side, housed a secure and steady little business. Such cloggers worked until 8 p.m. so that working men could get them 'ironed' and, perhaps, fitted with new, brass toe-caps out of working hours. Tom made and mended clogs on the ground-floor, while Roland, his brother, mended boots and shoes upstairs. The two workshops, for that is what they were, were joined by the most rickety and unsafe flight of board stairs I have ever encountered. At that age one was practically impervious to fear of unsafe structures, but those steps made me hesitate.

There was always the smell of leather, heel-ball, gas and human bodies in old clothes in that shop. It was best in the evening, when there might be half a dozen visitors, some for clogs, some just to talk, crowded into the tiny place while podgy Tom's stertorous breathing filled in as he hammered on clog-irons and toe-caps. The only light was a sputtering gas jet without mantle playing on weathered faces and long draw-knives hanging on the wall – a subject for Rembrandt, if it had not been so plebeian, perhaps more suited to Wright of Derby. This was one of the 'call 'oils' where all ages sometimes met. A frequent 'caller' was a young man who was considered to be only 'thrippence te t' bob'. Tom had to take a hammer from the latter occasionally.

The women of course, talked with effortless ease, incessantly, like drawing breath. In fact, there was a pub down New Road Side, at the junction with Carr House Gate, called The Quiet Woman, and the sign, which I must confess I never noticed, is said to have shown a woman lying in a coffin ! Walter Brook once went along Elizabeth Street to do a bit of shopping down New Road Side, and passed two women who had stopped in the middle of the street in the act of shaking a heavy, tabbed rug, and were busy 'callin'. When he came back, they were still holding the heavy rug between them and still 'callin'. He gave a scornful laugh and said, 'Aye, that's reight! Wimmin's wark's nivver dun!'

The women had no need of 'call 'oils', for they talked at work in the mill, over a cup of tea in their house, over the garden wall or when out shopping. They would have welcomed women's institutes and clubs as further places to gossip, but there was no real need for them, as they knew one another's routines and habits so well that they knew exactly when and where they could meet them. If a neighbour was ill, they would be alerted immediately by the fact that somebody else was doing their housework or their shopping.

The outsider might think that such inveterate gossips would have to sustain their flow of speech with arguments, debates and serious problems, that, in fact, such things would come naturally to them and that they would automatically be informed about life and the world in general in order to be able to sustain the talking. Nothing could be further from the truth! The only social layer I have talked about so far is the Little Tradition, the 'ordinary fowk', whose intellectual interest does not extend beyond family and the immediate community, so their conversation was confined to their own daily lives and that of their neighbours. *Nothing* that occurred in that sphere was left out of their conversation. They read certain parts of the newspapers, but rarely talked about what they had read unless their imagination was seized by the account of a natural disaster, a pit tragedy or something of that kind. Most dialects show a profusion of terms of criticism and abuse of their fellow men, and ours was no exception. By far the major part of their conversation consisted of laconic observations about local facts, happenings and developments, from Mrs X's new shawl or brooch to Fred Y's suicide or Sally Z's illegitimate pregnancy now just unmistakably showing. They could be devastatingly explicit about these things – devastatingly explicit! – but mostly they conveyed their opinions and attitudes, especially the women, by means of tone, pitch, gesture, facial expression, etc., the full range of extra-verbal expression, in fact.

Kidding

When A. E. Green writes: 'My main concern is not with the telling of jokes (i.e. the recounting of comic narratives with a punch line) but with the less obviously structured business of wisecracks, mockery, jocular insults and horseplay; in short, kidding,'[2] he is giving the word 'kidding' a meaning that does not agree with the usage of any of my Generations on Storr Hill Side. In the industrial West Riding the essence of humour was – and most frequently still is – the straight face, or what the outsider is inclined to call 'dry' humour. In our usage, a victim was an essential prerequisite of kidding, while the agent or perpetrator took up the challenge of keeping a sufficiently straight face to make the victim believe a tall story. This is the basis of kidding and it must never be confused with destructive wit, sarcasm, irony etc. The cult of the straight face was so strong that somebody who laughed at their own jokes or wit would evoke only a stony silence. Even recently, a young woman who had just started a new job, when asked if she was liking it and settling in, said that it was 'all right, but the boss is a Southerner – you know, he laughs at his own funnies!' The examples of comic and aggressive wit, the twitting and the ragging, quoted by Dr Green in his article, are of significance for his purpose, but they should not be designated as 'kidding' according to the usage of Storr Hill Side.

A good example of kidding, for which I fell completely and which I have since turned to good use, goes as follows: Immediately after the war there was a greenkeeper in Wyke Recreation Ground called John Willie Shooter ('Shooit' to his friends), a short, thick-set, chunk of muscle, jovial and popular. He was also a very good greenkeeper and won the award for the best-kept bowling-green in any Bradford Corporation park for some years in succession. Any unsuspecting stranger, even a reporter on the local newspaper or an experienced bowler, might be told that one of his secrets was a very small, very sharp scythe with which he pared the grass in the slight hollows which were bridged by the mowing machine and so remained uncut. The fact that he took so many people in with this tale, people who were far from gullible, was a great triumph for 'Shooit'; his ability as a kidder, as a straight-face performer had been demonstrated. The content of his kidding was only incidental.

As students we kidded a fellow student that it was possible to tempt a tortoise out of its shell with a really succulent leaf of lettuce if the temperature were right, and that it would go back into its shell as soon as the temperature dropped. He didn't completely fall for it, but he was observed the following morning to look up tortoises in the university library. There was also the bright salesman who, in the early days of television, told people that his firm was bringing out a television set that would operate from gas! In another part of the north, I once spent an evening in a dreary, dingy bar (to become a member of a certain bowling club), listening to a plasterer, who tried his best to convince me that if you suddenly lowered a canary in its cage from a table to the floor, the loss of altitude would give it a fatal heart attack! He still thinks that I swallowed it; I had been playing the game longer than he.

The bullies of the neighbourhood sought out the retarded and those of low intelligence as the victims of their kidding. They sought to hurt and humiliate through kidding. Charge-hands, foremen, overlookers, etc., especially in the mills, liked to show how superior to and how much cleverer they were than those under their command. This was easy, because their victims dared not answer back, and they could indulge their cruel wit with complete impunity. This is the same form of bullying as employed by many teachers, lecturers and professors, as well as barristers and judges. One or two men were pointed out to me in the streets as belonging to this category and one heard stories of the brothers and fathers of their victims putting a stop to this cruelty in no uncertain fashion. One such bully got a mongol son and never dared to go into a local pub again. There would always be somebody there who could make slit eyes and thick lips.

As Dr Green observes, the basic purpose of teasing and kidding was to assess the temperament of the victim, to find out whether he or she could take it in good part and thus to qualify as a stable and level-headed member of the community. The attitude of one's workmates depended very much on this; they had no time for someone who thought he or she was too good for such treatment. Frank tells how, when he kept the fish and chip shop down Storr Hill, the newly appointed, young and fresh-faced Salvation Army Lieutenant came in one evening to buy his supper. Gerry Pyrah, a Generation II 'character', in a jovial mood, arrived shortly after and he was barely over the door-sill when he called out: 'Atta still walking with the Lord, Frank?' It took Frank a lot of time and effort to assure the young man that no insult or aspersions against him were intended; and indeed, that he, Frank, was the object of the remark. But I know very well how the young man felt, having myself so often offended in exactly the same way. It is so easy to misunderstand the 'dry', straight-faced humour of our part of the world.

Repartee, verbal sticking-up for oneself, was much cultivated and highly appreciated. Some characters were renowned for their deadly tongues, and their triumphs would be recounted throughout the neighbourhood. There are numerous examples in my descriptions of the characters of Storr Hill Side, but one or two in this context will not come amiss.

I was shogging up the Tinkler with Seth, at his speed, when we were met by an old man, perhaps older than Seth, who must have been over seventy-five at the time. This old man was a notorious cadger with the reputation of having been work-shy all his life. As we came abreast there came from behind his beard, 'Es te a tanner, Seth?' The prompt reply was, 'Aye, en av iend it.' Neither of them checked their little stride, neither of them looked at the other, and that was all that was said. But when I told the story to people who knew them both (as I did for the next week!) it brought grins of satisfied, relaxed delight to their faces. Because they knew the protagonists, they could visualise every detail, and it rang so true! The work-shy were always considered to be fair game. One such came along as I was trimming a high hedge from the top of a step-ladder and cackled, 'Eh, eh, eh. That looks like wark, Donald! That looks like wark!' True to my upbringing, I replied, 'Aye, it is. How did you know?' Seth overheard this and everybody in the street must have heard of the encounter by nightfall. Similarly, shortly after the war, I was given a lift into Huddersfield by one of the great Generation II humorists of the district. It was a hot afternoon in summer. A lady driver in front of us was a bit slow to start up when the lights changed in our favour, but she moved quick enough when there came a great bellow from my driver: 'Come on, luv, it's bahn te be dark!'

The Sayings of Seth

From what I have written about the social life of my Generation I and their habits, notably their addiction to gossip, it is only to be expected that they placed a premium on pungent, vivid sayings and repartee. In this field Seth, being both intelligent and of a passionate disposition, was acknowledged as a star performer. Even the common epithets of command and abuse took on a new urgency when produced by Seth. At some time or other practically everybody in Elizabeth Street must have told me to 'ger aht o' t' pit ee' or 'tak thi ooks' or 'na, frame thisen', but these commands were never as effective as when Seth uttered them. In every such community words and phrases expressing an estimation of one's fellow men tend to be numerous. Seth had all the usual ones with a few of his own thrown in. Everybody used 'a bit lat', 'gormless', 'satless' (or 'sackless') and 'nobud thrippence te't bob'. But Seth's moral judgement and philosophy tended to be much more graphic and personal. That was his style.

Of unreliable people, the lazy and the neer-do-weel, he said simply: 'the' can't carry corn'; to somebody sprawled at ease in an untidy way he would say: 'idleness is nowt baht it's reight follered' (tended, looked after); the importance attached to industry and thrift as moral obligations was reflected in the saying: 'the' are nowt 'cos the' ev nowt, if the' wor owt the'd ev summet'. His grasp of industrial relations was far ahead of anything you will find in the press and media today: 'them as pays wages gives orders, an' them as gives orders pays wages'. Somebody of really bad character, a very wicked person in his eyes, had been 'gotten at twice an' put together cowd'.

Apart from normal expressions of degree, such as: 'deaf as a post' and 'grey as a badger', Seth had one or two that I heard only from him. When somebody took no notice of his advice or admonitions he would say: 'it taks as much od (hold) o' his clooathes as his carcase'; when he was very thirsty he would say: 'a'm as dry as a lime-burner's clog'. I never knew how the saying 'as drunk as a wheel-'eead' arose. Were the pit-head winding wheels notorious for not running true? Anybody who was making a poor attempt at a job or playing a poor, inept game at bowls or any game, would be 'framin' or 'laikin' 'like a gert lass i red stockings'. When he and Sarah launched out and bought a radio, he would listen intently to Paul Robeson, especially if he was singing a song he knew, like 'Old Man River' or 'Jericho' and then he would pass verdict: 'Same as if e'd swallered a organ!' Somebody who was very bowlegged 'couldn't stop a pig in a ginnel', and he could always get my Grandma into an indignant anger by saying of a woman who had put on a lot of weight: 'Shu's gooan as fat as a suckin pig'.

There were two expressions of triumph which stay in my memory: if he constructed or mended something that was very strong and secure he would claim: 'It'll stand t' drop o' York' (a reference to the gallows?) and if he could score off somebody by showing them a better way of doing something, a particular knack, perhaps, he would exult: 'That's afooa tha bowt thi shuvel'. We all shaved with cut-throat razors at Nos. 17 and 19 Elizabeth Street and were insistent on sharp edges on all cutting tools; Seth's verdict on a blunt knife or a chisel was: 'A c'd ride bare-arsed te Lunden o' that'. He and Ephraim were both pipe smokers of long practice, who used one match per pipeful if they were not working; Seth expressed his contempt, sometimes to their faces, of those who tried it (mostly with weak and scented tobacco) by way of wishing to appear either older, in the case of youths, or superior, in the case of older men, with the warning: 'Thee be careful, tha'll draw thi shirt lap up thi arse, if tha gues on like that!' All that he said to indicate that he found he was out of tobacco when he peered into the bottom of his pouch, was: 'It's a hard winter, lad.'

The code word for everything that was bad, wrong, unnatural or simply very unpleasant was 'shit'. Of a clique that was up to no good, but whose lies and frauds were impregnable he said: 'The' stick together like shit te a shuvel'. If a clumsy beginner like myself was struggling to use a hammer in a left-hand corner, I might be pushed to one side with the remark: 'Al use mi golek' – or – 'Come aht, al use t' shitten hand'; and if he was cheated when buying something or deceived in any way, it would be: 'Av been daubed' – or 'Av getten t' shitten end o't stick'. The only time Geoffrey and I remember a euphemism from him was when he dare not go out during an attack of diarrhoea and said that he was 'bun up o' a lowseness'. Occasionally, when he was bested in a slanging match or felt that further argument would be a waste of time, he might say: 'A ope tha guz ungri te shite'; and frequently, with greater finality, it would be: 'Tha c'n jump up an' bite a 'oil i' thi arse'. He could not bear to see me, or anybody, sitting on stone walls or steps, and would say: 'It'll tak sum time fer thy arse te warm that stuen through.' He expressed the height of wise caution in the telling admonition: 'Allus keep at t'back o' a shooiter en at t' front o' a shitter.' His version of 'More haste, less speed' was: 'There's nowt gotten in a 'urry nobbud 'ard knocks an' chonce bairns'. Seth was not the only one of his generation who expressed the resigned fatalism of their kind in the face of disappointment or tragedy with the saying: 'Ah weel, wi'sl live till we dee, if t'dogs dunt get us first.'

Chapter 14

Transport and Communications

From the Crown Hotel, before the war, public transport was available to take one to Bradford, Halifax, Huddersfield and Brighouse without changing, for Storr Hill Side lies at the hub of the towns which represented the very nucleus of the West Riding textile area. Leeds, to the east, was only a little more complicated to reach; the main road from Halifax to Leeds, now the A58, built 1832, passes the Red Lion in Lower Wyke.

Consequently, it is feasible to argue that the biggest single instrument of change in the history of Storr Hill Side was in the field of transport. The north-south route, the main road from Huddersfield to Bradford, has always been the most important, and it is little wonder that three roads, all serving this route at different times, can be traced through our neighbourhood, all of which are now largely obsolescent since the opening of the M62 and its Bradford spur, M606. The importance as a major freight road of the new turnpike road, part of which gave the name New Road Side to our small neighbourhood, would appear to have been relatively brief. That part which concerns us was a rationalisation of a particularly tortuous part of the old route joining Bradford and Huddersfield and, according to James Parker, it was built between 1825 and 1837. Parker gives a table of the tolls payable in 1825 for the distance of almost nine miles from Huddersfield to Odsal Top.[1] For that distance the tolls were, for instance, 5*d.* for a saddle horse, 1*s.* 6*d* for a coach, chaise or gig with one horse, 5*s.* if the vehicle was drawn by six horses. A waggon with six inch wheels pulled by one horse would pay 10*d.*, but with ten horses it would cost 7*s.* There was a similar table of tariffs for waggons with four and a half inch wheels and the same for waggons and carts with three inch wheels; in the case of four and a half inch wheels it would appear that nine or ten horses were never necessary on the flat four miles from Huddersfield to

Brighouse, and no more than six horses are given a scale for this stretch in the table for vehicles with three inch wheels. Driving a score of oxen from Huddersfield to Odsal would cost you 2*s*. 5*d*., sheep or pigs 1*s*. 6*d*. per score. Such activity and this kind of traffic down New Road Side, the road so familiar to us, defies the imagination.

In view of these tariffs, it can be assumed that, even allowing for the enormous cost of building railways and manufacturing rolling stock, it would not take long for the railways to take over most of the heavy freight and a lot of the passenger transport for distances of ten miles and more. How many waggons with six inch wheels and up to ten horses would be necessary to move the contents of one goods train for a distance of twenty miles? The cost of horses, their fodder and stabling, the maintenance of carts and the wages of so many teamsters, to say nothing of road tolls, would have been many times that of the railways. It cost a certain John Clay £10 for a round trip to London by mail coach in 1838.[2]

For short distances the horse still had a major role to play. Even between the wars most coal was delivered from the coal staithes and goods yards by horse and cart. On Elizabeth Street we had coal and milk delivered by horse power; the Co-op vegetable cart came round, as did Thompson and Pearson's soft drinks cart (with a board down the middle, above the load, proclaiming 'Drink T. & P. Table Waters!), and those smart little vans drawn by equally smart ponies brought Rington's Tea round. The last of these that I saw was striving against Storr Hill and looking less genteel and dignified than usual! The Account Book for the building of 17 and 19 Elizabeth Street in 1924 has several entries for the delivery of materials by horse and cart: e.g. 'To I. Garside for cartage of bricks, ashes, minion, cement & shovel: £3-7-6.' Occasionally, seeing that Irvine Garside was a neighbour and one of my closest playmates was his son, Stanley, I was given a ride on top of a load of clinker for hardcore or, even, on a load of coal! Men of means, who could have afforded cars but had been accustomed to a pony and trap, went in for smart turnouts of that kind. Altogether, there was still plenty of work for John Foster, the wheelwright and cartwright.

Although the horse and cart, or trap, was still a force in the field of transport when we were young, it cannot be denied that it was the railway that served and shaped the area, and until recently linked it with the rest of the country and sustained its trade. The West Riding Union Railway's line from Mirfield to Low Moor opened in 1848, and Low Moor Station was opened in 1849. The latter was closed for passenger transport in 1965 and for goods in 1966.[3] Its early days coincided with the heyday of the Low

Plate 28. A wagonette with: Left to right. Driver – wife of Edwin Lightowler; little girl unknown; wife of Dan Smith who kept the Rising Sun at Scholes; Sarah (nee Lightowler), wife of Seth Shaw; Eva, daughter of Seth and Sarah born 1902.

Moor Company, the Bowling Ironworks and an enormous expansion of the textile industry. The sale of coal to other parts of the country and abroad from the mines of the Low Moor Company started there. Between the wars, trains from the industrial areas of South Lancashire coming to Leeds or Bradford branched or divided at Low Moor, and it was thus a very active and important station.

About a mile away from Elizabeth Street in the other direction was the Wyke and Norwood Green station. The first edition of the 6" Ordnance Survey map, surveyed 1848-1850, shows the Halifax to Bradford Line of the Lancashire and Yorkshire Railway, including the latter station but calling it 'Pickle Bridge Station'. This was much enlarged in 1875, when it presumably assumed the name by which we knew it. These two stations were almost joined by the Wyke Tunnel, which started about 100 yards from the platform at Wyke Station and extended to within 500 yards of the platforms at Low Moor. The huge ventilation shaft serving this tunnel, which dominated the view from our front window in Elizabeth Street, is explicitly indicated on the 6" map of 1852. Above this tunnel, following its line from the top of Wilson Road to the end of Rawson Street, there is now Elizabeth Drive, built to provide access to the post-war housing built between Rawson Street and Elizabeth Street.

The daily life and all its activities were most influenced by the local, municipal, public transport, especially during the first half of this century.[4] Bradford Corporation took over all routes from the Bradford Tram and Omnibus Company on 1st February 1902, and new lines were laid. Electric trams first made their way to Wyke in that year, although there had been steam trams since 1892, but it was not until 1913 that the line was extended to Bailiff Bridge. The Wyke terminus was at the Board School, where the road forks at the Temperance Hall. From school children to old folks, all ranks and occupations were able to extend their spheres of work and leisure. I have dealt with the new opportunities for employment at a distance elsewhere; it also transformed education and leisure and health care. One of the most vivid memories of the older women of our family, as well as neighbours, was going to Bradford to queue for essential foodstuffs during World War I. From all quarters of Bradford, workers poured towards the centre, many alighting along the way to less central mills, many working in the mills, warehouses and commercial establishments in the centre, and many more taking a second tram to another outlying district. People shopped for everything that was then available, had their clothes made there, paid their rates, and supported the cinemas, theatres, swimming baths, libraries and markets of the city centre. All those young folk from our district who enjoyed secondary education before World War II, were taken there by tram or trolleybus.

Trams were the double-decker dreadnoughts of the roads, built like railway vehicles with iron wheels, steep stairs, lots of brass rods and rails (Ephraim had served his time as a brass-finisher, that is what it says on my birth certificate, and he worked for forty years at Thornbury Tramshed) and slatted, reversible wooden seats. Normally, they did not turn the trams round; the driver went from one set of controls at one end to another set at the other end. The space at the top of the stairs at each end was not enclosed; it was pleasant enough to sit there in warm weather, but otherwise you only sat there when the rest of the tram was full. As the illustrations in David Croft's book show, they were quite tall vehicles in relation to their wheelbase and, although we never had any real qualms about their stability, we got little thrills of apprehension as school-children when the conductor rushed upstairs and slammed the windows down on both sides as we rocked up or down the dual carriageway stretch between Low Moor and Odsal in a high wind! The specimen tram in the Bradford Industrial Museum was the last tram to run this route, I have heard; I would bet that

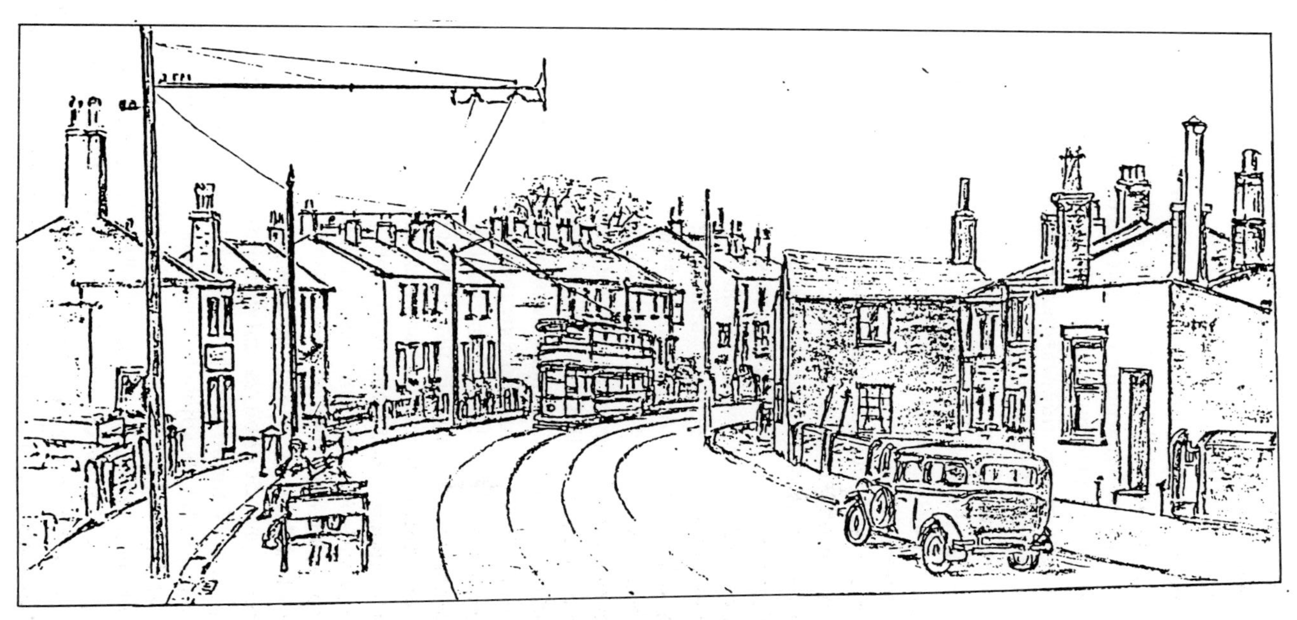

The Lower End of New Road Side, ca 1935. Drawn by Frank Wilkinson.

its upstairs windows still move freely. Instead of a horn, the driver stamped on a little iron disc in the floor of his cab to produce a nice musical clanging of the bell.

In this context, Bradford has a distinct claim to fame: the trolleybus, to us the 'trackless'. These used the same overhead cables and power supply as the trams but required no lines and were thus more manoeuvrable. As they were coach-built, more like a motor-coach in the body and ran on rubber tyres, the ride was much smoother and, on the whole faster. Bradford ran the first trolleybus service in Britain in 1914, and the last such vehicle ran in Bradford in March 1972. They had made a profit throughout! As the trolleybus never ran on the routes serving our part of the municipality, however, this is merely a remark in passing to complete a picture.

Talking about public transport in these terms may give a wrong impression of speed and convenience. From the early days of motor transport, 'chara' trips were immensely popular and remained so until well after World War II. Frank remembers a day trip to Blackpool at the age of 13-14 in a charabanc which ran on solid tyres, and took about four hours each way. This recollection reminded him of a bus service that I had never heard of before. Apparently a blue bus with solid tyres, Frank thinks it belonged to the Calder Bus Company, ran on a service from either the Crown Hotel or the Temperance Hill to the Harold Club, then turned right down Long Wall Side, straight down New Works Road as far as Low Moor Station and thence down to what later was the trolleybus terminus at Oakenshaw. It came back by the same route as far as the top of Carr Lane, then turned left down to the bottom of Storr Hill and started to climb the hill. But Frank swears that it never got further than the steep bit below Rawson Street, and had each time to reverse back down the hill and return up Carr Lane and Long Wall Side!

For the rest, transport since the war has followed the national pattern. Trams disappeared on most routes during the war and their place was taken by buses, which in turn were largely superseded by the private motor car. Both buses and cars travel faster than their predecessors and are more comfortable, but, especially since private car ownership became so prevalent, as adjuncts to national well-being and civilisation they are a catastrophe. They need petrol of which a large proportion must still be bought abroad; the houses of older areas such as Storr Hill Side may be good dwellings, but there is no room to garage or park so many cars; they make transport of both goods and passengers slower rather than quicker, especially in urban centres, and they are the major threat to life and limb in our lives today; very many of them are expensive status symbols, owned by the 'dead-weight' elements in our society. I suppose that I always feel much safer in other kinds of transport because such a large proportion of drivers of motor vehicles are amateurs, whereas ships, trains and aeroplanes are driven by professionals.

It is said that the dinosaur died out because its brain size was not up to feeding and managing its enormous bulk. This seems plausible, and it does not need to be true. Certainly, the proportions of brain to body-weight in the human being have proved to be about right for many more years than one can imagine, but when the human being grows a car-attachment, the proportions of brain to body become those of the dinosaur.

Chapter 15

Dress and Footwear

Practically all the men and quite a few of the women of Generation I and Generation II wore clogs on appropriate occasions down to World War II. When I took Sarannah's picture in 1954, she had come up Storr Hill to the Co-op in clogs and shawl as there were a few inches of snow on the ground. Whereas it was quite in order to wear clogs in school[1] and workshops which had wooden floors in the early twenties, by the end of the decade, with the old heavy industries being a thing of the past and more and more people using the trams to go to work, clogs were practically restricted to outdoor or wet or hot occupations. Early trams, before eight o'clock in the morning and those running about five o'clock or as darkness fell in winter, carried a fair sprinkling of forge workers, navvies, road-workers, fish and fowl dressers and so on, all wearing clogs.

Old habits died hard in those days, especially when they were as practical and economical as the wearing of clogs. Perhaps a third of the whole population, man, woman and boy (not girls) possessed a pair of clogs until after World War II. They were so much warmer and durable than shoes or boots! On a few occasions, when Seth was in his seventies, he asked me to cut inner soles for his boots with a fretsaw from thin plywood, because he felt better with wood under his feet. It was remarkable how quickly they assumed the contours of his feet. Men felt better in them when gardening, feeding the hens or cleaning them out, or just 'callin' on the street corner. Women who had worn them in earlier life in the mill or factory still preferred them for shopping on a cold day, or work on stone floors in cellar or wash-kitchen; and they had put their children into them when young because they themselves had worn them, and they knew that there was nothing to beat them for kicking tin cans in the street, climbing walls and fences, sliding on ice or any other smooth surface. Children could also have fun in adding up to nine inches to their height by balling repeated layers of wet snow between the irons – like the *cothurnus* of the Athenian actors in ancient Greece. We called them 'pattens', like the platforms that the ladies of Mrs Gaskell's *Cranford* wore to keep their fine shoes out of the mud. Even youngsters with some experience with clogs could get badly skinned ankles from a scrape with the side of an iron when running or breaking in a pair of new clogs, for the tops were made of harness leather; waxed kip is, I believe, the proper term.

Some men still bought good boots for Sundays, as well as for work, and both Ephraim and Seth took old boot tops which had come adrift at the welts to Tom Hoyle to be clogged. In the early fifties, I incurred the wrath of Annie by insisting on wearing Ephraim's gardening clogs to go to a Boxing Day match at Odsal Stadium. She expected me, as a young university lecturer, to take more care of my appearance and ignore frozen feet.

The style and manner of construction of our clogs was that common to the industrial north at the time.[2] I don't think that Tom Hoyle made his own soles in our day, although the walls of his shop were festooned with

Plate 29. The door in the corner opened straight in to Tom Hoyle's clogger's shop. His brother, Roland, repaired boots and shoes at the curtained window above. (John Nicoll)

large stock knives and draw knives; his soles were almost certainly factory made.

Clogs such as these were unsuitable for agricultural work for the simple reason that prolonged treading on soft surfaces such as earth or grass wore the wood away long before the irons, so that the sole wore paper-thin and split down the middle. Ephraim, who wore his clogs only in the garden and hen-pen, had a pair that wore really hollow between the irons, so that when his wedding ring dropped unnoticed into the litter of a hen hut floor, it stuck in the muck and peat lodged between the irons and was not discovered until he scraped his clogs before taking them off. And we had shifted the litter and muck almost grain for grain looking for it!

When I was in my early teens and the Low Moor Company's forge was still ticking over, one could hear from top to bottom the tread of a dozen men at a time climbing Storr Hill in their clogs. But most of the wives could tell who was in the group, whether it was time to put the pan or kettle on for her husband or son.

Right down to the Second World War, there were men who had their boots made to measure. This may have been a luxury for them, a habit acquired in their younger days, or they may have had very big or abnormal feet. It was usually possible to tell them by their beautiful finish and styling. Working boots were very heavy and usually hob-nailed, and, while it was possible to get lighter, waterproof rubber boots and wellingtons, these were rejected by most workers, especially in factories and wet workshops, because they said that they 'drew' their feet.

There was little change at first when boots gave way to shoes. They were still made entirely of leather, sometimes even with leather linings, the soles were sewn on them new and nailed on when repaired, but women's soles were sewn all the time. Well before World War II, stick-on rubber soles were frequently applied and rubber heels could be either stuck on with a rubber-based adhesive or nailed on. Rubber heels were especially a boon to women. I cannot recall children running around barefoot in our area, as they did in many of the inner cities of the North; even the poorest wore stockings that covered the calf and betrayed their poverty by wearing 'pumps' – lace-up gym shoes made of rubber and thin canvas, costing about 1*s*. 6*d*.

The rest of the story of footwear on Storr Hill Side needs no telling; the developments have been those common to the north of England and, in all significant details, to the whole of Britain. The picture has been completely changed by the introduction of new materials and new adhesives. Nowadays it is possible to make footwear that is light and warm, mass-produced by unskilled labour – plastic materials cut out by machines and glued together in jigs. It is not required to stand the amount of walking, often on very rough roads by modern standards, nor working in quarry or pit or on unmechanised building sites. Above all, it cannot be repaired other than by a specialist with special equipment; one cannot keep a last in the cellar and nail on new soles and heels as was possible with our pre-war boots, shoes and clogs. On the whole, the same applies to women's footwear.

One does not see the real, old leggings of any kind nowadays, their place having been taken by leg-warmers, wellingtons and women's high, fleece-lined boots. Leather leggings, such as those who worked with horses often wore in the nineteenth century, were quite frequent, and puttees, a legacy of the soldier's uniform of World War I, were sometimes seen. For children, especially girls, there were long cloth leggings with little buttons all the way up.

The clogs may have been the sartorial badge of the northern working man where he touched the ground, but the cap, the 'flat hat', was a more tenacious badge at the end which he held highest. Even today, it is not merely an important item of clothing but a necessary adjunct and a friend, to be discarded when almost or completely in pieces, and then mourned for weeks! My wearing it for thirty-three years as member of a select academic institution was not an affectation; with me, it was and is part of my inheritance, as though I had a cap-wearing gene. Students and professors alike tolerated this weakness in me without comment; I was merely wearing my badge, like the old professor of engineering whose first job every morning when he walked into his department was to don an old morning coat, beetle-green with age and with frayed tails! You can tell the difference between the headgear of a true-born cap-wearer and a 'county and rugby-union' cap because the latter has been added to the person; it is not part of him and is clean and fashionable.

It was much more than a head-covering to somebody born to the cap. Driving anything, from poultry to bullocks, saw it leave the head for the hand to be waved or applied as required, and I still catch the neighbour's rabbits and coax birds out of my greenhouse with it. You could get a hot pan or dish off the fire or out of the oven with it, or mop up spilt beer from a pub table; on it, you could sit on a stone wall and enjoy the view much longer, or use it as a kneeling mat, or as a receptacle for anything small that must not be lost, and when you went into a church or any place where politeness demanded that it be removed, it could be neatly folded and put into a jacket pocket. There are two incidents in the pages of James Herriot which bear testimony to his observation of the farmers of North Yorkshire and their men: the screw to hold a ring in a bull's nose was kept in a cap until required, and when Helen was to do the writing while James did the tuberculin testing – on their honeymoon! – the farmer scrubbed the top of the wall she was going to sit on with his cap.

It stands to reason that ease of putting the cap on and taking it off the head was vital. Maurice Priestley, with whom I played football for Belle Vue, and who played for England as a schoolboy, had erysipelas at the age of thirteen or fourteen and for a time was as bald as an egg. He played in his school-cap and snatched it off when he had the ball, replacing it as soon as he had got rid of it; when jumping to use his head, his cap came off halfway up and was replaced before his feet touched the ground! Many factory workers worked in them as a matter of course.[3] So, clearly, there were occasions when ease of removal was really urgent. I make this point because any cap wearer born to it abominates these caps with elasticated sides. True, you can't get a wrong size, they will fit any head, but you have to use two hands to put them on!

I know what Vera Smith means when she writes: 'Believe me if you have never had a strip wash in an old stone sink with only a bowl full of warm water and an icy wind blowing up the cellar steps right on to you, you have never lived!'[4] But I would reply: 'If you've never walked down Wilson Road into an east wind *in short pants*, you've never suffered!' When we were young there was no exception to being kept in short pants until a little before your fourteenth birthday at the earliest. They were stout and heavy, made to last in spite of many slidings down t'Clay Hill, just outside Carr Lane School, but they left young and fleshy knees very prone to painful chapping. Boys wore jerseys and shorts with stockings.

Nor did you wear underpants, briefs, or anything like that under them; I was aged twenty and had just had a slight kidney infection, when Annie was advised by Dr Brown to get me some underpants. When you got into long trousers, you were possibly taught by your father, as I was by mine, how to draw the long shirt laps through the legs until they overlapped. Shirts were large and warm, in those days. While on the subject of trousers, it must be recorded that a lot of trousers worn by working men of Generations I and II were lined. We are divided as to whether this was only to the knees or full length. As lads our short pants were always lined. This may have been to make them more hygienic, but I doubt it; in my opinion, it was simply for warmth, or it was to hold a ragged outer layer together as long as possible. Older men, however, wore 'long Johns' below their union shirts, winter and summer, and, often enough, dickeys.

Collars were rare in the garb of outdoor workers; the regular substitute was a 'necklath'.

For the rest, the men wore the ubiquitous garb of the northern industrial worker. Looking at a picture of a football crowd in the nineteen twenties, you will see serried ranks of men in caps and dark suits, or dark heavy overcoats in the colder weather. The suits were made of heavy worsted (many men, when boasting about the quality of a new suit quoted the ounces to the square yard), most often dyed navy-blue and consisting of trousers ('tight under the armpits!') a waistcoat and a jacket. The waistcoat was more important than might seem today; it had four handy little pockets for a watch and other small things, so when it was the best suit it was useful for displaying a silver or rolled-gold albert or medal won at some sport or other, and when it was no longer the best, for working clothes were always best clothes grown old and shabby, a man took off his jacket, rolled up his shirt sleeves, stuffed his pipe and matches into the waistcoat pockets and became a working man. I still have three-piece suits made! Boys' suits also had waistcoats.

Rank and affluence were reflected in dress. Managers and directors in the early days of the century were distinguished by wearing hats and immaculate suits, often of a lighter colour than the working man. They were also more likely to go bareheaded. Professional men, including my old headmaster at Belle Vue, Mr F. B. Fisher, often wore starched collars, and some of the older gentlemen wore starched wing-collars, which we called 'come-to-Jesus collars'.[5]

For a mere man, a discussion of women's clothes of yesteryear is an impertinence and fraught with danger, although it is one of the features of our age that televised fashion shows seem to feature as many men as women among the experts and designers. But the subject is certainly best left to women, and who better to talk about trends, models and, above all, materials, than Vera Smith? The general trend, of course, was related to the national, even international, fashion scene. When dating my photos of a wagonette of *circa* 1910, and the Sunday school group of about the same date, comparison of the clothes with those on photos from anywhere in the country at that time would be valid.

Two observations which are here in place come to mind. Corsets hung like sheets of pork ribs on all the clothes lines on Storr Hill Side. They seemed to be made of a strong canvas or webbing which could not be washed white, and they were truly all-embracing. This was not entirely motivated by vanity, although the women's weeklies could have led one to think so; the work that women did in factories in those days, and subsequent child-bearing without the benefit of modern care, made the support of corsets necessary for some women at an early age.[6]

My second point, which does not apply only to clothes, is contained in the following anecdote. A colleague, faced with half a dozen students who insisted on the omnipotence of science in the modern world and wanted to turn all knowledge into the sphere of the boffin, asked them what would be the most effective method of birth control of the future. This was when the Pill was quite new, and the answer he got was the obvious one. Slowly and regretfully he shook his head and with all the urbanity he could summon said, 'What? With women trying to look like men, without hips and flat chested, wearing trousers and check shirts, flat heels and all that, and men going in for higher heels, fancy colours, women's hair do's and scented toilet lotions? The last thing the next generation will be able to do is have children. The way things are going they'll be so confused they'll have lost the art!'

Since writing the above, it has occurred to me that a note on cosmetics might not be out of place. Perhaps the reason why I had omitted it was that it is one thing that has changed less than most in the period I am describing. Chemically, of course, things have changed enormously, but the extent of their use, the prices paid for them, their value in society, remain very much the same. Women loved to paint themselves just as much then, probably more so, as is the case today, but nowadays they prefer a more natural-looking colour but devote far more time and money to their hair. That is yet another change witnessed on Storr Hill Side, although not to the same extent as in more 'fashionable' parts of the land.

Chapter 16

Diet and Health Care

The preferences of Storr Hill Side in gastronomic matters were quite simple. What the men (and in this matter it was most definitely a man's world) were prepared to put in their stomachs had to be bland and satisfying, intolerably sweet or tasteless and far too heavy for the modern palate and digestion. The most 'tasty' combinations that fulfilled their requirements were compounded of fat and salt or fat and sugar. Working as they did and under the conditions of their daily lives, they needed comfort and sustenance; modern ideas of a healthy diet, even if there had been popular experts on the subject in their day, would have had no relevance at all in their view of life.

Meat and potatoes in all possible combinations, roasts, stews, hot pots, only slightly relieved by the addition of green vegetables or roots such as carrots and swedes, and plenty of pearl barley, were their staple when they could afford them. My Generation I had inherited from their parents, probably also their grandparents who had known harder times, a liking for tripe, cow-heel, trotters, udder, sheep's head, shin-beef, ox-tails (which were always referred to as 'cows' tails; we had no use for the word 'ox' in any context) and other less choice parts of the butcher's produce, which was all that many people could afford. Such as were suitable were made into stews and broths, which had to be boiled for a long time, leaving an unmistakable odour about the house that was enough to spoil the appetite of later, spoiled, generations. These were often eaten with bread. Some of Generation II carried on such dietary preferences, which were not only relatively cheap but supported one of the firm principles of Storr Hill Side: 'Waste not, want not.' Also, no doubt, because they sensed that they were wholesome and nourishing, as well as being cheap. They simply could not bear to think of them being thrown away and in the course of time the flavour had become perfectly acceptable to them. Dripping, rendered down from the meat, was a favourite with all generations, and I still have friends and contemporaries who yearn for 'mucky drippin', i.e. streaked and flavoured with the meat juices.

Meat was so cheap that most people could often, if not regularly, afford good lamb and pork, although they mostly had to be content with the less expensive cuts. Anyway, from my own experience, in a lot of cases the culinary skills of the Storr Hill Side housewife did not do justice to the more expensive cuts. Bacon and ham were favourites; the first was the breakfast food and was very often of the home-fed variety – ninety per cent fat! The fat from it was, of course, used in all dishes where it was thought desirable. Ham was the prestige food – what you offered your guests for tea and the hall-mark of a celebration meal or charity raiser in the local club or village hall; a 'ham tea' was a social concept. The local shops still boiled their own, and I was often sent to Harrison's the bakers (No. 1 on Map III) as they always seemed to have the best. The first thing Annie asked for when coming out of a bout of stomach trouble was boiled ham.

With poultry all around in such numbers, it is surprising that it was so expensive and regarded as a luxury by people who did not keep their own. There were always plenty of cock-chickens around for Christmas; later, as turkeys became more fashionable, they too were reared in the local hen-pens. Ephraim was inclined to regard meat as a status symbol, and he was very particular about securing the best quality he could afford, in spite of the fact that Annie and I shunned fat meat and would cut off even the minutest shreds and leave them on our plate. He insisted on buying the meat every week and, if we had no suitable birds ourselves, he would make a tour of inspection round his cronies' hen-pens in October to pick our Christmas dinner. As soon as the Christmas turkey became a status symbol and local poultry men, including us, bred and fattened them, we had to have a turkey for Christmas, even though the rest of the family sometimes complained that turkey-meat was 'dry' and would have preferred a cock-chicken. Two-year-old boiling hens that had run outside all their lives not only had plenty of flavour, they had layers of fat so thick that even our older people threw away most of it.

I don't know how old I was, when Ephraim came home from the Harold Club one evening with a dozen goslings, nearly feathered, in a basket. He had bought them as a present for me – to fatten for Christmas for the benefit of my savings bank account. It was easy! They simply ran out in the field, eating grass and stealing what they could of the mash and grain put down for the hens, until about six weeks before Christmas. By then I had only ten left; one had flown away and one had died. I took our wheelbarrow down to Ramsden's, the corn chandlers, and asked if I could sweep the floor. The knew me well and readily acquiesced, so I came away with well over a hundredweight of corn-meal, thirds, alfalfa, sack-labels, string, etc. The geese, who were looking quite good by this time, were penned into an area about five yards by five, I made a vee-shaped trough with two boards and mixed my mash with plenty of water, very sloppy. They put on weight daily. About a week before Christmas, Dad came in with the information that he had met a couple of colliers from either the Long Row or the Short Row, I forget which, who were out of work and trying to earn a little something by dressing poultry for Christmas. They were charging half a crown each if they came and killed, took them away and brought them back ready for the oven, and threepence less if the customer killed and took the birds to them. Anybody who has plucked a goose would recognise this as a real bargain, so they came and killed them – with me once more holding the storm lamp! – took them away piled on a hand-cart and brought them back two days later in clothes baskets wrapped in greaseproof paper and ready for the oven. They had all been spoken for, so I was a wealthy lad that Christmas. I can't remember eating a goose at home; Annie probably found them too fatty.

But there was one food *par excellence* that fulfilled the requirements stated above. Reay Tannahill writes: 'Who the genius was who first had the idea of marrying batter-coated, deep-fried fish to sturdy fingers of deep-fried potato remains a matter of sometimes acrimonious debate.' She names Lancashire, London and Dundee as claimants, the relevant dates falling between 1864 and 1874, and then goes on: 'Whatever the truth of its origin, the fish and chip shop made a valuable contribution to the protein consumption of the poorer urban worker from the latter years of the nineteenth century until the middle of the twentieth.'[1] Storr Hill Side bears out this latter assertion completely.

There were three shops selling fish and chips on Storr Hill Side between the wars, and it appears to me from perusing the maps that the premises in question were all there by 1894. The tiny, detached structure on open land just below the old library, on the right down Storr Hill, was certainly there. Throughout the war it was kept by my Aunt Eva and her husband, later by Frank Wilkinson for a while. It has never looked as smart as when he had it (Plate 30). The others were Greenwood's and Ellis & Wright's (see Map III), both of them down New Road Side. Each had its adherents, who insisted on the products of one or the other, if their favourite was

Plate 30. Fish and chips shop near the top of Storr Hill, Prop. Frank Wilkinson.

open at the time. Our family always seemed to favour the furthest away; I was invariably sent to 't' bottom shop', Ellis & Wright's, for their wares. But, such was the competition and the insistence on the best by the public, that I was usually sent down Wyke when any wet fish was required, to the Carr Road Fisheries, an old, low house that was entered by going down two or three steps into a flagged well. This shop sold the most delicious, large-flaked haddock cheaper than any other in the neighbourhood; although the price varied a little, one could sometimes get a six-ounce piece for 6*d*. – one old penny an ounce! Annie cooked it in the frying pan with a sprinkling of bread-crumbs or moistened with milk and butter and steamed between two plates over a pan of boiling water.

Keeping a fish and chip shop was decidedly not an easy life. You could make money and retire early, as many did, but there were also a significant proportion of fish and chip people who died young or were crippled in retirement. They had to get up early to go to market if they wanted good fish, most of them being there for 6 a.m. And it had to be good haddock, for no other fish was acceptable from a fish and chip shop anywhere in the district! It was a very long day for them, as there was no rest in the middle of the day, for they opened at midday to serve the mills and factories.

Apart from the heavy protein components of the old diet, the people of Storr Hill Side revelled in stodgy grain and meal foods. All kinds of steamed puddings, rice puddings, sago puddings, suet puddings, pies and dumplings were the order of the day in many households. Then there was the fat and sugar combination that resulted in tea tables laden with cakes and confectionery. Ephraim insisted on large, heavy fruit cakes, similar to Dundee Cakes but less fancy, at all times, and would eat a slice that 'stood up for itself' at the end of a big meal. He loved fruit pies and pasties and insisted on huge helpings of these too. Perhaps it was a good thing that Annie's pastry was decidedly on the hard and heavy side! But her sponge cakes, like those of her mother, were of a feathery lightness that I have encountered nowhere else.

New Road Side Co-op had a separate section, known as t'flahr 'oil', in which a row of bins occupied the full length of one wall. They contained various grades of flour, crushed oats, bran, etc., and it was the normal thing to get the week's groceries in the main shop and then go into 't'flahr-'oil' for a stone or half a stone of flour for the family bread. I don't remember when it was that Annie stopped baking our bread, having discovered that one could buy good bread at local shops. Teacakes, plain and currant, were a delight, especially when toasted on a fork and well buttered.

According to modern principles and practice, the diet of those days was disastrously short of vitamins and mineral salts. Salads were eaten as a garnish to ham and tongue, but they were not regarded as important. They could not compare in variety and quality with the garnishing of the average pub sandwich of today, being composed mainly of limp lettuce, a couple of radishes and a tomato. It was rare that even such a poor salad was eaten except in the season, when they could be produced at home or in a local allotment. Tomatoes were a speciality of those gardeners who were capable of managing a small, often unheated, greenhouse. Green vegetables were generally cooked to an unappetizing slime.

Of my sources only Cudworth sees fit to mention the state of health of the people of North Bierley, and of Low Moor in particular.[2] His informant on the subject was 'Dr Whitteron of Low Moor, than whom no one has a better acquaintance with the subject.' Whitteron House, in our day the house-surgery of Dr Harry Robinson, stood in Carr Lane Bottom, opposite the end of Kellet Buildings. People thought that Dr Whitteron had been a

Plate 31. Vincent Smith kept the post office and an off-licence, and sold everything – bacon, biscuits, buckets and mouse-traps. (John Nicoll)

relative of Dr Robinson. Cudworth describes the death rate in Low Moor as being lower than 'eighteen of the largest towns in England'; of the forgemen drinking large quantities of 'home-brewed', varying from one to three gallons per shift, he makes the point that '$2\frac{1}{2}$ lbs. is the ordinary amount of cutaneous exhalation in a day, but that in puddlers and slab-forgemen the amount is as high as 20 lbs.' Whereas factory operatives had a life expectancy of 43 years, the average age of a hundred deaths on which an enquiry had been based was 56.4 and the average age of pitmen was 51.7. He says: 'With regard to the prevailing forms of disease existing in the above classes, it has been ascertained that even colliers are less liable to chest disease of a tubercular nature than those employed in the neighbouring worsted mills.'

As in the rest of the country, especially in the northern industrial areas, conceptions of hygiene and health-care were either very primitive compared to today, or non-existent. Washing the hands after using the toilet was never mentioned by either parents or teachers. There were no facilities for washing in the outdoor 'necessaries', anyway, and at work toilet facilities were usually so disgusting that employees went to great lengths to avoid having to use them. Underclothes were worn for a week, often longer, and were changed on the occasion of the weekly ablution in a little tin bath before the fire. Few families bought toothbrushes or dentifrice. Annie always had Gibb's Dentifrice to hand but it could be ignored by all of us for weeks on end.

Nobody accepted that there was any danger in smoking, but some people, strict parents and teachers, frowned on it or forbade it as being a dirty habit and expensive for young people. Young men and lads couldn't wait to start smoking as a sign that they were grown up and acting like men. When I felt that I was smoking a few more than was good for me, and remonstrated with Annie for buying a bonus packet for me, her only reply would be: 'Well, you like it, don't you?' There was certainly no idea that cigarettes were so lethal in those days.

There were no electric fridges; not even the butchers had such things, but had to do their best with a cold-room or a cellar. Domestic cellars, however, did a very good job of keeping food in good condition. For the most part, this problem was left to the food retailers; housewives went shopping every day if necessary, provided they had the money. There were some women who had learned to use the term 'a balanced diet', which they had probably learned at night school, the St. John's Ambulance Brigade or the newspapers, but to them this meant little more than a bit of fruit and salad to relieve the meat, bread, cake and potatoes.

My Generation I and Generation II grew up and some of them grew old, before the days of antibiotics, cortisones, beta-blockers, infra-red and ultra-violet lamps, lasers, keyhole surgery, radio-therapy and all the other therapies as well as the plethora of analgesics and cold-cures that are now so readily available at a price that most of the population can easily afford. In those days, although there were plenty of patent medicines available at the chemists, a lot of folk-medicine still survived.

I regret very much having allowed the recipe for the famous salve to disappear, for which the Shaw family was known to most people of Generation I on Storr Hill Side and much further around. It looked like a sulphurous toffee in colour and consistency, and came in pieces like a big man's finger. Older people have told me of Seth's father, Shadrach Shaw, making and selling it in quantity. The only time I saw it being made was by Seth's brother Fred, at Scholes; he rolled it out on the table to the approved thickness and then cut it into lengths of 3-4 inches with the carving knife. Sores that threatened to go septic, angry spots and boils, were treated by melting some of the salve in the flame of a candle or taper until a large blob dropped on to a piece of rag, old shirting or handkerchief material. It was then clapped while still hot and liquid on to the spot. In those days pus was not attacked from within the body, you had to have something that 'drew' – the stronger the better![3]

There were also some curious analgesics which worked on the principle that one pain could be cured by introducing another pain to take the patient's mind off the first. I had a lot of trouble with my teeth when I was young, and I remember having been made to seek ease from toothache by clenching a wad of Bruno Flake on to the aching tooth. That was better than the vinegar and pepper plaster. The condiments were spread on a piece of brown paper and then held to the cheek. It was a treatment that made even a robust heathen youngster like me pray for Friday when Mr Rushworth, whose proper dentist's surgery was on Manningham Lane, came and attended to our dental troubles in the front room of a house at the bottom of Church Street. Such was the neglect of elementary dental care in those days, and so poor were my teeth, that he had taken out all my teeth bar seven by the time I was seventeen and filled the rest of my mouth with dentures. And while the subject is teeth, I can remember Seth coming into our house from next door one cold morning, as distressed as I ever saw him, with a length of string dangling from the very large tooth that he called his 'mutton bone tooth'. It was loose and had started to ache and he had tried without success to tie the other end of the string to the oven door and then slam the door. Many teeth were in fact drawn this way, but this time it did not work, and Annie managed to evade his demand that she should pull it out herself and got him to see a dentist.

Many of Seth's generation could make fun of their ailments in a way unknown today. I can remember a good cure for a sore throat: 'Tha mun tak' a sweaty sock an' put a piece o' bacon rind in it an' tee it rahnd thi neck'; someone who was 'a bit chesty' could be advised to rub his or her chest with the rough end of half a brick!

Three treatments come to mind that were more efficient than many of their modern equivalents, albeit not so comfortable and painless. Flu did not survive Annie's treatment for more than twenty hours, as far as I can remember. You got a hot mustard bath, a vigorous rub down and a glass of hot milk with brandy to wash down an aspirin tablet, and were then packed into bed with a hot-water bottle and covered with blankets and eiderdowns to a depth of at least six inches. No jockey or boxer ever wasted more efficiently! I dared not seek relief by sticking out a limb here and there – it would probably have been chopped off if Annie had caught me, for, in treating sick boys, she was efficient but brutal. But, by next morning, noon at the latest, the temperature was gone for good, the top blanket was wet through and the patient weighed a good bit less and was as weak as a kitten. It was a good thing that the older generations were pretty good at 'building up' a person after illness. The other efficient remedies that come to mind were senna pods and cascara sagrada, the last of which had the nastiest taste in the whole pharmacopoeia. Ugh!

One of the great episodes of Annie's life was her service in the St. John's Ambulance Brigade. I have the beautiful bronze pendant badge with her name and number on the back, above which are suspended, each on two links of bronze chain, service bars for the years 1917-1920 inclusive. She had vivid recollections of dressing the wounded and laying out some of the dead resulting from the Low Moor explosion in August 1916, in New Works School, which means that she must have been a member for some time before the service bars start. Perhaps some were lost before I got them. Her treatment of typical childhood complaints, as I remember them, was probably not learned in the Ambulance Brigade. If I cut a middle finger, she would apply a first-class dressing and bandage, but the two adjacent fingers would be severely sprained in the process, having been twisted into impossible positions so that Annie could get a proper job done! The slightest hint of a sore throat or bronchitis called for a good rubbing of the chest with a warming lotion, which Annie carried out with all her strength, standing behind one, rubbing up, and down, so that the

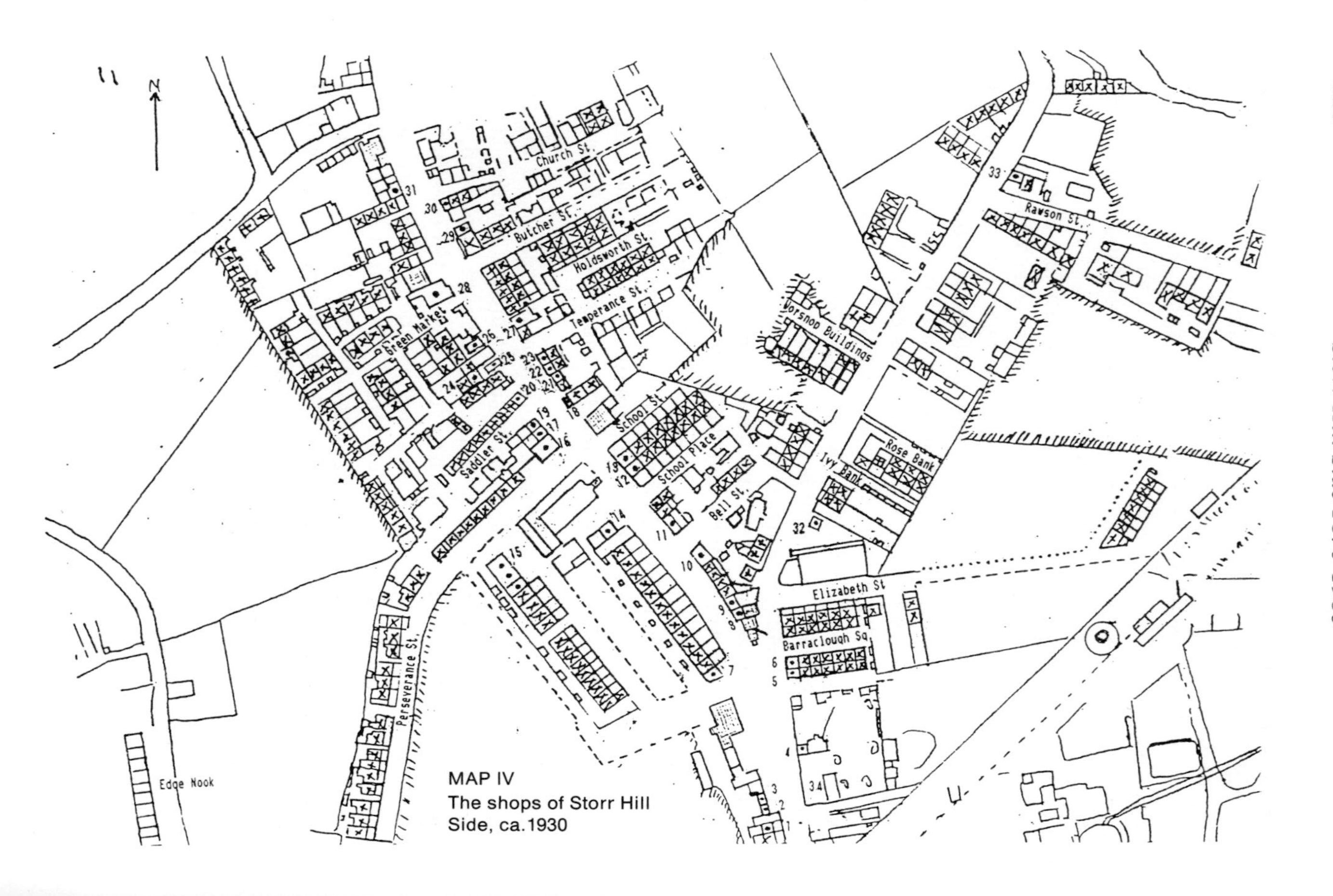

MAP IV
The shops of Storr Hill Side, ca.1930

KEY TO MAP IV

Shops
1 Harrison's – bakers and confectioners.
2 Matthew Mercer – cobbler (wooden hut).
3 Mr Jones – sweets and tobacco (wooden hut).
4 Morley's – junk, old wireless parts, etc. Later sweets, soft drinks, etc.
5 Jos. Terry – pork butcher and confectioner.
6 L. Atack – sweets and tobacco.
7 Thorpe's – grocers.
8 Tom Jagger, later H. Roebuck, barbers.
9 Mrs Benn – baker and grocer; later Sykes – health-shop.
10 Mrs Benn – confectioner (had moved from 9.)
11 Nathan Garside – greengrocer.
12 Pearson – watch and clock maker and repairer.
13 Law's – sweets and fancy goods.
14 Harry Garside – paints, wallpapers, paraffin.
15 Co-op – 15a Co-op butcher's dept.
16 Greenough – bakers.
17 Jim and Naylor Mitchell – butchers.
18 Miss Dodding – hairdresser; later Wheeler's.
19 Harry Broomhead – second-hand shop.
20 Moulson – cobbler.
21 Tom and Roland Hoyle – clogs, boots and shoes.
22 Hinchcliffe – newsagent; later bric-a-brac.
23 First, a greengrocer and then Wheeler of Wyke, electrician.
24 Healey's – sweets and tobacco.
25 J. Hinchcliffe – newsagent (wooden hut).
26 Greenwood's – fish and chips.
27 Miss Thorpe – haberdasher and draper.
28 Vincent Smith – post-office, bread, groceries, general stores.
29 W. Rawson – newsagent; earlier J. Holdsworth.
30 Haley – greengrocer; later a café.
31 Herbert Stobart – butcher.
32 Ellis and Wright – fish and chips.
33 Gartland's – bakers and confectioners.
34 Thornton's – fish and chips; later Frank Wilkinson.
35 Ainley's, later Mrs Tommis – grocers.
36 Mrs Benn – sweets and tobacco from house.
37 Mena Briggs – grocer and general store.
38 Reg Bennett – filling station and car repairs.

heel of her hand pounded one's Adam's apple with rhythmic ferocity! It was even more dangerous to move, evade or complain!

We got through the usual ailments of childhood, measles, chicken-pox, whooping cough and the like, with no more trouble than they had caused our parents and grandparents. There were two chemists in Wyke: Timothy White's & Taylor's and Hudson's down by the Post Office. They made up prescriptions and sold the full range of patent medicines of the day. Most people went to them direct with their troubles and were very often cured without going to the doctor. You stated your problem, anything from a baby that was teething to an arthritic grandparent, and something was made up that procured at least temporary relief. Shortly before the war we had a Dr Dalling in Wyke who was not satisfied with the branded aspirins then available and gave Mr Hudson a prescription to make what became known far and wide as 'Pink Tablets'. They did everything that aspirins did, only they did it better, and our family got to using nothing else. Students in the university hall of residence where I was a tutor swore by them for hangovers, and I was expected to stock up with them every vacation.

Doctors, at least those in Wyke, managed to seem human and approachable in those days. Their status in society was never questioned or threatened, they were never imposed upon by people who were not really ill, and they spent time, lots of time, on those patients who really needed them. Both Annie and Ephraim averred consistently that they owed their lives to Dr Brown, our large and genial family doctor, whose surgery was on Wroe Terrace. He was not always attending a patient when he called at our house; quite often he was there to ask Ephraim to mend yet another of his favourite pipes. It was surprising how often he broke the ebonite peg that held the two parts together, and Ephraim was the only man around who could bore out the mouthpiece and insert a new peg. This relative intimacy and its disappearance was yet another feature of life on Storr Hill Side that kept in step with the changes in the mode of transport. Annie used to tell about a Dr Dearden riding down Storr Hill on horseback to visit Seth when he had typhoid fever. The doctors were the first members of our local society to own a car and make regular use of it.

But tuberculosis was still a killer. The most saintly person I can recall was a Storr Hill mother who lost a husband and at least three sons with it and remained one of the most cheerful, generous and willing-to-help people we have ever known. Diphtheria also was still to conquer. I spent several weeks, I don't know how long, at the age of four in the North Bierley Isolation Hospital on Cleckheaton Road, and was one of the lucky ones. No visitors were allowed; my parents used to come and look in at me through the window! Those who, like me, survived such afflictions owed their lives to good and tireless nursing rather than the wonders of science.

The mere prospect of a death was sufficient to make people refer to the sufferer with a reverent lowering of the voice and brief, cryptic phrases. Cancer and, sometimes, TB, were never named but they were certainly present: 'E ez *it* i' t'throit.' As far back as I can remember, I picked up unmistakable but oblique references to colostomies.

They may not have been good church goers, the people of Storr Hill Side, but they liked to bury their dead decently and with style. Every Friday evening the man from the Prudential came along Elizabeth Street – and many other streets in the neighbourhood – collecting twopence from each household and solemnly writing it down in a little book, like a rent book. This was to pay for funerals. There would invariably be a collection among the neighbours for a wreath, and those not invited who did not have to work, women and old men, would be standing at their doors to pay their last respects when the cortège went past. Amos Petty's six black horses, by our time a little worn and slow with age and the other menial tasks they had to do, were still in demand by some families to pull the hearse.

In the case of most, if not all, deaths on Elizabeth Street and round about, the corpse was laid out in the home where they had died or the home of the children. Funeral parlours were quite rare and too impersonal for members of my Generations I and II. I remember this in the case of Seth in particular, as there was a convention that such a corpse must not be left alone in the house, and I had to keep this watch, while Grandma Sarah and other members of the family had their meals in our house next door. A funeral tea for him was held in the top room of the Harold Club; it was not as lavish as some that I have heard of because it was shortly after the war and there was still rationing. It was given exactly the right tone by the reunions of old people who had not seen each other for quite a long time, and their reminiscences, accompanied by smiles and chuckles of appreciation when his tricks and sayings were remembered.

Often there was no will, but this did not seem to cause the acrimony among those left behind that it does today. It did, however, make the obtaining of probate very tedious, because few on Storr Hill Side were prepared to pay a solicitor so much for such a trivial task.

Chapter 17

A Summing Up

At the beginning of my period of the history of Storr Hill Side the landscape was dotted with tall chimneys and the primitive headgear of scores of small pits. Roads were cobbled and the railway carried the real traffic, both passengers and goods. There were no motor vehicles on the roads and consequently no garages or filling stations. Horse-drawn trams were about to give way to steam trams and these were soon to be superseded by electric vehicles. There were no aeroplanes in the sky; even fifty years later, in the middle of my period, we used to rush out of the house and gape up at the sky when we heard one.

There were no houses built of brick and roofed with tiles on Storr Hill Side, no toilets inside the houses and water-closets outside were only just becoming the norm. Inside, there was no hot water from a tap and the only source of heat in the house was a single large coal fire, which baked the bread, heated the water, dried the clothes and the people and consumed almost all the rubbish. The fire-back boiler for hot water was still quite a long way off. There were tabbed rugs on the stone floors, or perhaps nothing at all.

Labour was still typically manual labour, the exercising of human muscle and brain, although steam power was by then well able to manage the heavy loads and keep the textile machinery turning. Not only the workshops of the artisan but every department of the pit, the mill or the forge was served by manual operators. Hurriers did the job in the narrower seams of coal which pit ponies did in the thicker seams; there were no endless belts. Holidays with pay and unemployment benefit were both unknown concepts.

Babies were born at home with the help of the midwife and there was no pre-natal care, no clinics. Infant mortality was high. Both sexes, as young children, wore dresses. The responsibility for education was slowly being accepted by the state and the church schools and private dame-schools were being assimilated into the control of the school boards. There were no school meals, no outings, no school uniforms except at the old-established grammar schools, which represented the only form of secondary education. Provincial universities were being envisaged and a start was being made in some cities as a matter of civic pride. Infants and primary pupils in many schools learned to write with special pencils on slates until the middle of my period. Nowadays many pupils are being introduced to word-processors and computers at the same age.

Hospitals were just starting to be established in the area; there was no NHS and doctors were self-employed. Until World War II there were no antibiotics and tuberculosis (called 'consumption' on Storr Hill Side) diphtheria, polio, pneumonia, typhoid, and others which have now been mastered, were still potential killers. Sticking-plaster was still a long way off.

There were no fridges or freezers, no radios or television sets, no cinemas, no motor cars, no electric cookers, no fans, no safety-razors or electric shavers, and no zip-fasteners. The telephone did not exist at the beginning of my period and made its way slowly into domestic use between the wars. Photography was still in its infancy, a fascinating pursuit for the relatively well-off. Some primitive, not very versatile, plastics made their appearance in everyday use after World War I, but it was not until after the Second World War that plastics featured in almost all aspects of our lives, most notably in the shape of man-made fibres for textiles.

Women, while having more rights than they still have in many parts of the world and under some religions, were nevertheless, in practice, in the position of being second-rate creations – not merely second-class citizens. They had no vote, no access to the professions and were only just being allowed to study but not to take degrees. They could not show their legs or wear trousers, and their bathing costumes were as unattractive as they could be made.

Materially then, there has been enormous progress, but has it made people on Storr Hill Side happier? It was a society that had evolved its own standards and world-picture without reference to the irrelevant élitism of the national culture. The word 'culture' evoked in the people of Storr Hill Side the impression of something foreign and effete, something that was 'all show' and no substance. Instinctively, they rejected the moral hypocrisy of the 'superior' culture. How could there be any good in something so far away and so strange, and which did nothing to foster either their bodily needs and comforts or their sense of security? In their experience, the only agent that did this was work; by working they could secure all that they needed, and this was the only way to do that, as far as they could see. So work became to them not only the source of their physical well-being but also the foundation of their dignity, because this depended on their confidence in being able to make their own way in life and provide for their dependants. Only through work were they able to meet what they had been taught to regard as their obligations to society. The old device of the City of Bradford, *Labor omnia vincit*, was a clear and direct expression of the work ethos. Its place has been taken by a slogan: 'Progress, Industry, Humanity', which sounds good, but is open to as many interpretations as 'New! Dazzling! Biological!' on packets of soap-powder.

The feature most frequently omitted from social histories of the late nineteenth and early twentieth centuries is the natural dignity and composure of working people. By the standards of those who write social history, they had no dignity at all, and, of course, they have none today. They had none of the necessary trappings, no office carrying a title, no letters after their name denoting a specialised education, no titles or decorations deriving from the monarch or the government and they were not pictured in the papers wearing top hats and morning suits nor in big wigs or walking in procession in medieval costume. Such things represented a life that was totally incomprehensible to them because it was obviously a planned, organised display of wealth and power. The social historians and analysts of the Victorian working classes are wont to emphasise the squalor, poverty and cruelty of the life they were forced to live; they make great play with the long hours of work on starvation rations, with the cold, the damp and the disgusting lack of sanitation of their dwellings, and with the high rate of infant mortality and the short expectancy of life. They ignore, however, the type of character that these conditions produced in a large percentage of working people who suffered under them.

As far as I know, none of our modern academics and experts has produced a clear, brief and explicit explanation of the factor I have in mind, and yet again we must have recourse to the wordly wisdom of the Ancient World of Greece and Rome. Seneca puts it, loosely translated, like this: 'Poverty with joy is not poverty at all. The poor man is not one who has little, but one who thinks he should have more.' This is precisely the impression I retain of the best of my Generation I, and, although there were many to whom it did not apply, I still think that this formulation is as good a signature for their generation as can be offered. To them, poverty and its attendant circumstances was normal and inevitable. They were not subject to the pressures of an élitist upbringing and education whose purpose was to inculcate an unlimited desire to 'get on in life', to place professional and social ambition at the top of their priorities and to cultivate and esteem only those who might possibly be of use in the attainment of these ambitions. My Generations I and II, taken as a whole, regarded it as natural and knew that it was expected of them to cope, to find a way to manage, whatever circumstances and trials they might encounter in the course of their daily life. The principle of 'make do and mend' that was a central feature of the outlook is still present on Storr Hill Side to an appreciable degree, and even those of us who have left the neighbourhood long ago cannot quite shed it. Our houses will always be cluttered up with things that 'might come in some day'.

They could devote all their efforts to earning the respect of their fellows in the community by conforming to the group ethos of reliability and hard work and not seeking to impress with their individual superiority. In genuine people this happened automatically, without trying, as a natural result of their upbringing – and their dignity was founded on this one fact: that they could afford to be natural and naive in all things. One of the main results of this was that they were not shackled by the chains of the expert, the 'authority' in all that they did. Accountants were not able to earn a lot of money by telling them how to save a few pounds; the women had no need to go to night-school to learn how to iron or cook; they did not feel it necessary to consult the opinions of medical experts, gynaecologists, keep-fit experts, dieticians and child psychologists before having babies, and they lost neither sleep nor money over the choice of education for them as they grew up. For my people possessed as a birthright that natural power of achievement without strain and neuroses – albeit of limited achievement by modern standards – that our older universities have claimed and with which they have in vain struggled to impress us throughout the last hundred years. This is why a dignified élitist, one reared and educated to compete and surpass, is a contradiction of terms.

Not every inhabitant of Storr Hill Side was possessed of this dignity, of course; in fact, it was merely the signature of my Generation I. My Generations II and III saw its erosion to the point I have described at the end of my chapter on Law and Order. Even Generation I had its brutal drunks and wife-beaters, men who would worry and kill a rat with their teeth, their hands tied behind their back; and drabs who would descend to any degradation in the pubs. But these were exceptions and very much in contrast to the morality and outlook of the vast majority, and they were retailed in the local gossip mostly with disgust and rejection. The other side of the coin, is represented by the account in *Low Moor in Times Past* (p.42) of the origin of the name 'T' Drop' for the Victoria Hotel in Low Moor. According to this account, the name arose because a landlord at the beginning of the century, Squire Hodgson, on pay-days asked men if they had been home (and, presumably, handed over the housekeeping money) before coming to his pub. If the answer was, 'No', he would only let them have 'a drop', and then they had to leave.

Socially, the quality most esteemed was, without doubt, solidarity, a positive acceptance of and belonging to the community *as it was*. The greatest offence was to put on airs of superiority, to be 'holier than thou', to boast of greater experience, greater affluence, greater talent and to 'talk down to folk'. Not that this gives the society of Storr Hill Side any claim to being different; it is a common feature of small communities in which generation has followed generation in the same way of life. In fact, the best definition I have found of this aspect of a small community applied to a very rural village in the Cotswolds, the place where Laurie Lee grew up.

The astuteness admired by the locals in Laurie Lee's village was also an essential feature of the ethos of Storr Hill Side. But, as in the Cotswolds, this astuteness had to be harmless if practised on an accepted member of the community. Proving one's astuteness (it was expressed as being 'fly' in our day) was not approved, although it did happen, if it damaged one of the community, especially a weaker member.

The most valued and respected members of the community were first and foremost workers who were good at their trade and reliable, men and women who did their best and kept their word, and who faced up to the trials and vagaries of life without complaints and self-pity. In the words of Frank Wilkinson: 'They knew that the work had to be done, and they did it.' Their main, central ambition was to be as comfortable as possible, but they were prepared to make reasonable, honest efforts for it. It didn't matter to them that they lived with their family in a one-roomed low house like No. 68 Storr Hill if, without killing themselves with hard work, they and their family could keep warm and dry and be well fed there. What is nowadays called 'the quality of life', which demands a display of affluence – a posh house of a size that people do not need, furnished and decorated according to the latest women's magazines; a large, showy car that costs a fortune in petrol, taxation and insurance; private or grammar-school education for their children; expensive food and drink habits, foreign holidays which impress the neighbours – these, and many more attributes of the modern ethos, have proved impossible to realise to any satisfactory degree on Storr Hill Side. New houses there are, which look modern and attractive, but earning a mortgage for them, while observing the above canons of 'quality living', wears people out almost as quickly as did the Low Moor Company's pits in its heyday. The vital factor is that, even in their young days, the earning of such affluence and the regimentation of their initiative, humour and taste by the media, turns them into state- and commerce-designed robots.

Compared to those days of steady, if arduous, work in the immediate locality, when work and the social life of the community were as one, the present residents on Storr Hill Side, while still placing comfort high on the list of their priorities, are now concerned to gain as much material affluence as possible with as little effort as possible. Parents throughout the land require nothing more of schools than that they should equip their children to pass examinations and thus get jobs that are physically less arduous and, at the same time, financially more rewarding. After all, this ambition has been regarded as the most laudable objective in life throughout my lifetime, and has become yet more pronounced since World War II. This search has produced an unsettled population; people move at short intervals as 'better' opportunities of employment offer themselves, and the accumulated traditions of the generation necessary to cement communal relationships no longer exist. The 'quick buck' and the 'free lunch' fallacies, which their grandparents would have treated with suspicion or completely ignored, have taken over, and the result is runaway inflation, political lies, corruption, terrorism, fraud, mugging and drugs. Even those vices and crimes which existed in the days of Generation I, were not allowed to become so blatant, overt and even applauded as they are in our present 'enlightened' age. Most of the young people have found that the approved ambitions of their generation cannot be realised on Storr Hill Side and have gone elsewhere; of the families that we knew there in the twenties and thirties, very few are still represented.

attributes of the modern ethos have proved impossible to realise to any satisfactory degree on Stony Hill [illegible]. New houses there are, [illegible] [illegible]

[illegible]

[illegible] unknown and ethnic [illegible] [illegible] [illegible] [illegible] and [illegible] [illegible] [illegible] [illegible] [illegible] [illegible] [illegible] [illegible] [illegible] and [illegible] [illegible] [illegible] [illegible] and [illegible] [illegible] [illegible] [illegible] [illegible] [illegible]

Appendix I

The government of the day published in 1842 a Report to the Commissioners on the Employment of Children prepared by Mr S. S. Scriven. (British Parliamentary Papers. Industrial Revolution, Children's Employment. Session 1842. No. 8). From his Report on the Collieries in the West Riding of Yorkshire, I take some of his remarks concerning the hurriers in pits close to Storr Hill Side, including some which employed girls from the age of eight. Mr Scriven, in his report on a number of pits around Halifax (p.74), is particularly concerned about the plight of girls down the pits: 'In almost every instance I have found that their introduction has been compelled either by the avarice or improvidence of their parents, who as colliers receive better wages than most other labourers when they *will* work, and are less liable to the fluctuations of prices for what they do.'

He gives numbered, verbatim reports of some of his interviews:

105. Esther Craven (No. 75) says: 'I have cried many a time afore now for coming into pit; but I have got used to it, and think nought about being brayed by the getters a bit.' In the statistical part, which Mr Scriven appends to his report, this Esther Craven is aged 14.1 and has been employed for 5 years. She is 4ft. 7½ in. high with a circumference of 2ft. 1in.; her physical condition is given as 'at par', which is next to the bottom grade in Mr Scriven's notation. She can neither read nor write.

106. Mary Barrett (No. 72) – aged 14.6, having been down the pit for 3 years, stands 4ft. 7in. high, with a circumference of 2ft. 4in. and is described as 'muscular'. She can neither read nor write. She says: 'I do not like working in pit, but I am obliged to get a living. I work without stockings or shoes, or trousers; I wear nothing but my shift.'

At Messrs. Foster and Lassey's Clewes Moor Pits, depth 210 feet, where these two girls worked, there were three girls out of a total of nine hurriers.

Mr Scrivens pulls no punches in his report:

> The estimation of the sex has ever been held a test of the civilization of a people. Shall it then be said that in the very heart of our own country – from which missions are daily sent to teach God's law, and millions upon millions have been generously poured forth for the manumission of hosts in a distant land – that there shall exist a state of society in which hundreds of young girls are sacrificed to such shameless indecencies, filthy abominations and cruel slavery as is found to exist in our coal pits? Chained, belted, harnessed like dogs in a go-cart, – black, saturated with wet, and more than half-naked, – crawling upon their hands and feet and dragging their heavy loads behind them, they present an appearance indescribably disgusting and unnatural.

In the following paragraph he singles out by name two proprietors who have given evidence, a Mr Emmet and a Mr Rawson, junior,

> whose desire was to make known to me that they knew nothing – literally nothing about them [child hurriers]; it was enough that they paid the 'getters' so much a ton or dozen, who found the children. As to the time when children came to work in the morning or left in the evening – whether they stopped to take a meal, or had any at all – whether they were educated or debased – they professed to be profoundly ignorant, and appeared to attach to themselves neither responsibility nor care, so long as they enjoyed the comforts and affluence that their daily toil brought them.

On the surface, it would appear that Mr Scriven did not labour in vain. His Report was not suppressed and not ignored, for, one year later, 1843, it was made law that women and girls should not be allowed to work underground. Nevertheless, there is plenty of evidence that the Mr Emmets and the Mr Rawsons experienced no difficulty when it came to breaking the law, and that girls and little boys worked in the conditions just described for many years afterwards. In the 1871 Census Returns, Edwin Lightowler, later landlord of the Patent Hammer, is given as a collier, aged 11. See also letter to *Dalesman*, March 1991, p.1074.

Mr Scriven examined one hundred and twenty-four hurriers in the pits of the Low Moor Company. The paternalism of the Company seems to have held good here also, to the extent that there were no girls among them. There were, however, many boys who had started down the pit at the age of seven or eight and several who, aged 15-17+ were rated as 'muscular' or 'very muscular' but whose height was well short of 5ft. Of the 124 examined, the only two to reach 5ft in height measured 5ft. 2in. (aged 17); and 5ft. 1in. aged 16.1. Peter Benn, in the Soldier's Green Pit, stood 4ft. 4in. at the age of 17.2 and had been employed for ten years. Averages for the eighteen hurriers at the Soldier's Green Pit were: aged 12 yrs. 8m.; time employed 4 yrs. 9m.; started down pit aged 7 yrs. 11m. The average height was 4ft. 4in. and their 'circumference' was 2ft. $2\frac{1}{2}$ ins.

One of the pits examined was on Storr Hill Side, and the Ordnance Survey 26" Map surveyed in 1849 includes a pit in Church Street, behind where the fish and chip shop of Ellis and Wright later stood, 'Messrs. Akroyd and Co's New Road Side Pit, 285ft.'. For topical interest as the most relevant item in the Report, I give the following details. There were only six hurriers down this small pit. None of them could read or write: Edward Clough (aged 14; 4ft. $7\frac{1}{2}$ in. high, circumference 2ft. 4in.; muscular; employed for 5 years). Jesse Butterfield (aged 16; 4ft. $8\frac{1}{2}$ in. 2ft. 7in.; very muscular; employed 7 years). William Shaw (aged 11.10; 4ft. $1\frac{1}{2}$ in., 2ft. 5in.; very muscular, employed 3 years). Eli Crabtree (aged 12.6; 4ft. $4\frac{1}{2}$ in., 2ft. 3 in.; Par; employed 1.6 years). Dawson Crabtree (aged 10.0; 3ft. 9 in., 2ft. $0\frac{1}{2}$ in.; Below par; employed 1.6 years). James Shaw (aged 10.0; 3ft. 8 in., 2ft. $0\frac{1}{2}$ in.; Par; employed 6 months).

Appendix II

The Census Returns for the year 1881 reveal the following picture of Perseverance Street and its inhabitants:

Four of the infants listed below were known to us personally, as adults, around the year 1930: Willie Thirlwell (the family called itself Thurwell), (Census No. 88), Fred Barraclough (Census No. 90), Luther Wade (Census No. 92) and John Hanson (Census No. 101) were still living in the same houses as heads of families. The first three lived in houses numbered 9, 11, and 13 respectively and the latter at No. 22. In each case the gaps between these numbers are the same as those in the enumeration of the 1881 Census, if one allows for the splitting of No. 16 into two dwellings. It would seem reasonable, therefore, to assume that we are able to insert actual house-numbers into the returns of the Census. This I have done in brackets beneath the number given by the census enumerator.

The 1881 Census of Perseverance St., Wyke, Bradford.

Ref. RG 11/4426, 29v. -32v.

No.	*Name*	*Relat.*	*Cond.*	*Age*	*Occupation*
	(New Rd. Side)				
75	Robert Gadsby	Head	mar.	24	Ironstone-filler, forge
	Susannah "	Wife	"	28	
	Annie "	dau.		8	Scholar
	Matilda "	"		6	"
	William "	son		4	"
	Charlotte E."	dau		1 mth	

	Name	Relation	Condition	Age	Occupation
	(Birkby St.)				
76	William H. Wood	Head	mar.	32	Draper & Milliner
	Jane "	Wife	"	32	
	George W. A. "	son		4	Scholar
	Marion E. "	dau.		2	
	Florence E. "	"		4 mths	
	Betty Briggs	serv.	unm.	15	Domestic servant
77	Squire Brook	Head	mar.	39	Dyer
	Mary A. "	Wife	"	38	
	Sarah A. "	dau.	unm.	18	Worsted weaver
	Adam "	son		16	Coal miner
	Mary J. "	dau.		8	Scholar
	Janice "	"		1 mth	
	Mallinson Garside	nephew	unm.	20	Coal miner
78	George Parish	Head	mar.	44	Agric. labourer
	Mary "	Wife	"	42	
	Frank "	son	unm.	20	Worsted mill hand
	Hannah "	dau.	"	17	" " "
	William "	son		14	Coal miner
	Frances "	dau.		11	Scholar
	Henrietta "	"		8	"
	Emily "	"		4	"
	John H. "	son		2	
79	Harriet Kershaw	Head	Wid.	66	Housekeeper
	Walter "	son	unm.	25	Iron roller
	Charles "	"	"	23	Dyer's Overlooker
	Mary A. Massey	boarder	"	26	Domestic servant
80	Ezra Garside	Head	mar.	42	Ironstone miner
	Ann "	Wife	"	40	
	Lydia "	dau.	unm.	12	Worsted spinner
	Fred "	son		9	Scholar
	James "	"		6	"
	Elizabeth A."	dau.		3	
	Sam "	son		2	

Three empty houses in Birkby St. recorded.

	(Perseverance St.)				
81	Thomas Worsnop	Head	mar.	28	Brass moulder
(2)	Mary "	Wife	"	27	
	Arthur "	son		5	Scholar
	Herbert "	"		3	
	Walter "	"		1	
82	Mary A. Seed	Head	Wid.	68	
(3)	John "	son	unm.	31	
83	Joseph Shaw	Head	mar.	30	Joiner, Organist &
(4)					Choirmaster
	Ann "	Wife	"	24	
	George "	son		4	Scholar
	Sarah J. "	dau.		2	
	Amy A. "	dau.		1	
84	John Harker	Head	mar.	35	Forge man
(5)	Nancy "	Wife	"	36	
	Sarah J. "	dau.		9	Scholar
	Annie "	"		8	"
	Edith "	"		6	"
85	Squire Mitchell	Head	mar.	34	Engine tenter
(6)	Emma "	Wife	"	34	
86	Ruth Kellet	Head	Wid.	33	
(7)	Naomi "	dau.	unm.	15	Worsted spinner
	Olive "	"	"	14	" "
	Harry "	son		11	Errand boy
	Irvine "	"		9	Scholar
	Harriet A. "	dau.		7	"
	Caroline "	"		5	"
	James "	son		2	"
	Benjamin Seed	Boarder	unm	30	Joiner
87	Richard Priestley	Head	mar.	60	Engine tenter
	Elizabeth "	Wife	"	55	
88	George Thirlwell	Head	mar.	41	Iron puddler
(9)	Menetta "	Wife	"	39	
	Willie "	son		11	Scholar
	Arthur "	"		5	"

89	Clifford Grey	Head	mar.	30	Coal miner
(10)	Lavinia "	Wife	"	39	
	Martha A. "	dau.		8	Scholar
	Emily "	"		2	
90	James Barraclough	Head	mar.	39	Forge man
(11)	Mary A. "	Wife	"	35	
	Thomas H. "	son		14	" "
	Mary E. "	dau.		11	Scholar
	Fred "	son		7	"
	Frances E. "	dau.		4	"
	Ethel "	dau.		1	
	Martha Bywater	mother-in-law	Wid.	56	
91	Ephraim Hardwick	Head	mar.	34	Plaisterer
(12)	Mary M. "	Wife	"	34	
	Lucy "	dau.		7	Scholar
	Arthur "	son		5	"
	Julia "	dau.		3	
	John G. "	son		10 mths	
92	Daniel Wade	Head	mar.	47	Blacksmith
(13)	Hannah "	Wife	"	45	
	Bramwell "	son		13	Worsted mill-hand
	Clara "	dau.		12	Scholar
	John Luther"	son		10	"
	Lydia "	sister	unm.	43	Worsted weaver
93	Luke Belfield	Head	mar.	46	Coal miner
(14)	Harriet "	Wife	"	49	
	Squire "	son	unm.	21	" "
	Martha Bywater	mother-in-law	Wid.	76	
94	Michael Booth	Head	mar.	46	Forge man
(15)	Elizabeth "	Wife	"	43	
	Alice "	dau.	unm.	17	Worsted mill hand
	James "	son		14	" doffer
	Martha E. "	dau.		12	" spinner
	Sarah "	"		10	Scholar
	Hiram "	son		8	"

	William "	"		4	"
	Annie "	dau.		4	
95	Paul Thornton	Head	mar.	58	Forge-labourer
(16)	Hannah "	Wife	"	54	
	Martha "	dau.	unm.	25	Worsted weaver
	John "	son	"	22	Overlooker (unemployed)
96	Watson Lightowler	Head	mar.	39	Engine smith
(16a)	Alice "	Wife	"	38	
	Holdsworth "	son	unm.	16	Worsted spinner
	Mary H. "	dau.		7	Scholar
97	Mary A. Bottomley	Head	Wid.	55	
(17)	Mary "	dau.	unm.	20	Worsted weaver
	John "	son		17	Coal miner
	Sam "	"		14	Hurrier
	Levi "	"		11	Coal miner
98	Richard Holdsworth	Head	mar.	49	Coal miner
(18)	Rebecca "	Wife	"	49	
	Ellen "	dau.		16	Worsted weaver
	Sarah "	"		10	Scholar
99	John Greenwood	Head	mar.	48	Coal miner
(19)	Harriet "	Wife	"	47	
	Ann "	dau.	unm.	22	Worsted drawer
	Joseph "	son	"	21	Coal miner
	Manasseh "	"	"	19	Joiner
	Martha E. "	dau.	"	17	Worsted spinner
	Benjamin "	son		15	Clogger
	Edith "	dau.		12	Scholar & Mill hand
	John "	son		11	"
	Emma "	dau.		7	"
100	Jonathan Mitchell	Head	mar.	39	Iron puddler
(20)	Hannah "	Wife	"	35	
	Fred "	son		17	Worsted overlooker
	Mary E. "	dau.		14	Dressmaker
	Harry "	son		11	Scholar
	Sarah E. "	dau.		8	"

101	George Hanson	Head	mar.	36	Carter
(21)	Mary A. "	Wife	"	37	
	Hannah M. "	dau.		14	Worsted spinner
	Charles "	son		12	? – illegible
	Esther A. "	dau.		10	Scholar
	Emma "	"		9	"
	John "	son		5	"
	Eliza "	dau.		3	"
	Annie "	"		1	
102	Ellen Alderson	Head	Wid.	66	
(22)	Harriet Moore	dau.	mar.	40	Worsted weaver
	Charles Alderson	son	unm.	30	Steam hammer driver
103	Benjamin Marsh	Head	mar.	46	Waggoner
(23)	Ann "	Wife	"	45	
	George "	son	"	20	Carter
	Ruth "	dau.-in-law		20	
	Annie "	dau.		11	Scholar
	Elizabeth "	"		9	"
	Benjamin "	son		2	
	Walter "	"		1 mth	
104	Thomas Faraday	Head	mar.	66	Carpenter
(24)	Elizabeth "	Wife	"	66	
105	William Barmby	Head	mar.	56	Coal waggoner
(25)	Mary "	Wife	"	48	
	Squire "	son	unm.	24	Carter
106	Thomas Holdsworth	Head	mar.	44	Grocer & Joiner
(26)	Mary "	Wife	"	45	
	Sam "	son	unm.	22	Joiner
	Fred "	"	"	20	Teacher

Appendix III

When Ephraim and Seth bought land on Elizabeth Street, sometime in 1923, it fell to Ephraim to keep an account of the money involved, a rough record of where money came from and how it was spent. The little exercise book in which the record was kept has survived, (Facsimile pp. 105-6) and I append here samples of a few pages, in which I retain the lines, spelling and punctuation of the original. As they are not numbered and the sequence is rather haphazard, the pages are taken at random.

Expense

	£.	*s.*	*d.*
For land in Elizabeth Street, Wyke			
May 9th 1923 Paid to Uram Jagger on account	10	0	0
To Harold Stead Solicitor	232	0	0
June 29th Wooden spars for fencing	2	0	0
July 6th " " " "	6	16	6
" 7th carting of wood 2/3. nails 1/6		3	9
nails 1/11. allowance to carter 1/-. Saw 6/-		8	11
" 2/7. wood 3/6. tar 1/-. wood 4/-. tar 5/-		16	1
" 2/0. cartage 2/6. wood £5 12*s*.	5	16	6
" 3/9. wood for gate 12/4		16	1
Tar 4/-. nails 6*d*. gate hangings 1£	1	4	6
Conveying fees £5 7*s*. 6*d*.	5	7	6
wood 3/-. saw file 11*d*. saw sharpening 6*d*.		4	5
for bricks, 5£ on account to A. Chew	5	0	0
Barrow 24/-. sharpening tools 6d.	1	4	6
in settlement for bricks to A. Chew 3£ 11/-	3	11	0

	£.	s.	d.
Commission per W. Law 10/-		10	0
Carting of bricks, etc. to I. Garside 5£ 1*s*.	5	1	0
Spars, door & frame £2. 9*s*. Parallel rule 1/7	2	10	7
To I. Garside for minion 18/-		18	0
	284	9	4

A little further on, a page reads:

	£.	s.	d.
Brought forward expense	355	2	4
Postage 2/- Bricks £9-0-0	9	2	0
damp proof per W. Birkby 3/6		3	6
A. Wilkinson £2-3-10. W. Barker £2-0-0	4	3	10
S. Shaw £2-18-1-. W. Barker 5/-	3	3	10
" " £3-14-1. A. W. £2-12-7	6	6	8
4 air bricks 6/-. iron rods 3/4. ins. stamps 26/7	1	15	11
Grant, Foster & Co. £13-13-0. Cement £3-10-10	17	3	10
Jagger Bros. £13-16-11. I. Garside £6-14-1	20	11	0
Best bricks Brighouse £14-5-0	14	5	0
Scaffoldings £3-7-3. Taylor & Parsons £1-6-9	4	14	0
Haulage per Goldthorpe £1-16-0	1	16	0
Bfd, Bricks £9-0-0 S. Shaw £3-7-1	12	7	1
A. Wilkinson £2-7-7 Ins. stamps 4/10	2	12	5
Backings £1-7-6. 1 doz scaffold ropes 14/-	2	1	6
Iron 6/- S. Shaw £3-15-10 A. Wilkinson £2-3-10	6	15	8
Ins. stamps 4/10 postage 2/- Workmen's Ins. £1-7-6	1	14	4
Bfd. Bricks £9-0-0. Air bricks 3/-	9	3	0
A. Wilkinson £2-12-0 S. Shaw £3-13-2½	6	5	2½
Ins. stamps 14/6 120ft scaffolding & pudlocks £3-6-6	4	1	0

On the appropriate Money in Hand page, the entries for part of the above page appear as follows:

	£.	s.	d.
(Brought forward)	140	1	4
Deposit E. A. Barker £5-0-0	5	0	0
	145	1	4
	9	2	0
	4	3	10
	3	3	10

	£	s	d
	6	6	8
	1	15	11
	13	13	0
	106	18	1
sods 2/-	3	10	10
	20	11	0
	82	12	3
	14	5	0
corrected Balance	68	11	3
	4	14	0
	1	16	0
	62	1	3
	12	7	1
	2	12	5
	47	1	9

Appendix IV

The Shaw Family of Wibsey

- Joseph SHAW, b. *ca.* 1735-40, m. Martha Bairstow, 26th June 1760
  - James SHAW, bapt. 12-4-1762, 5-8-1782m. Deborah Greenwood (bapt. Dec. 1766)
    - Joseph 1785
    - James SHAW, bapt. 25-3-1787, m. Charity Fletcher, 19-4-1808 (bapt. 1787)
      - Joseph SHAW, bapt. 2-6-1811, m. Nancy Mitchell 13-7-1833
        - Shadrach SHAW, b. 1836, m. Martha Wood 14-12-1856, d. *ca.* 1905
          - Sarah 1861
          - Seth SHAW, b. 28-6-1865, m. Sarah Lightowler 11-7-1891, d. 15-4-1947
            - Annie SHAW, b. 5-5-1893, m. Ephraim A. Barker 15-12-1920, d. 28-7-1974
            - Harry 1896, killed in action 1916
            - Eva 1902, d. 3-6-1971, m. Walter Thornton
          - Rhoda 1871
          - Rose 1875
          - Fred 1880
          - Walter *ca.* 1881-1960
        - Sarah 1834
        - Naomi 1838
      - John *ca.* 1820
      - Benjamin 1826
      - James 1827
    - Hannah 1789
    - David 1794
    - Ann 1798
    - Enoch 1805
    - Peter 1808

Various sources – census returns, certificates of baptisms, marriages, etc. confirm that all the Shaw generations listed above, from Joseph, b. 1735, to Seth, b. 1865, were born at Slack Side, Wibsey.

Notes

Introduction

1. *Workers' Housing in West Yorkshire 1750-1920* (Royal Commission on the Historical Monuments of England, etc., 1986) p.33.
2. Laurence Sterne, *The Life and Opinions of Tristram Shandy* (Penguin, 1967) p.339.
3. Robert Redfield, *Peasant Society and Culture* (Chicago, 1956) pp.70-72.
4. Laurie Lee, *I Can't Stay Long* (Penguin, 1985) p.44.

Chapter 1: Location and Climate

1. James Parker, p.124 (1902).
2. James Parker, p.245 (1904). Unless otherwise stated all references to Parker's work comes from the book of 1904.
3. Percy Nudds, p.43.
4. Wright's Shop (the older form Reet's Shop was often rationalised to Reid's Shop) was a low, factory-like building at the bottom of Abb Scot Lane, opposite the Harold Club. As its name suggests, it was originally the maintenance centre for the Low Moor Company's vehicles and other equipment.
5. James Parker, pp.244-50.
6. J. N. L. Myres, *The English Settlements* (OUP, Oxford, 1986) p.233.
7. *The Concise Oxford Dictionary of English Place-Names* ed. Eilert Ekwall (Clarendon Press, 4th edition, 1964).
8. Gordon Manley, *Climate and the British Scene* (Fontana New Naturalist, 1972) p.251.

Chapter 2: Work on Storr Hill Side

1. Census reference: R.G. 11/4426.
2. Percy Nudds, p.5.
3. Unpublished essay in Reference Section, Bradford Central Library (B625 DIC) : *Low Moor Ironworks Railways* by J. Dickinson, 5B Hipperholme Grammar School.
4. Dodsworth, p.127.
5. Dodsworth is in error in stating that both the Long Row and the Short Row have gone. The Short Row is still there and inhabited, cf. *Workers' Housing in West Yorks*, p.32. My photos of it, (Plates 38, 39) were taken in September 1985.
6. Dates of the Patent Hammer Inn. The brewery has lost all records concerning this public house, but Miss Willmott was able to find it mentioned in a trade directory of 1879/80 although one for 1877 did not include it. Dodsworth, p.143, writing in 1979, says that it still existed, but I could not find it in 1985.
7. Dodsworth, p.144: 'However, by 1869 the acreage being worked in the Wyke area had been extended, with royalty payments of £70 per acre for Black Bed coal, £60 for the ironstone, and £50 per acre for the Better Bed coal.' I can find no trace on the maps of 'Wyke Colliery'. Was this composed of a group of pits centred on the Westfield Pit?
8. Marion Yass, *Britain Between the World Wars, 1919-1939*, p.17.
9. Cudworth, *Worstedopolis*, p.29.
10. ibid., p.38.
11. ibid., p.57.
12. ibid., pp.63-4.
13. These figures are taken from a substantial brochure issued by the Bradford Branch of the Anglo-South American Bank, Ltd. in 1920, on the occasion of it entering fine new premises at 61 Market Street, opposite the bottom of Ivegate.
14. Cudworth, *Round About Bradford*, p.78.
15. I am obliged to John Nicol for these dates.
16. Nudds., p.51. All references to the Hind family are from this page.
17. James Parker, p.242.
18. Cudworth, *Worstedopolis*, p.67.
19. ibid., pp.67-71. Vera Smith's *All Muck and Nettles* is valuable on this subject, but I obtained it too late for its contents to be used here.
20. Directory of Chester and North Wales 1874.
21. The French textile manufacturers were Bradford's most serious competitors in the middle of the nineteenth century.

22. Sharp's dyeworks; see Cudworth, *Round about Bradford*, p.87; and the careful account of its demise in Grace Carter, *Wiche is Wyke*, pp.37-43.
23. I am assured that Percy Nudds, p.44, was absolutely right in his statement that R.N.O. stood for 'Restoring Nature's Own'! It was a reference to the R.N.O.'s waterproofing process. The trademark was a duck!
24. Cudworth, *Round About Bradford*, p.87.
25. This must refer to the North Bierley Waterworks mentioned by Parker, p.226. He quotes a price of 2*s.* 6*d.* per 1000 gallons in 1867.
26. Marion Yass, *Britain Between the World Wars, 1918-1939* (London, 1975).
27. Yass, p.19.
28. See picture of uniformed station staff in 1912, *Low Moor in Times Past*, p.37.
29. Cudworth, p.49.
30. Mr Scriven's Report, p.74.
31. Dodsworth, p.142.
32. Cudworth, *Worstedopolis*, p.42.
33. ibid. p.41.
34. From: *Report of an Enquiry by the Board of Trade into Working-Class Rents and Retail Prices Together with the Rates of Wages in Certain Occupations.* Extracts from Reports of 1908 (p.104ff.) and 1913 (p.136).

Chapter 3: Education On Storr Hill Side

1. Jennifer Davies, *The Victorian Kitchen Garden* (BBC, 1987), p.90.
2. For the whole of this chapter the national background is admirably presented by G. A. N. Lowndes, *The Silent Social Revolution* (2nd ed., 1969), especially the first two chapters.
3. Parker talks about 'Wright's School' in Wibsey in his earlier book, (1902), p.76.
4. Parker, p.241.
5. *Low Moor in Times Past*, pp.22-3.
6. ibid. pp.19-21. See Lowndes, pp.57-60, on the subject of subsidies for voluntary schools from the School Boards. The one penny per pupil per week would not bring Miss Briggs the £40 per annum quoted as the minimum by Lowndes. Her school was probably classed as a denominational school or voluntary school and subsidised accord-

ingly by the local School Board and later by the Bradford Municipal School Board.

7. We do not understand Cudworth's statement, p.83, *Round about Bradford*. Speaking about Wyke church and schools attached to it, he says: 'The National Schools, erected in 1850, are situated near the church, and a new Infants School of neat construction will shortly be opened at Storr Hill.' It is likely that he refers to the school opposite the Temperance Hall, on the corner of Worthinghead Road, which is now a Welfare Clinic, but we would never have considered this to be 'at Storr Hill'.
8. Parker, pp.233-4.
9. See Nudds, pp.46-7, on the history of libraries in Wyke.
10. See *Dalesman*, April 1991, pp.38-9.
11. The Grammar School was there certainly before 1553 and possibly earlier. Scruton, *Pen and Pencil Pictures*, p.77.
12. See Appendix III.
13. For information about the curricula of the schools of present-day Wyke I am indebted to Mr Geoffrey Antcliffe, Deputy Head of Wyke Manor School.

Chapter 4: Some People

1. See Appendix I, *British Parliamentary Papers 1842. Reports to the Commissioners on the Employment of Children.* pp.74-9.
2. See also *Dalesman*, March 1991, p.1072.
3. See the Shaw genealogical tree, Appendix IV.
4. 19th January 1937. Small Montana won.
5. Who had once been landlord of the Patent Hammer, I am told.
6. See James Parker, pp.229-32. In the 1881 Census, William North, son of John o' Judy's and his son, Samuel North, are both shown as living down Storr Hill. William is given as 'landscape gardener', aged 61; Parker, p.232, says he died that same year. Samuel is given as 'landscape gardener and grocer', aged 35. The topography of Storr Hill suggests that William lived at the house with the large front garden just above the end of Rawson Street, while the linking of 'grocer' to Samuel makes it almost certain that he lived at what we knew as Tommis's shop and his garden was the open patch down to Rock Side.
7. Cudworth, *Round About Bradford*, pp.54-64.
8. Columella, *De re rustica* (Loeb Classical Library, 1927) Translated by H. B. Ash. p.37. 'And, as I have stated, not even those aids, nor

the constant toil and experience of the farm overseer, nor the means and willingness to spend money, avail as much as the mere presence of the master; for if his presence does not frequently attend the work, all business comes to a standstill, just as in an army when the commander is absent.' This was written about 70 AD in a manual on agriculture.

9. Parker (1902), p.123.
10. The Tom Jagger mentioned on p.101 of *The Low Moor Explosion*.

Chapter 5: Housing on Storr Hill Side

1. *Granny's Village*, p.178.
2. *Workers' Housing*, p.4.
3. ibid. pp.31-3.
4. Figures from *Bradford 1847-1947*. Pages not numbered – under Building Laws.
5. Cudworth. *Round About Bradford*, p.79.
6. ibid. p.52.
7. ibid. p.78.
8. *Bradford 1847-1947*.
9. *Workers' Housing*, p.100, Fig. 40.
10. Faxfleet Development. See drawing of scullery on p.133 of *Workers' Housing*.

Chapter 6: Perseverance Street

1. Census Reference: RG 11/4426, 29v.-32v.
2. British Parliamentary Papers. Session 1842, No. 8. Reports to the Commissioners on the Employment of Children, p.79.
3. Cudworth, *Round About Bradford*, p.87; Parker, p.242.
4. Cudworth, *Worstedopolis*, p.50.
5. *Workers' Housing*, p.79.
6. ibid, pp.132-3.
7. East Bowling Reflections, pp.24-5.
8. C. C. Robinson (?), *The Dialect of Leeds and its Neighbourhood, etc.* (London, 1862). No author is given but Joseph Wright attributes it to C.C.R.

Chapter 7: Religion and Morality

1. For the attitudes towards religion, the pattern of development and the interaction of the denominations in Bradford during the nineteenth century, see the contribution by Tony Jowitt, 'The Pattern of Religion

in Victorian Bradford,' in *Victorian Bradford.* City of Bradford Metropolitan Libraries Division, 1982. pp.37-61.
2. James Parker devotes a lot of space to Wibsey Chapel, pp.190-201, and reproduces interesting documents concerning its history.
3. Nudds, pp. 8-9.
4. See Table 2, *Victorian Bradford*, p.43.
5. Cudworth, *Round About Bradford*, p.83.
6. James Parker, p.210.
7. Donald Barker, 'Walking to Church', in *Old West Riding,* Vol. 2, No. 2. Winter 1982, pp.11-12.
8. *Victorian Bradford*, p.37.
9. Cudworth, *Round About Bradford*, pp.46-7.
10. Parker, p.241.
11. I am grateful to Miss Willmott for the following information: The 1904 Year Book of Bradford Education Committee states that the New Road Side School was opened as a Board School in November 1899 when the City incorporated the district, and a new temporary iron building was opened for the infants the following year. The school is not listed in the 1905 edition of the Year Book, and the First Annual Report of the City of Bradford Education Committee for the year ending 31st December 1904 states that 'the opening of the new schools at Grange Road and Wyke has enabled the Committee to discontinue the use of the temporary premises at Princeville, New Road Side and Westfield, Wyke.' Local directories at least as late as 1924 list New Road Side Wesleyan Chapel and Schools. Perhaps this reference is to Sunday Schools?
12. *Wiche is Wyke*, p.74-5. The whole of the chapter 'Christian Worship in Wyke' is instructive on this subject.
13. There is a picture of the St. Mark's choir of *ca.* 1936 on p.28 of *Low Moor in Times Past*; and of Holy Trinity choir in early 1900s on p.10. Laurence is fifth from the right on the photo of St. Mark's; he informs me that, of the 37 on the picture, there were occasions when as few as four turned up for a service.
14. Nudds, p.52.
15. There is no doubt about the spontaneous piety expressed in the books of, for instance, Grace Carter, Vera Smith, Martha Heaton and others. It was, in our young days and theirs, far more frequent among women than men, and it seems to have been more deeply rooted in the purely textile quarters of the city.

Chapter 8: Law and Order

1. Cudworth, writing in 1876, *Round About Bradford*, p.87: 'It is a fact that, notwithstanding the absence of educational facilities, the tone of morality of Wyke was generally good, robberies being especially rare.'
2. I hope to make available transcriptions of extracts from the Sid Smith tapes, made by John Nicoll, when time permits.
3. *Granny's Village*, p.111.
4. *A Portrait of the Bradford District. Poverty, Health and Disadvantage* (City of Bradford Metropolitan Council, 1986), pp.35-6.

Chapter 9: Spare Time and Play

1. 'The Pursuit of Leisure', in *Victorian Bradford*, p.199.
2. Michael Parkinson, *Parkinson's Lore*, p.2.
3. In *Victorian Bradford*, p.200, it is stated that it was outlawed nationally in 1834. But the *Encyclopaedia Britannica* Vol. 6, p. 2 states categorically that 'cockfighting was prohibited by law in Great Britain in 1849'.
4. Parker, p.137. See also the attempt at a revival featured in the *Telegraph & Argus*, 27th March 1991, p.3.
5. *Oxford Companion to Classical Literature*, ed. M. C. Howatson, p. 76, 'Athletics'. See *Dalesman*, August 1993, p. 58.
6. I still have the woods made for Ephraim by Sykes of Horbury about 1920. At that time, he and Seth paid £3 each for a set of two woods and a jack.
7. See James Parker, pp.212-13, for founding, architects, opening ceremony in 1883, and Annual General Meeting report for 1904.
8. For the hold that rural and impromptu cricket could have on both sexes and all ages see *Wiche is Wyke*, p.24.
9. Parker, p.150: 'History of the Wibsey Park Sports and Gala Committee, 1892-1904'.
10. See pp.207-9 in *Victorian Bradford.*
11. For details of areas, prices, donors, dates of opening, etc. see Parker, pp.113-14.
12. Cudworth, *Round About Bradford*, p.48.
13. For an exhaustive description of a typical tide, see *Bowling Tidings* by the East Bowling History Workshop. There is an enthusiastic account in *Wiche is Wyke*, p.58.
14. It was always referred to by this name in our immediate vicinity; but many people who knew it, as well as James Parker and Percy Nudds, mention the club without apparently knowing this name.

15. *Victorian Bradford*, p.214.
16. For an account of culture in the raw in Wyke see the item on Wyke Temperance Band in *Victorian Bradford*, p.216. I assume that Nudds is talking about the same band, which he calls Wyke Old Band, p.49.
17. Martha Heaton, *A Tale That Is Told*, p.52.
18. *Victorian Bradford*, p.204.
19. *All Muck and Nettles*, p.93. Vera Smith went to the New Victoria Ballroom and to Gledhill's in Westgate; an informant in *Textile Voices*, p.79, tells of dancing at the Ideal Ballroom at Bankfoot; Laurence danced at the Harold Club, and the Beacon Hall School of Dancing, with occasional visits to the Ideal. Maggie Newberry, too, liked to dance: *Reminiscences*, p.71.
20. Nudds, p.43, is in error about both the date and the name. The old Zion Chapel was certainly functioning as a cinema before 1930, and it was known throughout our young days as Wyke Hippodrome, not as the Star Cinema.

Chapter 10: Children at Play

1. *Dalesman*, March 1991, p.1072; and Edwin Lightowler 'collier, aged 11' in the 1881 Census.
2. See in Doris Beer *T'Weaver's Web* the poem 'Pur 'Em Up', p.29.

Chapter 11: Women's Activities

1. There are full details of these works in my main bibliography.
2. *All Muck and Nettles*, p.115.
3. *Wiche is Wyke*, p.59.
4. See picture of women's football team of *ca*. 1918, *Textile Voices*, p.79.

Chapter 13: Talking, Kidding, Sayings

1. James Herriot, *It Shouldn't Happen To a Vet* (Pan Books, 1973) p.186.
2. A. E. Green, 'Only Kidding: Joking Among Coal Miners' in *Language, Culture and Tradition. Papers Presented at the Annual Conference of the British Sociological Association* (April 1978) pp.47-76.

Chapter 14: Transport and Communications

1. Parker, p.250.
2. Parker, p. 249.

3. Nudds, pp.17-18.
4. For all information about Bradford Tramways see D. J. Croft, *Bradford Tramways* (1976).

Chapter 15: Dress and Footwear

1. See front row of 1922 class at Carr Lane School! p.40. Only Frank is shown wearing boots, and he swears to this day that his was the only mother who knew that the photograph was to be taken that day! Compare the photo of children of the same age taken in 1933.
2. It is excellently described in *Clogs and Clog-Making* by Jeremy Atkinson, Shire Album 113, especially p.2 and p.8.
3. See picture of man perching wearing a cap, *All Muck and Nettles*, p.90; there are several plates illustrating this point in *Textile Voices*. The Works outing on p.75 shows both men and women in 'better ner Sunda clooas', and for caps see p.53.
4. *All Muck and Nettles*, p.84.
5. In *Bygone Bradford* there are many pictures showing stiff, starched collars. Even the young scholars at Green Lane Board School in 1901 wore them! – p.25. I have found only one picture in that book of what we called a 'come to Jesus collar' – on the front row of the founders of the Bradford Independent Labour Party, p.38. See also Vera Smith's description of the collars worn by her first schoolmistress, *All Muck and Nettles*, p.19.
6. *Textile Voices*, p.24.

Chapter 16: Diet and Health Care

1. On fish and chips see Reay Tannahill, *Food in History*, p.287; and *All Muck and Nettles*, pp.76-7.
2. Cudworth, *Round About Bradford*, pp.51-2.
3. For other such cures see *All Muck and Nettles*, p.15.

Bibliography

The amount of historical information about the last hundred years in Wyke and Low Moor is quite surprising considering the small size and relative unimportance of the area. Most of the records contained in the sources centre around Royds Hall and the Low Moor Company, with the textile trade and the leaders of local society not far behind. The following are interesting and informative about our district:

Grace H. Carter. *Wiche is Wyke* (Prod. in Saltaire by A.S.A.P, 1988).
William Cudworth. *Round About Bradford* (1876, Reprint 1968 by Mountain Press, Queensbury).
C. Dodsworth, 'Low Moor Ironworks', *Industrial Archaeology VIII*, (1971), pp.122-164.
D. Lingard and C. & J. Nicoll, *Low Moor in Times Past* (Countryside Publications, Chorley, Lancs, 1983).
Percy Nudds, *Past & Present History of Low Moor, Oakenshaw, Wyke, Norwood Green and Wibsey.* (Privately published, 1974). Typescript.
James Parker, *Illustrated History of Wibsey, Low Moor, Oakenshaw, Wike, Norwood Green, Judy Brig, Royds Hall, Coley, Shelf* (J. Feather & Sons, Bradford, 1902).
James Parker, *Illustrated History of Thirty Villages from Hipperholme to Tong* (Percy Lund Humphreys, Bradford, 1904). Unless indicated, all references to James Parker come from this book.
British Parliamentary Papers, Industrial Revolution. Children's Employment. (Session 1842). No. 8 pp.74-79.

Only in the first two of the above titles and *Low Moor in Times Past*, which is based on some old photographs of the area, is there a significant proportion of reference to ordinary people and everyday life. James Parker gives an enormous amount of information about institutions, contracts, dates and celebrities, but needs an index. Percy Nudds brings the story of Wyke and Low Moor almost up to the present, but he is very selective and not always accurate.

In recent years, mainly through the initiative of the Libraries Division of Bradford Metropolitan Council, the story of the ordinary people of Bradford and their everyday life during the last hundred years has been told in great detail in a series of autobiographies and monographs:

Textile Voices. Mill Life this Century, Ed. Olive Howarth, Bradford Heritage Recording Unit, 1989).
From Mill to Microchip. Bradford in the Making (Bradford Heritage Recording Unit. City of Bradford Metrop. Council, 1986).
Kathleen Binns, *A Family Affair. My Bradford Childhood, 1900-1911* (Bradford Libraries and Information Service. 1988).
R. Blackwell, *The Low Moor Explosion of August 21st 1916* (Private, 1987).
East Bowling History Workshop, *Bowling Tidings* (City of Bradford Metr. Council Libraries Div. Local Studies Dept. Occasional Local Publ. No. 2, 1979, Repr. 1980). Also by the East Bowling Workshop: *East Bowling Reflections* (1980).
William Cudworth, *Worstedopolis. A Sketch History of the Town and Trade of Bradford, the Metropolis of the Worsted Industry* (Bradford, 1888).
Gary Firth, ed. *Bygone Bradford* (Dalesman Publishing, 1986).
Martha Heaton, *A Tale That Is Told* (Bradford Libraries Division, Occasional Local Publications No. 5 1983).
Maggie Newbury, *Reminiscences of a Bradford Mill Girl* (Bradford Libraries Division. Occasional Local Publications, No. 3, 1980, Repr. 1981).
Vera Smith, *All Muck and Nettles. The Early Life of Burler and Mender No. 57* (Bradford Libraries and Information Service. 1990).
Bygone Bradford is a collection of photographs by Christopher Pratt accompanied by quotations from J. B. Priestley and historical notes by Gary Firth. The pictures really do represent the essence of Bradford of the past, especially if seen in conjunction with the text of Vera Smith's *All Muck and Nettles*.

More traditional historical sources on Bradford and district that have been found helpful are:

The Legacy, The Challenge, Poverty, Health and Disadvantage (City of Bradford Metropolitan Council, 1986). Based on 1981 Census.
Board of Trade. *Enquiry into Working-Class Rents, Housing and Retail Prices* (1908). Extract of section on Bradford, pp.104 ff.
Board of Trade. *Enquiry into Working-Class Rents, Retail Prices and Rates of Wages in Certain Occupations* (1913). Extract dealing with Bradford.
D. J. Croft, *Bradford Tramways,* Locomotion Papers 9 (Oakwood Press, Blandford, Dorset. 1976).
Joseph Fieldhouse, *Bradford* (Bradford Metropolitan Council Libraries Division, 1978).
Horace Hird, *Bradford in History* (1968).
Horace Hird, *How a City Grows. Historical notes on Bradford and its Corporation* (Bradford, 1966).
Edward Hotspur Johnson, *The Bradford Almanack* (Bradford Libraries and Information Service, 1990).
William Scruton, *Pen and Pencil Pictures of Old Bradford* (1st ed. 1890. 2nd ed. 1891. Repr. 1985 by Amethyst Press, Otley. Introd. by Jack Reynolds).
D. G. Wright & J. A. Jowitt, *Victorian Bradford* (City of Bradford Metropolitan Council Libraries Division, 1982).

All the above represent different angles of approach to the history of Bradford, ranging from the popular appeal of *The Bradford Almanack* to the thorough, academic treatment of clearly defined themes by local scholars in *Victorian Bradford.*

The incapsulation of Wyke and Low Moor into Bradford, into Yorkshire and into Great Britain, have made it necessary to consult some works which deal with a wider scheme:

Lucy Caffyn, *Workers' Housing in West Yorkshire, 1750-1920.* Royal Commission on the Historical Monuments of England. (H.M.S.O., 1986).
G.A.N. Lowndes, *The Silent Social Revolution. An Account of the Expansion of Public Education in England and Wales.* 2nd ed. (Oxford University Press, 1969).
Gordon Manley, *Climate and the British Scene* (Collins, Fontana New Naturalist, 5th Imp. 1972).

Ordnance Survey Map, 26" : 1 mile. First surveyed 1893; 1908 edition used.
Ordnance Survey Map, 6" : 1 mile map. Sheet 231. Surv. 1849, Publ. 1854.
Ordnance Survey Map, 6" : 1 mile map. Sheet 216. Surv. 1847-1850. Publ. 1852.
W. J. Reader, *Victorian England* (Batsford, London; Putnam, New York (1964, 1973, 1974).
Marion Yass, *Britain Between the World Wars, 1918-1939* (Wayland, London, 1975).

Other works, of no immediate relevance to my subject, but from which I have quoted occasionally are:

Anthony Burton, *The Miners* (Andre Deutsch, London, 1976).
Columella (Lucius Junius Moderatus), *De re rustica*. Transl. H. B. Ash, E. H. Forster and E. Heffner, 3 vols. (Loeb Classics, Heinemann, London, 1977-79).
Jennifer Davies, *The Victorian Kitchen Garden* (B.B.C. Books, 1987).
Ian Dewhurst, *Yorkshire Through the Years* (Batsford, 1975).
Laurie Lee, *I Can't Stay Long* (Penguin Books, 1977).
Laurie Lee, *As I Walked Out One Midsummer Morning* (Penguin Books, 1971).
J. N. L. Myres, *The English Settlements* (Clarendon, Oxford, 1986).
Michael Parkinson, *Parkinson's Lore* (Michael Joseph, 1981).
Robert Redfield, *Peasant Society and Culture* (Chicago, 1956).
Laurence Sterne, *The Life and Opinions of Tristram Shandy* (Penguin, Hardmonsworth, 1967).
Reay Tannahill, *Food In History* (Paladin Press, 1975).